Cross-Platform Desktop Applications
Using Electron and NW.js

Cross-Platform Desktop Applications

USING ELECTRON AND NW.JS

PAUL JENSEN

MANNING

SHELTER ISLAND

For online information and ordering of this and other Manning books, please visit
www.manning.com. The publisher offers discounts on this book when ordered in quantity.
For more information, please contact

    Special Sales Department
    Manning Publications Co.
    20 Baldwin Road
    PO Box 761
    Shelter Island, NY 11964
    Email: orders@manning.com

Manning Publications Co.   Development editor: Cynthia Kane
20 Baldwin Road   Technical development editor: Kathleen Estrada
PO Box 761   Project editor: Karen Gulliver
Shelter Island, NY 11964   Copyeditor: Corbin Collins
   Proofreader: Katie Tennant
   Technical proofreader: Clive Harber
   Typesetter: Dennis Dalinnik
   Cover designer: Marija Tudor

ISBN: 9781617292842
Printed and bound by CPI Group (UK) Ltd, Croydon, CR0 4YY
1 2 3 4 5 6 7 8 9 10 – EBM – 22 21 20 19 18 17

To Fiona

brief contents

contents

foreword

The Electron framework was born in 2013, when Node.js was just becoming popular. The community was excited about JavaScript running on both the client and server sides, and there were various attempts to write desktop apps using JavaScript.

I was excited about JavaScript, too, and GUI programming was my favorite area. I wrote a few modules for Node.js to provide bindings for popular GUI toolkits with JavaScript, but they were no better than existing tools and didn't attract much attention.

Then I found an interesting Node.js module called node-webkit: a simple module that could insert Node.js into WebKit browsers. I had the idea of using it to develop a full-featured desktop framework: I could use Chromium to display web pages as windows, and then use Node.js to control everything!

Development for node-webkit was inactive at that time, so I took over and rewrote the module to make it a complete framework for desktop apps. When I had finished my initial development, it worked incredibly well for small, cross-platform apps.

In the meantime, GitHub was secretly developing the web technology–based Atom editor and was eager to replace Atom's subpar web runtime with a better tool. GitHub tried to migrate Atom to node-webkit but encountered many problems; I met with the developers, and we agreed that I would write a new framework for writing desktop apps with browser techniques and Node.js, and help them migrate Atom to it.

The new framework was initially called atom-shell; it was renamed Electron a year later when it became open source. Electron was written from scratch with a completely different foundation than node-webkit, to allow developers to create large, complex apps. (Today, node-webkit is being actively developed and maintained by others. The module is now known as NW.js, and it's used widely.)

Because Electron made it easy to quickly write sophisticated cross-platform desktop apps, it attracted attention from many developers and underwent rapid improvements. Now big brands are releasing products based on Electron, in addition to small startups building their business around the platform.

Writing desktop apps with Electron and NW.js requires developers to understand a number of new concepts. Desktop development is different from front-end programming in ways that can make it difficult for beginners. That's where this book can help.

Cross-Platform Desktop Applications will walk you through the rich APIs of Electron and NW.js and help you get started developing desktop apps. You'll learn the details of desktop development with JavaScript, from building and shipping apps to in-depth tricks for integrating apps with the desktop. The book also covers advanced topics like debugging, profiling, and publishing apps on various platforms—even experienced developers can learn a lot from these pages.

I recommend this book to anyone who wants to work in desktop development. You'll be surprised how easy it is to write a cross-platform desktop app using JavaScript and the web techniques outlined here.

CHENG ZHAO
CREATOR OF THE ELECTRON FRAMEWORK

preface

A few years ago, I was at a company called Axisto Media, and for a health conference we needed to produce a desktop app that contained videos, session information, and posters from the conference. We developed the app with Adobe AIR. But building the app wasn't simple, and customers had to go through a few steps to get the app running on their computer. There had to be a better way—and, thankfully, there was.

I came to learn about NW.js (back then known as Node WebKit) around the end of 2013. I realized that NW.js could make it easier for customers to use the desktop app because they wouldn't have to install Adobe Flash Player or fiddle with locating files on the USB to load the app. They could simply double-click the app. Not only that, we could also offer support for Linux, and harmonize our tech stack within the business, as we were using Node.js in quite a few places.

I took the opportunity to re-create the desktop app with NW.js, and never looked back. It made things so much simpler, and with the ability to reuse HTML, CSS, and JS from the web app for the conference website, we could make the look and feel of the app more consistent. It was a massive win.

I was so pleased with the framework that I decided to give a presentation about it at the London Node.js User Group meetup in June 2014. I then put the slides online. A couple of months later, I noticed that the slides on SlideShare had quickly accumulated some 20,000 views. It was nice, and I thought that would be that.

But it wasn't.

In December of 2014 I received an email from Erin Twohey at Manning Publications asking me if I'd be interested in writing a book about Node WebKit. It felt too good to pass up. I jumped at the chance and embarked on writing this book.

Lots of things happened during that time. The Node.js community created a fork of the project called IO.js to get features into the platform more quickly, and subsequently merged the fork back into Node.js. The Node WebKit framework switched to using IO.js, and as it was using Blink rather than WebKit, was renamed to NW.js. A year passed, and the book was nearing completion, when we noticed that there was another Node.js desktop app framework in the space called Electron. Taking a closer look, we realized that it was quite similar to NW.js, and it turned out that the author of Electron had previously worked on NW.js. We therefore decided to include the framework in the book.

Writing a book covering two Node.js desktop app frameworks was a challenge, but here it is. The book covers the fundamentals of building desktop apps across both NW.js and Electron. It doesn't cover everything there is to know about the frameworks, but enough to acquaint you with a wide range of features and uses, so that you can pick a framework that suits your needs and build desktop apps with it.

This is a great time to be a developer, and with tools like NW.js and Electron, it's never been easier to make a desktop app. I hope you enjoy this book, and if you find you want to ask me about the frameworks, you can contact me at paulbjensen@gmail.com. You can also find me at @paulbjensen on Twitter.

PAUL JENSEN

acknowledgments

Writing a book is one of the hardest projects you can take on. It requires an incredible amount of time, energy, and dedication. It also requires the support of a sizeable group of people. I have a lot of people to thank for helping me, and for good reason.

I'd like to start by thanking the team at Manning publications: Erin Twohey, Ana Romac, Candace Gillhoolley, Rebecca Rinehart, Aleksandar Dragosavljević, Toni Bowers, Mehmed Pasic, Karen Gulliver, Katie Tennant, Janet Vail, and Lynn Beighley. You can't imagine how much work goes into making a book, and they have been great at helping me through the process of creating and promoting it. I would also like to thank technical proofreader Clive Harber and the following reviewers: Angelo Costa, Daniel Baktiar, Darko Bozhinovski, Deepak Karanth, Fernando Monteiro Kobayashi, Jeff Smith, Matt Borack, Nicolas Boulet-Lavoie, Olivier Ducatteeuw, Patrick Regan, Patrick Rein, Robert Walsh, Rocio Chongtay, Stephen Byrne, Toni Lähdekorpi, William Wheeler, Yogesh Poojari, and Marcelo Pires; and Natko Stipaničev, for his diagram help.

I thank Marjan Bace for giving me the chance to write this book. It's a privilege to have written for Manning; there were already a number of their books in my collection, so it's been fantastic to add to their collection. I also thank Michael Stephens for his work at the beginning of this process to help me form the outline of this book, to cope with my delays in getting material across, and for being understanding when I navigated some personal difficulties.

I thank my development editor, Cynthia Kane. She accomplished the difficult job of prompting chapters out of me, and as this is my first book, you can imagine how painful that process has been. I have an archive of some 150+ email threads that she sent to me during the writing phase, times when I was writing in London, Amsterdam, Iceland, Italy, New York, then Amsterdam again, and finally, back in London. During a very difficult 2016, Cynthia kept gently prodding me along to get this book done, and knew when to offer support when times got tough. I am eternally grateful; so, Cynthia, I thank you.

I thank Roger Wang and Cheng Zhao for having built NW.js and Electron—without their efforts this book would not have existed in the first place.

I thank Edwina Dunn and Clive Humby at Starcount in London. It has been a privilege working for them, and I am grateful for the support that they have given me.

I thank Stuart Nicolle at Purple Seven. Stuart took me on board and showed me the possibilities of what could be gleaned from the world of arts and theatre analytics.

I thank my family: my mum Jette, my sister Maria, her partner Mark, my late Gran Lis, and Brenda and Jim. They have helped me to become the person I am and supported me in discovering the path I am on.

I want to especially thank Fiona. She has had to endure all that has come with writing this book, and much more. The successful completion of this book is a testament to her support and love.

Finally, I want to mention my father, Willy, who was a hardware and software engineer—a smart man, a difficult man. Though we don't see eye to eye, I thank him for playing his part.

about this book

NW.js and Electron are desktop application frameworks powered by Node.js. They allow developers to create cross-platform desktop apps using HTML, CSS, and JavaScript. They offer web designers and developers a way to take their existing skills for crafting web apps and interfaces, and apply that to building desktop apps. The frameworks also support shipping apps for Mac OS, Windows, and Linux from the same codebase, meaning that developers can save time and energy when creating desktop apps that all OSs can use.

NW.js and Electron come from a shared history, and have some similar approaches to app features. This book covers both frameworks topic by topic, helping you to see what they have in common, and where they differ in their approaches. This will help you to decide which framework is best for your needs. We'll cover a broad range of apps and features together, to spark your passion and interest, as well as provide ideas for things you might want to build but don't know how.

I hope you enjoy the book, and that you get to make something great with it.

Who should read this book

Anyone who has experience with HTML, CSS, and JavaScript can pick up this book and get to grips with it right away. Experience with Node.js is not a requirement, but experience will come in handy. If you're completely new to HTML, CSS, and JavaScript, then it would be best to get acquainted with those technologies before you begin to read this book.

How this book is organized

This book has 18 chapters, organized into 4 parts.

Part 1 is an introduction to the frameworks:

- Chapter 1 introduces NW.js and Electron, describing what they are, how they came about, what a Hello World app looks like in both frameworks, and some of the real-world apps that have been produced with them.
- Chapter 2 then explores a direct comparison of the frameworks by building a file explorer application in each one.
- Chapter 3 continues to flesh out some features of the file explorer application.
- Chapter 4 rounds off part 1 by building executable versions of the app for different OSs.

By the end of the first part, you'll have seen how to build a full-feature app with both frameworks.

Part 2 (chapters 5-6) looks at understanding the internals of NW.js and Electron from a technical perspective:

- Chapter 5 looks at Node.js, the programming framework behind both NW.js and Electron. It covers how Node.js works, how asynchronous programming is different from synchronous programming, and the use of callbacks, streams, events, and modules.
- Chapter 6 looks at how NW.js and Electron operate under the hood in terms of how they combine Chromium with NW.js, and how they handle state between the back end and front end.

This will help demystify the magic that NW.js and Electron perform to make their frameworks operate, and provide a useful guide to Node.js for those new to the framework.

In part 3 of the book, we'll look at how to start fleshing out specific features of desktop apps with NW.js and Electron:

- Chapter 7 looks at controlling how the app can be displayed, in terms of the window dimensions and different screen modes, and how to toggle between them.
- Chapter 8 explores how to create tray applications that sit in the tray area of desktops.
- Chapter 9 shows how to build app and context menus for integrating into your apps.
- Chapter 10 introduces dragging and dropping files into your app, and being able to craft the UI to have the same look and feel as other OSs.
- Chapter 11 uses your computer's webcam to build a selfie app and to save the photos to your computer.
- Chapter 12 looks at ways in which you can store app data for your apps, as well as how to retrieve it.
- Chapter 13 shows how to use the clipboard APIs of both NW.js and Electron to copy and paste contents to and from the OS's clipboard.

- Chapter 14 uses a 2D game to demonstrate how to add keyboard shortcuts to your apps, as well as how to program global shortcuts that are accessible across the entire OS.
- Chapter 15 rounds off the part by exploring how to implement desktop notifications for a Twitter streaming client.

This part demonstrates a broad range of features that both NW.js and Electron support, helping you to see how the frameworks go about providing those features, and giving you a chance to evaluate which framework suits your needs best.

In the final part of the book, we'll look at things you can do to prepare your app for production: writing tests, debugging code, and finally, producing executable binaries for shipping to your customers:

- Chapter 16 looks at ways you can approach testing your desktop apps, and at different levels. It introduces the concepts of unit, functional, and integration testing, using Cucumber to document how your app features work, and using Spectron to automate testing your Electron apps at an integration level.
- Chapter 17 explores ways you can debug your code to help spot performance bottlenecks and bugs, and covers tools like Devtron to help inspect your app in greater detail.
- Chapter 18 finishes off the part by looking at various options for building executable binaries of your app, as well as creating setup installers for the different OSs.

By the end of this part, you should be in a position to test your apps, debug any issues that may occur with them, and finally get them built and shipped to your customers.

About the code

This book contains many examples of source code, both in numbered listings and in line with normal text. In both cases, source code is formatted in a `fixed-width font like this` to separate it from ordinary text. In many cases, the original source code has been reformatted; line breaks have been added and indentation reworked as necessary to accommodate the available page space in the book. Additionally, comments in the source code have often been removed from the listings when the code is described in the text. Code annotations accompany many of the listings, highlighting important concepts.

Source code for the book's examples is available for download from the publisher's website at www.manning.com/books/cross-platform-desktop-applications and at http://github.com/paulbjensen/cross-platform-desktop-applications.

Author Online

Purchase of *Cross-Platform Desktop Applications* includes free access to a private web forum run by Manning Publications where you can make comments about the book, ask technical questions, and receive help from the author and from other users. To access the forum and subscribe to it, point your web browser to www.manning.com/ books/cross-platform-desktop-applications. This page provides information on how to get on the forum once you are registered, what kind of help is available, and the rules of conduct on the forum.

Manning's commitment to our readers is to provide a venue where a meaningful dialog between individual readers and between readers and authors can take place. It is not a commitment to any specific amount of participation on the part of the authors, whose contribution to the forum remains voluntary (and unpaid). We suggest you try asking him some challenging questions lest his interest stray! The Author Online forum and the archives of previous discussions will be accessible from the publisher's website as long as the book is in print.

about the author

Paul Jensen is a Senior Pre-Sales Consultant at Starcount in London, UK. He has a history of working in startups, the web agency New Bamboo (now part of Thoughtbot), AOL, and his own consultancy, Anephenix Ltd. He has spoken at a number of events (London Ruby User Group, Cukeup 2013, London Node User Group), created his own real-time dashboard (Dashku), and was the project lead for the Socketstream web framework. He enjoys ale and cycling, and can be found on Twitter as @paulbjensen.

about the cover

The figure on the cover of Cross-Platform Desktop Applications is captioned "Man from Murcia." The illustration is taken from a collection of dress costumes from various countries by Jacques Grasset de Saint-Sauveur (1757–1810), titled *Costumes de Différents Pays*, published in France in 1797. Each illustration is finely drawn and colored by hand. The rich variety of Grasset de Saint-Sauveur's collection reminds us vividly of how culturally apart the world's towns and regions were just 200 years ago. Isolated from each other, people spoke different dialects and languages. In the streets or in the countryside, it was easy to identify where they lived and what their trade or station in life was just by their dress.

The way we dress has changed since then, and the diversity by region, so rich at the time, has faded away. It is now hard to tell apart the inhabitants of different continents, let alone different towns, regions, or countries. Perhaps we have traded cultural diversity for a more varied personal life—certainly for a more varied and fast-paced technological life.

At a time when it is hard to tell one computer book from another, Manning celebrates the inventiveness and initiative of the computer business with book covers based on the rich diversity of regional life of two centuries ago, brought back to life by Saint-Sauveur's pictures.

Part 1

Welcome to Node.js desktop application development

Two frameworks prevail when it comes to building desktop applications with Node.js: NW.js and Electron. In the first part of the book, you'll be introduced to those frameworks and what advantages they have compared to other app frameworks, build a quick Hello World application with both NW.js and Electron, and then see what kinds of applications have been built.

In chapter 2, we'll begin to put those frameworks to use by building a file explorer app. We'll flesh out the skeleton of the app and add features to it, and explore the different approaches that NW.js and Electron take.

In chapter 3, we'll continue to iterate on the file explorer app by adding more features such as search and opening files. We'll then round up the app in chapter 4 by building executable versions for Mac OS, Windows, and Linux. By the end of part 1, you'll have gotten to know both NW.js and Electron, and put your knowledge to practical use in a real-world application.

Introducing Electron and NW.js

This chapter covers

- Understanding why Node.js desktop apps are the rage these days
- Previewing Node.js desktop application frameworks Electron and NW.js
- Using these frameworks to build cross-platform desktop apps with Node.js
- Comparing the frameworks
- Identifying real-world applications built with Electron and NW.js

Node.js is known as a programming framework that lets developers build server-side applications in JavaScript. Since its creation in 2009, it has spawned a variety of popular web frameworks like Express and Hapi, as well as real-time web frameworks like Meteor and Sails. It has also allowed developers to create isomorphic web apps using tools like Facebook's React, a UI library that has had a huge impact on web development in recent years. It's fair to have the impression that Node.js is purely about web apps, but the truth is that Node.js is far more than that.

Node.js can be used to build cross-platform desktop apps, and chances are you're using one of them today. If you've ever used Slack at work, edited code using Atom from GitHub, or watched a movie using Popcorn Time, then you've used a Node.js desktop app. It's becoming a popular choice for developers, in particular web developers with little experience in desktop application development—even Microsoft has built and shipped an IDE (Visual Studio Code) using Node.js.

In the Node.js ecosystem, there are two major frameworks for creating desktop apps: NW.js and Electron. Both are supported by major businesses (NW.js by Intel and Gnor Tech, and Electron by GitHub), both have large communities around them, and both share similar approaches to building desktop apps. This book shows how to build cross-platform desktop apps with both Electron and NW.js. You may be pleasantly surprised by how much they have in common—in fact, they have something of a shared history, but we'll get to that later. For now, we'll explore some of the reasons why Node.js desktop apps have taken off and where they might be useful for you and your work.

1.1   Why build Node.js desktop applications?

To answer this question, you have to see how software has changed over the past generation and visualize where it is going.

1.1.1   Desktop to web and back

At the beginning of 2000, most software was available as desktop apps in shrink-wrapped boxes that you could buy from stores like Best Buy. You'd need to check the system requirements and make sure that it would work on the operating system (OS) you were running (which was Windows, for the majority of people). You'd then grab a CD-ROM out of the box, and install the software on your computer that way.

Over time, that began to change: improvements in web browsers, greater internet speeds and access, and the movement toward open source software resulted in a major shift in how software was created and distributed. The advent of AJAX spawned a new era of delivering software as web apps. These apps didn't require downloading anything onto the computer, and they could run across multiple OSs. Companies like Google and Facebook signaled the rise of the web as a powerful platform in the industry, and as people became accustomed to using apps online for a monthly fee, traditional software houses adapted and began to offer their software online.

It seemed like the web had won, but then mobile computing came along, leading to the rise of native apps for Apple iPhone and Android mobile devices. The industry changed again, and developers found themselves needing to adapt their business to support those devices too.

If reflecting on 16 years of software development shows anything, it's that there's a lot of change in the industry, and that we as developers will probably find ourselves supporting multiple computing platforms for years to come: desktop, web, mobile, and more. We're in the age of multiplatform computing.

Where does that leave desktop apps? Desktop apps have become one of a number of computing platforms that we use in our day-to-day activities. But what has changed since the 2000s is that where Microsoft Windows was the dominant OS for desktop computers back then, Apple has pared back that dominance with the popularity of its computers among creatives and professionals. Not only that, but Google's Chromebooks were the best-selling laptops in the U.S. in the first quarter of 2016. The year of the Linux desktop may have finally arrived. The point is this: you can't afford to develop desktop apps that work on only Windows these days—there's a need for developing apps that work across Mac OS and Linux as well.

Cross-platform desktop apps aren't a new concept; frameworks like Mono and Qt have provided a way to develop desktop apps that run across all three of the major OSs. Usually, developers with a background in programming languages like C, C++, and C# could come to grips with these frameworks and develop software for them. Other developers, like web developers, would need to learn a new language alongside a framework, and this would be a barrier to them developing desktop apps.

When NW.js and Electron came about, they offered an opportunity to build desktop apps with the same code used to create web apps—and not only that, these desktop apps could operate across Windows, Mac OS, and Linux. It was a massive win for both code and skills reusability and unleashed a wave of new apps.

In addition, the popularity of Node.js has meant that developers have been able to leverage a huge ecosystem of open source libraries to build their apps with. Node.js developers and web developers alike could suddenly make desktop apps, and some of the apps out there are truly fantastic. One that comes to mind is WebTorrent by Feross Aboukhadijeh, shown in figure 1.1.

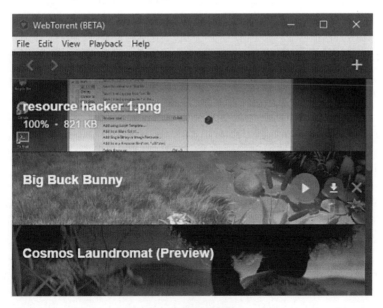

Figure 1.1 WebTorrent by Feross Aboukhadijeh

WebTorrent is a desktop app that allows you to upload files for other users to download, much in the same fashion as BitTorrent. It uses WebRTC to enable peer-to-peer connections, and to show you how portable the code is, the library used in the desktop app is the same as the one you can use in a web browser. It's a truly fantastic piece of work.

The ability to support multiple OSs but write the software in a common and popular language has lots of pros because, as mentioned, desktop computing is still a major part of how people use computers today, even as new mobile computing platforms emerge. That's why Node.js desktop apps have become an interesting way to deliver software. The next section elaborates on some of the reasons why you may consider building Node.js desktop apps over web apps.

1.1.2   *What Node.js desktop apps offer over web apps*

Web apps have thrived for a number of reasons:

- Internet speeds improved and access increased, and, importantly, the cost of internet access went down, making the user base grow massively, unlike most other communication channels.
- Web browsers have benefitted from increased competition. As appealing alternatives to Internet Explorer emerged, new features were added to those browsers, which in turn enabled web apps to do new things.
- The relative ease of learning HTML, CSS, and JavaScript lowered the barrier of entry for developers to make web apps, as opposed to learning lower-level languages like C and C++.
- The rise of open source software meant that the cost of distributing and obtaining software declined significantly, meaning that developers with a bit of cash, time, and the right level of skill could build their own web apps.

When you look at all this, you can see why the web is such an important platform for developers to make software for. That said, there are still things that challenge and limit the ability of web apps today:

- Internet access is not always available. If you're on a train and you go under a tunnel, chances are you'll lose internet access. If your web app depends on saving data, hopefully it will be able to store a local copy of the changes and allow for them to be synchronized via the internet when access resumes.
- If your app has a lot of features, the amount of data it will need to transfer over the internet to run the app could be large and may slow down the loading of the app. If it takes too long, people load something else—something proven by research into the impact that slow web page loading times have on e-commerce transactions.
- If you're working with large files (such as high-resolution images and videos) that are sitting on your desktop computer, then it might not make sense for them to be uploaded to the internet in order for a web app to edit them.

- Because of the security policy of the web browser, there are limits to what hardware/software features of the computer the web app can access.
- You have no control over what web browsers a user may use to visit your web app. You have to use feature detection to cater to different web browsers, which restricts what features your app can use. The user experience (UX) can vary wildly.

Web apps are essentially restricted by the limits of internet access and browser features. It is in these circumstances that a desktop app may be preferable to a web app. Some of the benefits include the following:

- You don't require internet access to start and run the app.
- Desktop apps start instantly, without having to wait for resources to download from the internet.
- Desktop apps have access to the computer's OS and hardware resources, including access to the files and folder on the user's computer.
- You have greater control over the UX with the software. You don't have to worry about how different browsers handle CSS rules and what JavaScript features they support.
- Once a desktop app is installed on a user's computer, it's there. It doesn't depend on you running web servers to support the app, where you need to offer 24/7 support in case your web app goes down, or worse, your web-hosting provider encounters technical difficulties.

Usually, desktop apps have required developers to be proficient in languages like C++, Objective-C, or C#, and knowing frameworks like .NET, Qt, Cocoa, or GTK. For some developers, that can be a barrier to entry and may discourage them from considering the possibility of building a desktop app.

The great thing about Node.js desktop application frameworks like Electron and NW.js is that they have significantly lowered that barrier of entry for developers. By allowing developers to create apps using HTML, CSS, and JavaScript, they've opened the door for web developers to also be desktop app developers, with the added benefit of being able to use the same code across both the web app and desktop app platforms.

Now it's time to introduce the frameworks. As mentioned earlier in the chapter, Electron and NW.js have something of a shared history, so I'll touch on the origins of both frameworks and then cover each in some detail.

1.2 The origins of NW.js and Electron

Back in 2011, Roger Wang managed to find a way to combine WebKit (the browser engine behind Safari, Konqueror, and Google Chrome at the time) with Node.js, so that you could access Node.js modules from the JavaScript code running inside a web page. This Node.js module was given the name node-webkit. He continued to work on the project at Intel's Open Source Technology Center in China, which gave its support to the project by letting Roger work on it full time. Not only that, he was allowed to hire others to work on it too.

In the summer of 2012, a senior college student named Cheng Zhao joined Intel as an intern to work on node-webkit. He worked with Roger to help improve its internal architecture, which involved changing how Node.js and WebKit were combined. As the code evolved, node-webkit moved from being a mere Node.js module to becoming a framework for desktop apps. Node-webkit was given interesting uses within third-party apps. The Light Table editor was the first to make use of node-webkit to deliver its functionality and helped to promote the framework to other developers.

In December of the same year, Cheng left Intel to work at GitHub as a contractor. He was tasked with helping to port GitHub's Atom editor from using Chromium Embedded Framework and native JavaScript bindings to using node-webkit.

The efforts to port Atom to node-webkit encountered difficulties (see https:// github.com/atom/atom/pull/100), so they abandoned that approach. Instead, they decided to create a new native shell for Atom, which they called Atom Shell. This approach to combining WebKit with Node.js differed from the approach taken by node-webkit. Cheng Zhao focused all of his efforts into working on Atom Shell, which GitHub later open sourced shortly after open sourcing its text editor, Atom.

During this time, Node.js was going through a period of splintering—members of the Node.js community created a fork of Node.js called IO.js in order to get updates into the project faster, and in the WebKit community, Google announced that it was going to fork the WebKit project for Google Chrome into a variant called Blink. The combination of these changes led to renaming node-webkit as NW.js, and GitHub renamed the Atom Shell framework as Electron. Over time, Electron quickly acquired a number of admirers and was being used in high-profile apps like Slack and Visual Studio Code. It eventually became a juggernaut of its own creation, distinct from its original purpose as a tool for delivering Atom.

Although NW.js was the first Node.js desktop application framework, Electron has quickly emerged as a popular framework that has overshadowed NW.js, although both have been heavily worked on by the same developer at different points in time and share a lot of common code in terms of how users use their APIs for creating app features. Each has evolved a different approach to its internal architecture and has spawned separate communities that actively promote their respective projects.

In this respect, this book essentially covers two frameworks that do the same thing in slightly different ways. It's a fairly unique situation in that the frameworks share so much history and are similar enough to merit being evaluated together. There's a natural inclination to pick whichever is the bigger of the two and go with that, and the answer to that would be Electron (if you go by popularity and momentum), but some prefer NW.js to Electron for its relative simplicity in how you execute code and load the app, as well as for supporting computing platforms like Google Chromebooks, and because of other matters of programming opinion. I prefer to provide the information and let you decide what you want to use. It's more ground to cover, but you'll be better informed.

If you're interested in digging into the history of both projects a bit more, the following links provide helpful pointers:

- http://cheng.guru/blog/2016/05/13/from-node-webkit-to-electron-1-0.html
- https://github.com/electron/electron/issues/5172#issuecomment-210697670

If you're looking for posts that compare and contrast the frameworks, here are some good links to look at as well:

- http://electron.atom.io/docs/development/atom-shell-vs-node-webkit/
- http://tangiblejs.com/posts/nw-js-and-electron-compared-2016-edition

That's a brief history of the two projects and how their paths have formed over time. We'll now dive into each framework, starting with the first framework to emerge on the scene: NW.js.

1.3 Introducing NW.js

To recap, NW.js is a framework for building desktop apps with HTML, CSS, and JavaScript. It was created back in November 2011 by Roger Wang at Intel's Open Source Technology Center in China. The idea was that by combining Node.js with WebKit (the web browser engine behind Chromium, an open source version of Google Chrome), you could create desktop apps using web technologies. This was the basis for the framework's original name, node-webkit.

By combining Node.js with Chromium, Roger found a way to create apps that could not only load an HTML file with CSS and JavaScript inside an app window, but also could interact with the OS via a JavaScript API. This JavaScript API could then control visual aspects like window dimensions, toolbar, and menu items as well as provide access to local files on the desktop—things web apps couldn't do.

To give you an idea of what this looks like, let's walk through an example Hello World app for NW.js.

1.3.1 A Hello World app in NW.js

This example application will give you a better understanding of what Node.js desktop apps are like with NW.js. Figure 1.2 show a design of the app we'll build.

Figure 1.2 Design for the Hello World app we'll build

The code for this app is available in the GitHub repository for this book at http://mng.bz/4W7Y.

If you want to get the code to run the app and see it in action, follow the instructions in the README.md file there. It's ready-made to go. But if you want to see how the sausage is made, then read on and we'll build the app from scratch.

The first step is to check whether you have Node.js installed. If you already do, great—move on to the next section, "Installing NW.js," but if not, you'll find instructions for installing Node.js in the appendix.

INSTALLING NW.JS

Node.js comes with a package management tool called npm that handles installing libraries for Node.js, and NW.js can be installed using it. On your computer, open the command-line program for your OS (Command Prompt or PowerShell on Windows, and Terminal on both Mac OS and Linux).

After you've opened your command-line program, run the following command:

```
npm install -g nw
```

This will install NW.js on your computer as a Node.js module available to all of your Node.js desktop apps.

CREATING THE HELLO WORLD APP

The app is so small that you can create the files by hand. At the bare minimum, you only need two files:

- *A file named package.json*—This contains configuration information about the app, and is required by NW.js.
- *An HTML file*—This file will be loaded by the package.json file and displayed in the app window. In this case, it's a file called index.html (but it can be named something else, such as app.html or main.html).

Start by creating a folder for the app's file. On your computer, go where you like to store your project source code and create a folder named hello-world-nwjs. Then you can create the package.json file that will be stored inside the hello-world-nwjs folder.

In your text editor/IDE, create a file named package.json inside the hello-world-nwjs folder and insert the following code into it:

```
{
  "name" : "hello-world-nwjs",
  "main" : "index.html",
  "version" : "1.0.0"
}
```

The package.json file consists of some configuration information about the app: its name, the main file to load when the app starts, and its version number. These fields are required by NW.js (though the version field is required by npm). The name field must contain lowercase alphanumeric characters only—there can be no space characters in the name.

The main field contains the file path for the entry point of your app. In the case of NW.js, you have the option of loading either a JavaScript file or an HTML file, but HTML files tend to be the common choice for NW.js apps. The HTML file is loaded into the app window, and to demonstrate this, you'll create an HTML file called index.html that will be loaded.

Inside the hello-world-nwjs folder, create a file named index.html and insert the code in the following listing.

Listing 1.1 Code for the Hello World app's index.html file

```html
<html>
  <head>
    <title>Hello World</title>          ⊲—  Sets title of app
    <style>                                  window with title
      body {                                 element
        background-image: linear-gradient(45deg, #EAD790 0%, #EF8C53 100%);
        text-align: center;
      }

      button {
        background: rgba(0,0,0,0.40);
        box-shadow: 0px 0px 4px 0px rgba(0,0,0,0.50);
        border-radius: 8px;
        color: white;
        padding: 1em 2em;
        border: none;
        font-family: 'Roboto', sans-serif;
        font-weight: 100;
        font-size: 14pt;
        position: relative;
        top: 40%;
        cursor: pointer;
        outline: none;
      }

      button:hover {
        background: rgba(0,0,0,0.30);
      }
    </style>
    <link href='https://fonts.googleapis.com/css?family=Roboto:300'
     rel='stylesheet' type='text/css'>          ⊲—  Links to font provided by
    <script>                               ⊲—      Google fonts for the button
      function sayHello () {
        alert('Hello World');
      }
    </script>
  </head>
  <body>
    <button onclick="sayHello()">Say Hello</button>
  </body>
</html>
```

Annotations:
- **Sets title of app window with title element**
- **Inline stylesheet included to give background and button element a nice look**
- **Links to font provided by Google fonts for the button**
- **JavaScript function embedded that prints "Hello World" in alert dialog**
- **Body element contains button element that calls JS function sayHello when clicked**

Once you've saved the index.html file on your computer, you can run the app on your computer. Inside the hello-world-nwjs folder, run the following command on your terminal:

```
nw
```

If you're running on Mac OS, figure 1.3 shows what you should see.

Figure 1.3   The Hello World app running on Mac OS. This screenshot of the app is almost identical to the design, the only difference being size dimensions.

If you're running Linux, figure 1.4 shows the same app running on openSUSE 13.2 (Linux has many distributions, and openSUSE is one of the well-known distributions).

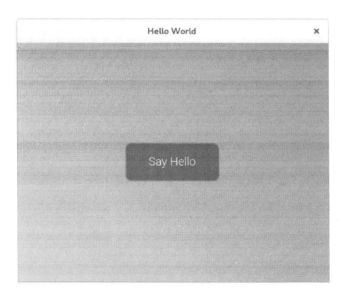

Figure 1.4   The Hello World app running on openSUSE 13.2. It looks fairly identical to the Mac OS variant of the app, although the window title bar looks different, the color profiling is slightly different, and the font rendering is noticeably different.

The Windows 10, Mac OS, and Linux versions of NW.js all share the same way to get the app started, which is handy. Type the same command in your Command Prompt, and you should see something like figure 1.5 on a Windows 10 computer.

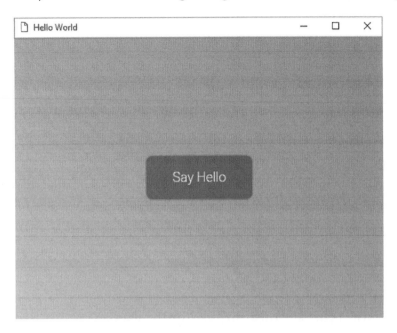

Figure 1.5 The Hello World app running on Windows 10. The app looks almost identical to the app running on openSUSE Linux (minus the app window and a slight difference in font rendering).

If you click the Say Hello button in the middle of the app screen, you'll see an alert dialog that says "Hello World." If you were to take the index.html file and load it in a web browser such as Google Chrome, Microsoft Edge, or Mozilla Firefox, you would see the same screen and get the same result. That's the point—you can take an HTML page for a website and turn it into a desktop app with NW.js without having to change the code.

At this point you might say, "Well, if that's the case, why don't I use a desktop app template that renders an HTML page inside a window and make do with that?" That's not a bad question, and some apps have taken this approach.

The reasons against such an approach could boil down to ease of development. You might not know C++, or if you do, you may not want to be compelled to compile code every time you make a feature change. Also, you might want to use features that are only available natively to the desktop framework and are beyond what an HTML file embedded inside of an app window shell would be able to access. The other major reason is that as desktop app frameworks, both Electron and NW.js provide a rich feature set to support you in developing desktop apps, covered in the next section.

1.3.2   *What features does NW.js have?*

NW.js has a set of features that makes it appealing for developers to use when building desktop apps. In a generic overview, they are as follows:

- A JavaScript API for creating and accessing native UIs and APIs to the OS: control windows, add menu items, tray menus, read/write files, access the clipboard, and more
- The ability to use Node.js inside your app as well as install and use a huge library of Node.js modules via npm
- Being able to build executables of the app for each OS from a single codebase

I'll explain each bullet point in more detail in the next sections.

ACCESSING OS NATIVE UI AND API VIA JAVASCRIPT

A good desktop app integrates well into the user's OS: a music app will work with the media keyboard shortcuts on a user's keyboard, a chat app may have a menu icon in the tray area of the OS, and a productivity app may provide notifications when actions have completed.

NW.js provides a large API for getting access to OS features, which do the following:

- Control the size and behavior of the app's window
- Display a native toolbar on the app window with menu items
- Add context menus in the app window area on right-click
- Add a tray app item in the OS's tray menu
- Access the OS clipboard, read the contents, and even set the contents
- Open files, folders, and URLs on the computer using their default apps
- Insert notifications via the OS's notification system

As you can see from the preceding list, there are a lot of things you can do within NW.js that web browsers cannot do. For example, web browsers don't have direct access to files on the desktop or the contents of the clipboard due to security restrictions that web browsers implement to protect users from sites with malicious intent. In the case of NW.js, because the app runs on the user's computer, it's granted a level of access where the user trusts the app. This means that you can do things like access the files that are on the user's computer, create new files and folders, and more. These features allow the developer to create desktop apps that fit well with the user's OS and do things that web apps can't do (or at least not as easily)—and the user trusts the app to be responsible and not do anything malicious.

USING NODE.JS AND NPM MODULES INSIDE YOUR APP

NW.js provides access to the Node.js API in the app, as well as uses modules that are installed with npm. This means that you can install npm modules for use with your desktop apps, and you can even access them and Node.js core modules from the same code that's interacting with the front end of the desktop app.

For example, you could write a bit of embedded JavaScript in the index.html file that uses the Node.js filesystem module to get a list of files and folders in a given directory, and then list those files as list items in the HTML. This shared JavaScript context between the front-end and back-end parts of the desktop app is an intriguing aspect of the way NW.js combines Node.js with Chromium. It's something to keep in mind when you're working with NW.js applications (as opposed to Electron applications). It's quite different from how web apps work, as figure 1.6 demonstrates.

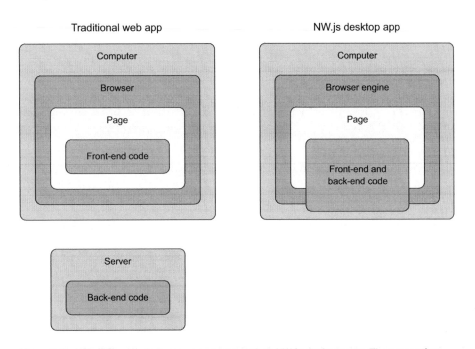

Figure 1.6 The difference between a web app and an NW.js desktop app. The separation between front-end and back-end code in an NW.js desktop is blurred, as the JavaScript context is shared between both parts of the code.

To explore this a bit further, consider how traditional web apps work. Web apps tend to have a client/server model where the client requests a web page or makes an API request, and the server executes some code to then serve that data back to the client. The client in this case is a computer running a web browser. The web browser then loads the data, where, if it's HTML, the rendering engine turns it into a web page; or, if it's data like XML or JSON, the rendering engine displays it in raw form. The server does its job of executing back-end code to serve HTML pages or API requests, and the computer client running the web browser does its job of making HTML/API requests and rendering the response in the web browser. The web browser applies a strict security model to ensure that the front-end code executes within the context of the web page and nothing else. There's a clear separation of application state and responsibility.

In an NW.js app, the app window is essentially like an embedded web browser, but with the distinct difference that the code inside the web page has access to the computer's resources and can execute server-side code. There's no separation of app state and responsibility. This means you can write code that's calling out to DOM elements in the web page and executing server-side code accessing the computer's filesystem in the same place. Not only that, you'll be able to use npm modules in your code as well.

Being able to install npm modules and require them in your desktop app means you have access to over 400,000 libraries (as of January 2017) for use in your code. You'll have plenty of options when it comes to using third-party libraries in your app. In fact, both NW.js and Electron have spawned a number of dedicated libraries for use with desktop apps, all of which you'll be able to find at http://npmjs.com, and at https://github.com/nw-cn/awesome-nwjs and https://github.com/sindresorhus/awesome-electron.

BUILDING YOUR APP FOR MULTIPLE OSS FROM A SINGLE CODEBASE

One of the most useful features of NW.js is that from a single codebase for your desktop app, you can build native executable apps for Windows, Mac OS, and Linux. This is a time saver when you're developing an app that has to work across multiple platforms. It also means you can have greater control over how the app looks and feels, more so than you can when trying to support a website for multiple web browsers.

The native executable is able to run on its own and doesn't require the user to have any other software installed on their computer. This makes it easy to distribute the app to users, including on stores like Apple's App store and the Steam store, where some NW.js apps and games are sold.

The process of building an app for a specific OS involves a few command-line arguments, but there are some tools that simplify the process for you, such as the nw-builder tool, illustrated in figure 1.7.

Taking an example desktop app, I'm able to use nw-builder's `nwbuild` command in step 1 to automate the steps of turning our desktop app's code into executable binaries for both Mac OS and Windows, as shown in step 3. This can save a lot of time (if you have to make both 32-bit and 64-bit builds of the app) and prevent mistakes when building the app.

In the next section, we'll turn our attention to Electron: how an example app works and looks with it, and what features it has.

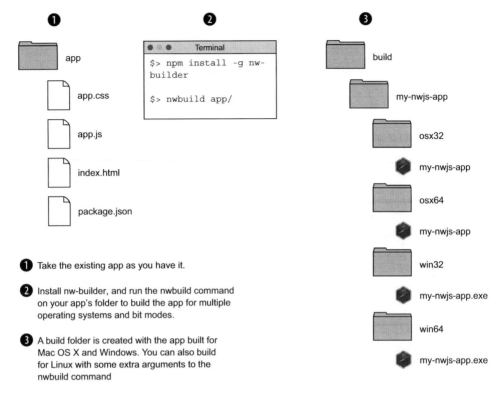

1 Take the existing app as you have it.

2 Install nw-builder, and run the nwbuild command on your app's folder to build the app for multiple operating systems and bit modes.

3 A build folder is created with the app built for Mac OS X and Windows. You can also build for Linux with some extra arguments to the nwbuild command

Figure 1.7 **The nw-builder tool can build native executables of an NW.js app for both 32-bit and 64-bit versions of Mac OS and Windows.**

1.4 *Introducing Electron*

Electron is a desktop app framework from GitHub. It was built for GitHub's text editor Atom and was originally known as Atom Shell. It allows you to build cross-platform desktop apps using HTML, CSS, and JavaScript. Since its release back in November 2013, it has become popular and is used by a number of startups and large businesses for their apps. Electron is used not only in Atom but also in the desktop clients of a chat app called Slack (www.slack.com), a startup that was valued at $3.8 billion as of April 2016.

1.4.1 *How does Electron work and differ from NW.js?*

One of the things that Electron did differently from NW.js was the way it got Chromium and Node.js to work together. In NW.js, Chromium is patched so that Node.js and Chromium are sharing the same JavaScript context (or *state*, as you may call it in programming). In Electron, there's no patching of Chromium involved; instead, it's combined with Node.js through Chromium's content API and the use of Node.js's node_bindings.

The implication of this approach is that Electron works differently from NW.js in terms of how it handles JavaScript contexts. Where NW.js maintains a single shared JavaScript context, Electron has separate JavaScript contexts—one for the back-end process that kicks off running the app window (referred to as the *main* process), and one for each app window (referred to as the *renderer* process). This is an important difference between the frameworks, and one that will be elaborated on further in the book through various examples.

Another important difference between NW.js and Electron is that where NW.js usually uses an HTML file as the entry point for loading a desktop app, Electron uses a JavaScript file instead. Electron delegates the responsibility of loading an app window to code that's executed inside the JavaScript file. You'll see this in greater detail as we explore the Hello World app in Electron in the next section.

1.4.2   *A Hello World app in Electron*

Like the Hello World app in NW.js, I've also created the app that we'll run through now. If you want to boot that up and play with it, you can grab a copy of the source at http://mng.bz/u4C0.

Follow the instructions in the README.md file to get the app up and running. Alternatively, if you want to bake the cake rather than merely eat it at the end, we'll walk through that now.

Assuming that you've already installed Node.js on your computer (if not, see "Installing Node.js" in the appendix of this book), let's start by downloading a copy of Electron via npm. In your terminal or at the Command Prompt, run the following command:

```
npm install -g electron
```

This will install Electron as a global npm module, meaning that it will be available to other Node.js applications where you want to use it. Once you have installed the Electron module, we can take a look at what an example Hello World app's files consist of. Here's the bare minimum number of files required to run an Electron app:

- index.html
- main.js
- package.json

You can create a folder named hello-world-electron to store the app's files. Create a folder with the suggested name, and then you'll add the required files inside it.

We'll start with the package.json. Here's what an example package.json looks like:

```
{
  "name"    : "hello-world",
  "version" : "1.0.0",
  "main"    : "main.js"
}
```

You might notice that package.json looks almost identical to the package.json file used to load the Hello World app in NW.js. The only difference is that where an NW.js app's package.json field expects the main property to specify an HTML file as the app's entry point, Electron expects the main property to specify a JavaScript file.

In Electron, the JavaScript file is responsible for loading an app's windows, tray menus, and other items, as well as handling any system-level events that occur in the OS. For the Hello World example, it looks like the following.

Listing 1.2   main.js file for the Hello World Electron app

Creates reference to Electron's Browser-Window class

Add event listener that quits the app when all windows are closed (except in Mac OS)

Loads Electron module from npm

Creates reference to Electron's application object

mainWindow variable stores reference to app's window

Creates new app window and assigns it to main window variable to prevent it being closed by Node.js garbage collection

Loads index.html file in app window

When app window is closed, unassigns app window from main window variable

```javascript
'use strict';

const electron = require('electron');
const app = electron.app;
const BrowserWindow = electron.BrowserWindow;

let mainWindow = null;

app.on('window-all-closed', () => {
  if (process.platform !== 'darwin') app.quit();
});

app.on('ready', () => {
  mainWindow = new BrowserWindow();
  mainWindow.loadURL(`file://${__dirname}/index.html`);
  mainWindow.on('closed', () => { mainWindow = null; });
});
```

What you can see in listing 1.2 is that where NW.js points to an HTML file in the package.json file, Electron requires a bit of code configuration to achieve the same result.

The JavaScript code looks a bit funny

If you're fairly new to Node.js and haven't touched JavaScript in a while, you may notice some new language features like the use of `const` and `let` for variable declaration, as well as `=>` as a function shorthand. This is the next version of JavaScript, also known as ES6. It's a fairly new version of JavaScript that's now integrated into Node.js and is actively used in Electron. To learn more about ES6, you can visit https://babeljs.io/learn-es2015/, http://es6-features.org, and https://es6.io/.

If you prefer the traditional style of writing JavaScript, you can continue to use it for your Electron applications. The internet is full of opinions, but that doesn't mean that you have to adopt them. My suggestion is to find what works for you and go from there.

Having created the main.js file that's the entry point to your app, you'll now create the index.html file that the main.js file loads in an app window. Create a file named index.html, and insert the code shown next.

Listing 1.3 index.html for the Hello World Electron app

```
<html>
  <head>
    <title>Hello World</title>
    <style>
      body {
        background-image: linear-gradient(45deg, #EAD790 0%, #EF8C53 100%);
        text-align: center;
      }

      button {
        background: rgba(0,0,0,0.40);
        box-shadow: 0px 0px 4px 0px rgba(0,0,0,0.50);
        border-radius: 8px;
        color: white;
        padding: 1em 2em;
        border: none;
        font-family: 'Roboto', sans-serif;
        font-weight: 300;
        font-size: 14pt;
        position: relative;
        top: 40%;
        cursor: pointer;
        outline: none;
      }

      button:hover {
        background: rgba(0,0,0,0.30);
      }
    </style>
    <link href='https://fonts.googleapis.com/css?family=Roboto:300'
     rel='stylesheet' type='text/css' />
    <script>
      function sayHello () {
        alert('Hello World');
      }
    </script>
  </head>
  <body>
    <button onclick="sayHello()">Say Hello</button>
  </body>
</html>
```

This is the HTML file that will be loaded into the browser window by the main.js file. It's the same code that's used in the NW.js example app's index.html file (so we can compare the examples across both frameworks). With the files saved in the application folder, you can now run the app from the command line.

To execute the app from the command line, cd into the hello-world-electron directory, and run the following command:

```
electron .
```

Once you've run the command, click the Hello World button, and you can expect to see something like figure 1.8.

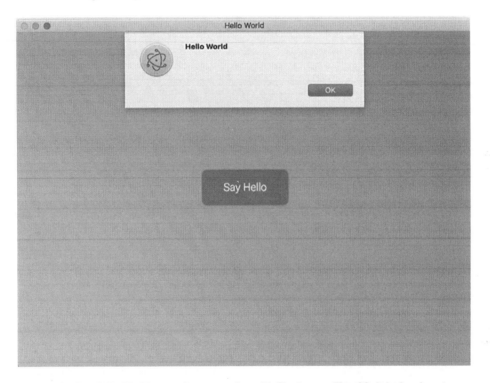

Figure 1.8   The Hello World example app running with Electron on Mac OS. It looks almost identical to the NW.js equivalent, except the window dimensions are different.

The app for the most part looks identical to the one running on NW.js, with a few slight differences. In figure 1.9, you can see how it looks running on OpenSUSE Linux 13.2.

The Hello World Electron example app looks a bit different from the version that runs on a Mac. This is because Mac OS handles displaying menus differently than Windows and Linux apps do. Where menus are attached to app windows on both Microsoft Windows and Linux apps, Mac OS displays a single menu in the OS's toolbar that applies to all app windows, as shown for the Hello World Electron app's Mac OS example in figure 1.10.

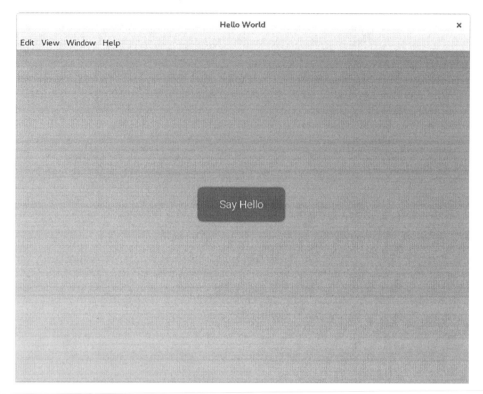

Figure 1.9   The Hello World example app running with Electron on OpenSUSE Linux. Notice how the app displays a menu bar with some menu items by default.

Figure 1.10   Application menu on Mac OS. The application menu for the Hello World example app uses the same default menu items.

If you open the app in Windows 10, you can expect to see a result similar to the one displayed for the Linux app example, as shown in figure 1.11.

The Hello World app with Electron and Windows 10 again looks quite similar to the app equivalents on Linux and Mac OS, minus where the application menu is displayed. The ability to write an app and have it work across three different OSs is a nice feature to have, though, and it's one of the reasons why developers have been flocking to Electron for their desktop apps.

Besides what's been shown so far, Electron has some other features to offer that make it a compelling choice, described in the next section.

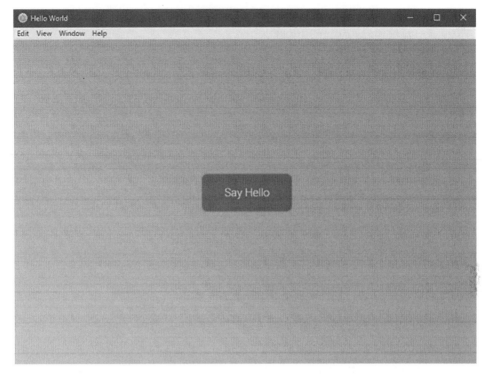

Figure 1.11 The Hello World app running on Electron and Windows 10. Like the Linux app example, the Windows example displays a menu in the app window.

1.4.3 What features does Electron have?

Although Electron is relatively young, it has managed to accumulate a number of useful APIs and features for building desktop apps:

- Creating multiple application windows with ease, each with its own JavaScript context
- Integrating with desktop OS features through the shell and screen APIs
- Tracking the power status of the computer
- Blocking the OS from going into power-saving mode (useful for presentation apps)
- Creating tray apps
- Creating menus and menu items
- Adding global keyboard shortcuts to the app
- Updating the app's code automatically through app updates
- Reporting crashes

- Customizing Dock menu items
- Operating system notifications
- Creating setup installers for your app

As you can see, a lot of features are on offer, and that isn't an exhaustive list of all of the framework's features. In particular, the crash-reporting feature is unique to Electron—there's currently no equivalent to it in NW.js. Electron has also recently come up with dedicated tools for app testing and debugging, called Spectron and Devtron, covered in later chapters.

> **A COOL WAY TO EXPLORE ELECTRON'S FEATURE SET** Demonstrating what Electron does and how it does it, the team behind Electron created a desktop app for demoing Electron's APIs. It's a neat way to browse through Electron's APIs in a practical fashion, and can be downloaded from http://electron.atom.io/#get-started.

The next section looks at what apps can be made with NW.js and Electron.

1.5 What apps can you make with NW.js and Election?

Although Electron and NW.js are relatively young in terms of software, their use in professional cases is rich and varied. On the NW.js GitHub repository, there's a long list of example apps that have been built with NW.js, and for Electron there's the Awesome Electron GitHub repository providing a long list of apps and resources at https://github.com/sindresorhus/awesome-electron. In this section, I discuss a couple of well-known examples that have been commercially successful, as well as ones that demonstrate the potential for what Electron and NW.js can do. We'll start with one of the biggest success cases for Electron: Slack.

1.5.1 Slack

Slack (slack.com) is a workplace communication and collaboration tool for businesses. Slack uses Electron to provide the desktop app and is advertising jobs for desktop app engineers who have experience with using Electron. The desktop user interface (UI) is practically identical to the web app interface—a shining example of what Electron can achieve. The app has expanded its feature set to allow for audio and video calls. Figure 1.12 shows Slack in use (note, I blanked out some of the message content and channels for privacy reasons).

Slack recently expanded its offering with support for an app directory for Slack, allowing users to install third-party apps that run inside Slack. The company seems to have a good future ahead.

Figure 1.12   Slack running on Mac OS

1.5.2   Light Table

Light Table (lighttable.com) is a code editor that takes a different approach to the IDE. It was developed by Chris Granger and raised over $300,000 through a campaign on Kickstarter. It was also the first third-party usage of NW.js and was credited with helping promote the framework in the early days of the project.

The code editor initially supported Clojure but went on to support JavaScript and Python. The philosophy behind Light Table was to rethink how to approach the task of editing code. Rather than having to think of code as lines within files, the focus should be on providing a kind of workspace in which the code is executed live, and documentation is displayed in place rather than searched for in another window, as shown in figure 1.13. It was meant to be a kind of workspace for the developer to be able to write code and see the results immediately, rather than in isolation. Originally made with NW.js, it was recently ported to Electron.

Figure 1.13   Light Table, a live interactive code editor. A 3D visualization written in JavaScript is being edited in the left-hand panel, and the results are being rendered live in the right-hand panel.

1.5.3   Game Dev Tycoon

Game Dev Tycoon is a simulation game in the spirit of old simulations like Transport Tycoon and SimCity, but in this case themed around running a game development studio (an irony, given that it was created by a game development company). Behind it is a small company called Greenheart Games, founded in July 2012 by Patrick and Daniel Klug.

The game was unique (and even more ironic) in its attempts to fight off piracy. Patrick anticipated that the game would eventually be pirated and countered this by releasing a cracked copy of the game onto Torrent sites, but with an interesting twist: people playing the game would find themselves losing in the game. As they played the game, they would find that suddenly their games would stop making money, because they were being pirated. Eventually they would go bankrupt as a result and lose. This antipiracy tactic attracted a lot of amusement and attention.

Since its founding, the company has grown to five employees, and the game is being sold on the Steam game store. Shown in figure 1.14, it's one of the best showcases for using NW.js to build a successful commercial project.

Figure 1.14   Game Dev Tycoon, a game studio simulator

1.5.4   *Gitter*

Gitter is a service that provides chat rooms for open source projects on GitHub, including the official chat room for NW.js. It allows users to sign in with a GitHub account and to then access chat rooms based on projects and organizations. It's seen as a popular alternative to Slack.

As a chat service, Gitter is available both via its website (gitter.im), as well as via desktop apps for Windows and Mac OS, which are built using NW.js. The app's look and feel is an exact replica of what you see in the web app and well demonstrates the principle of code reuse. During the beta period, Gitter attracted almost 25,000 developers to the service, delivering over 1.8 million messages, and is currently hosting over 7,000 chat rooms. It now offers paid plans for chat rooms, and the company is working on getting a version of the app to run on Linux as well.

The main chat room for NW.js can be found on Gitter, a nice example of a product being used to support itself (figure 1.15).

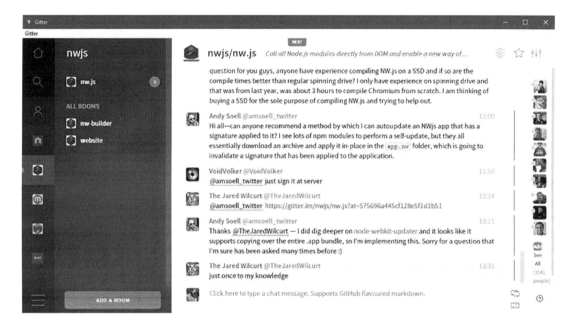

Figure 1.15   Gitter, a chat room client that's integrated into GitHub

1.5.5   *Macaw*

Macaw (macaw.co) is an innovative WYSIWYG web design tool. It allows web designers to create a visual design for their websites, as they would normally do in an image editor, and generates the underlying HTML and CSS for that design. It helps eliminate the step of converting a visual design into a real website by automatically creating the website code. As a WYSIWYG web design tool, Macaw differs from predecessors like Microsoft FrontPage and Adobe Dreamweaver by outputting semantic HTML and CSS from the visual design.

Founded by Tom Giannattasio and Adam Christ, the product (figure 1.16) was funded through a Kickstarter campaign that raised over $275,000 from more than 2,700 backers. Since March 2014, Macaw has gone on to become a product sold directly through Macaw's website.

Since I began writing the book, I'm pleased to say that Macaw was acquired by another web design application company called InVision—yet another example of a real-world desktop app becoming a success story.

Figure 1.16   Macaw, a WYSIWYG web design tool that lets designers create websites using visual design features

1.5.6   *Hyper*

Hyper (hyper.is) is a minimal-looking terminal app authored by Guillermo Rauch, a well-known figure in the Node.js community for his work on the Node.js websocket library, Socket.io, and for the real-time hosting service Now. As a terminal app written in HTML, CSS, and JavaScript, Hyper is an extensible app that can be configured to look and behave in lots of different ways. Developers have created plugins (such as hyperpower) that animate the text as it's typed into the app and enable users to open URLs from within the terminal window. Figure 1.17 shows Hyper in use.

It's one of the more unique types of desktop apps reimagined with Electron and shows Electron's minimal style title bar in use.

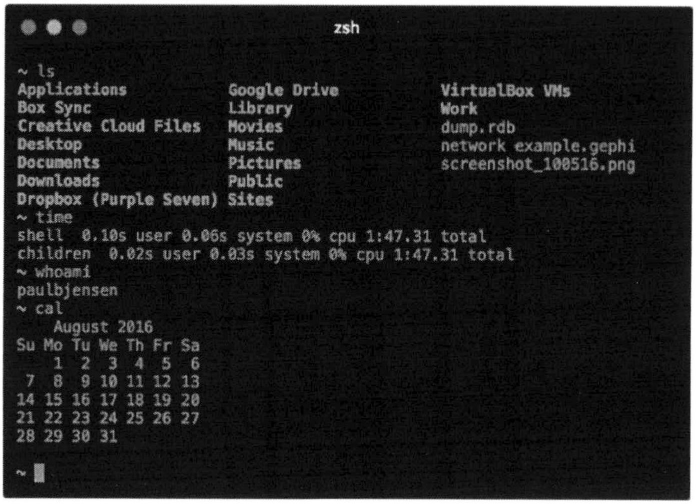

```
● ● ●                        zsh

~ ls
Applications              Google Drive          VirtualBox VMs
Box Sync                  Library               Work
Creative Cloud Files      Movies                dump.rdb
Desktop                   Music                 network example.gephi
Documents                 Pictures              screenshot_100516.png
Downloads                 Public
Dropbox (Purple Seven)    Sites
~ time
shell  0.10s user 0.06s system 0% cpu 1:47.31 total
children  0.02s user 0.03s system 0% cpu 1:47.31 total
~ whoami
paulbjensen
~ cal
      August 2016
Su Mo Tu We Th Fr Sa
    1  2  3  4  5  6
 7  8  9 10 11 12 13
14 15 16 17 18 19 20
21 22 23 24 25 26 27
28 29 30 31
~ █
```

Figure 1.17   Hyper running on Mac OS

1.6   Summary

This chapter introduced you to NW.js and Electron and explained how they help web developers build desktop apps. We explored reasons why you might want to prefer Node.js desktop apps over building a web app, and how those frameworks help web developers by letting them use the same tools and technologies they're already familiar with.

We then looked at the way that a simple Hello World app works and looks with different frameworks, across different OSs. This gave you a chance to understand how easy it is to take a web page and turn it into a desktop app.

We examined the features that make NW.js and Electron great frameworks for desktop app development, such as their use of the popular Node.js framework and the npm ecosystem, and the way they provide native executables for the different OSs from a single codebase. Finally, we explored a couple of real-life examples of NW.js and Electron in the wild and saw how apps have been successful in their own domains. This shows you what's possible with Node.js desktop apps, and hopefully provides inspiration for any app ideas that you have.

In the next chapter, we'll get our hands dirty and start building a file explorer desktop app with both NW.js and Electron. This will help you understand how you go about building desktop apps with those frameworks as well as how they compare in their approaches to desktop app development.

Laying the foundation for your first desktop application

This chapter covers

- Building a file explorer in both NW.js and Electron
- Setting up your application
- Structuring your application's files
- Understanding how the user interface of the application works
- Accessing the filesystem in Node.js

As developers, we often forget how lucky we are to work in an industry where the tools are readily available and free or relatively inexpensive to get ahold of. In this chapter, we'll get to grips with building desktop applications through creating a file explorer application. We'll look at how the app is built with both NW.js and Electron so that we can compare and contrast the ways in which they approach desktop applications.

Grab a cup of tea or coffee, a pen and paper, and settle in for some programming.

2.1 What we're going to build

Whether you use a Windows PC, a Mac, or Linux, there are a few things common to all of them—they store files organized in folders, and they all have their own take on how to organize files in folders, as well as how you find and display those files to the user. This isn't a problem for people who use only one OS, but those who have to learn to use a new OS (such as when going to work at a new organization) can struggle to get their head around how to do simple tasks like rename a folder, or find out where the file that they saved to their computer is located.

It feels fitting to approach the idea of making a file explorer that works the same across all OSs, so that's what we'll build: a file explorer.

2.1.1   *Introducing Lorikeet, the file explorer*

There's a common joke in developer circles that says naming things is the second hard problem in computer science (caching being the first hard problem). Sometimes it's nice to take inspiration from nature, so we'll name the file explorer Lorikeet, after the colorful native Australian bird.

Lorikeet is a file explorer with the following goals:

- Allow users to browse folders and find files
- Allow users to open the file(s) with their default app

These are relatively simple goals, but implementing features to support them will provide enough scope to help you become familiar with building a desktop application. Building Lorikeet will also help demonstrate the different approaches that NW.js and Electron offer for developing desktop applications.

Building a desktop application is a lengthy process consisting of many steps: constructing user journeys, creating wireframes, writing tests, fleshing out the wireframes, writing code, and making sure that the app works as intended. For the sake of learning about NW.js and Electron, we'll work off of the basis that we have some user journeys and wireframes for the file explorer and focus on building a functional version of it.

You'll flesh out the features in the wireframes one by one, which helps to provide a natural flow to building the app, and gives you a chance to see where the code lives and what it does. Figure 2.1 shows a wireframe.

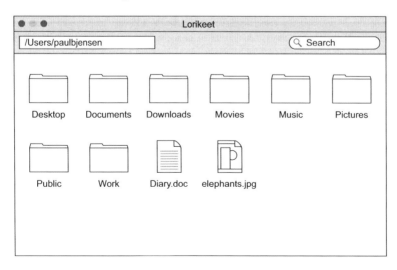

**Figure 2.1
Wireframe of the
file explorer app
you'll build**

With this wireframe, you take the app and break it down into separate features, helping you to implement the app one feature at a time. The first feature to work on is where the user begins to use the app—in this case, the start screen. But before you can do that, you need to create an app to store the code in.

2.2 Creating the app

As you saw in chapter 1, it's relatively easy to get started with creating desktop applications with either NW.js or Electron. Regardless of which framework you begin to build the app with, you'll need to have Node.js installed (a quick and simple process you can do in a minute). To see how to install Node.js on your computer, see "Installing Node.js" in the appendix.

Once you have Node.js installed on your computer, the next step is to install both of the desktop application frameworks on your computer (if you haven't already).

2.2.1 Installing NW.js and Electron

If you've already installed NW.js and Electron as explained in chapter 1, please skip to section 2.2.2. If not, you can run the following commands in the Terminal. For NW.js, run the following command to install NW.js as a global module:

```
npm install -g nw
```

For Electron, run the following command to install Electron as a global module:

```
npm install -g electron
```

Once they're installed, you can proceed to build the NW.js version of the Lorikeet application.

2.2.2 Creating the files and folders for the NW.js-powered app

The next step is to create a folder that will store the code for your app. Choose a location on your computer where you like to store your code work, and run the following command to create a folder named lorikeet-nwjs:

```
mkdir lorikeet-nwjs
```

Once the folder (or directory, as some developers call it) is created, the next step is to create a package.json file for the app. This is Node.js's equivalent of a *manifest* file, where you store configuration information for the app. First, create the file inside the application folder:

```
cd lorikeet-nwjs
touch package.json
```

Running on Windows?

If so, there isn't a `touch` command. What you can do instead is simply create the file using a code editor such as Notepad++ or even GitHub's Atom.

Now that you have a package.json file that you can edit, you can use whatever text editor you like to open the package.json file and insert the following code into it:

```
{
  "name": "lorikeet",
  "version": "1.0.0",
  "main": "index.html"
}
```

The package.json file follows the same conventions used for creating modules that are then used in Node.js applications via npm. The `name` field has the name of the application, and must not contain spaces. The `version` field contains the version of the software, which we call 1.0.0 in accordance with a versioning format known as *semantic versioning* (also known as *SemVer*). The `main` field is used to tell NW.js what file to load when it's booted—in this case, the index.html file. These are the minimum requirements that NW.js has for the package.json file before it can load an application. You haven't yet created the web page that's loaded by NW.js, so you should probably create that next.

The index.html file is a pretty standard example for the moment. To create it, run the following command in your command-line tool (or create the file with Notepad++/Atom in Windows):

```
touch index.html
```

Once that's done, using your favorite text editor, insert the code in the following listing into the index.html file.

Listing 2.1 Adding the index.html file's contents for the NW.js app

```
<html>
  <head>
    <title>Lorikeet</title>
  </head>
  <body>
    <h1>Welcome to Lorikeet</h1>
  </body>
</html>
```

Now that the index.html file is created, you're in a position to make NW.js run the app. To do that, simply run the following command in the Terminal, or your Command Prompt/PowerShell in Windows:

```
nw
```

This will load the NW.js app. Because no further arguments were passed to the command, NW.js will inspect the files located in the current working directory where the command was run (in this case, the lorikeet-nwjs folder) and search for a package.json file. When it finds the package.json file, it will then load that file. The package.json file's `main` field will indicate to NW.js to load the index.html file in the app, which it then does, and you should see the screen shown in figure 2.2.

Figure 2.2   NW.js running a bare-minimum app. The app displays the contents of the index.html file, which means it's working as expected so far. Later in the chapter, you'll replace this simple HTML with the UI that makes up the app.

The title of the app window is loaded from the value inside the `<title>` element in the index.html file. You can edit the value of that field, save the change to the file, and run the application again from the command line to see the changes.

> **Can I load the index.html file in a web browser?**
> You can try, but any code that's calling out to NW.js's APIs or to Node.js code will result in a JavaScript error, so it's best not to. Even though NW.js apps appear to be running inside an embedded web browser, the app is more sophisticated because it has access to both Node.js/NW.js APIs and the DOM in the same JavaScript context.

With one folder and two files in that folder, you have the main skeleton code that will get a bare-bones version of the application up and running. At this point, you can adjust the contents of the index.html file to change the UI that's displayed by the application, but before you do any more on the NW.js version of the application, let's take a look at how you can achieve the same bare-bones application version with Electron.

2.2.3   Creating the files and folders for the Electron-powered app

The Electron version of the application starts off very much in the same fashion. You'll begin by creating a folder named lorikeet-electron. You can do this by running this command in the Terminal/Command Prompt:

```
mkdir lorikeet-electron
```

This will create a folder named lorikeet-electron. This is the main application folder for the application, and inside it will be the application's files. Now you'll create the next file needed by the application, the package.json file. In your terminal or via your text editor, create a file named package.json inside the lorikeet-electron folder:

```
cd lorikeet-electron
touch package.json
```

Once you have an empty package.json file, you'll move on to populating the file with the configuration needed by Electron. Inside the package.json file, add the following JSON configuration:

```
{
  "name": "lorikeet",
  "version": "1.0.0",
  "main": "main.js"
}
```

The package.json file looks almost identical to the package.json file used by the NW.js version of the application, with one exception: the main property is different. In NW.js, the file that's loaded is an HTML file. In Electron, the file that's loaded is a JavaScript file. The file you load in the case of the Electron version of the application is called main.js.

The main.js file is responsible for loading the Electron application and any browser windows that it will display as part of that application. In your terminal or your text editor, create the file main.js and insert the following content.

Listing 2.2 The main.js file for the Electron app

```
'use strict';

const electron = require('electron');        ◁── Electron is loaded via npm
const app = electron.app;
const BrowserWindow = electron.BrowserWindow;

let mainWindow = null;                        ◁──

app.on('window-all-closed',() => {            ◁──
  if (process.platform !== 'darwin') app.quit();
});

app.on('ready', () => {
  mainWindow = new BrowserWindow();
  mainWindow.loadURL(`file://${app.getAppPath()}/index.html`);
  mainWindow.on('closed', () => { mainWindow = null; });
});
```

mainWindow variable keeps application's main window in JavaScript context, so garbage collection, which would close application window, doesn't remove it

Mimics UX of Windows and Linux applications — closing only application window for app quits app; on Mac OS, closing application window doesn't close app

When app is ready to run, tells main window to load index.html, and when that window is closed, sets mainWindow variable to null

The main.js file will result in loading the index.html file. Here, you create the index.html file and put the following contents into it:

```html
<html>
  <head>
    <title>Lorikeet</title>
  </head>
  <body>
    <h1>Welcome to Lorikeet</h1>
  </body>
</html>
```

Once you've saved the index.html file, you're in a position to run the Electron application from the command line. Go to the Terminal or Command Prompt and type the following command inside the lorikeet-electron folder to run the application:

```
cd lorikeet-electron
electron .
```

If you run the application now, you should see something like figure 2.3.

Figure 2.3   The Lorikeet app running on Electron. This is what Electron apps look like by default—pretty much like the NW.js variant.

The Electron app looks almost identical to the NW.js app. The index.html file is exactly the same as the one used for the NW.js variant of the Lorikeet app, and to load the application from the command line is practically the same.

Having built the Lorikeet app's bare-bones application structure in both NW.js and Electron, you can see that they share some similar coding conventions—after all, as mentioned, Cheng Zhao worked on both NW.js and Electron. But they differ in terms of how they go about loading the app.

So far, I've shown you how to build and set up the Lorikeet app's skeleton of files and folders with both frameworks. The next stage is to start working on the first feature of the application that the user sees, as shown back in figure 2.1.

We'll continue to compare and contrast the approaches taken with both frameworks but share code where it's possible.

2.3   *Implementing the start screen*

The start screen has a number of components to it. We'll start with the display of the personal folder, as shown in figure 2.4.

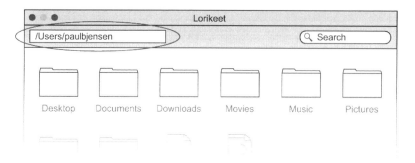

Figure 2.4   The Lorikeet wireframe. Notice the circled item in the wireframe. This is the item you want to build first.

This is the first feature you'll flesh out in the UI and then implement in both versions of the Lorikeet app.

2.3.1   *Displaying the user's personal folder in the toolbar*

Three parts comprise this feature:

- The HTML that makes up the toolbar and the personal folder
- The CSS that applies the layout and styling of the toolbar and the personal folder
- The JavaScript that will discover what the user's personal folder is and display it in the UI

The good news is that the HTML, CSS, and even the JavaScript needed for this feature are exactly the same in both the NW.js and Electron versions of the Lorikeet app. In this case, you'll be able to show it once but use the same code in both applications. Let's start with the HTML.

ADDING THE HTML FOR THE TOOLBAR AND PERSONAL FOLDER

The index.html file is the main screen for both the NW.js and Electron versions of our applications. For both versions of the application, open the index.html file in a text editor and change it to what you see in the next listing.

> **Listing 2.3   Adding the toolbar and personal folder HTML to the index.html file**

```
<html>
  <head>
    <title>Lorikeet</title>
  </head>
```

```
<body>
    <div id="toolbar">
        <div id="current-folder"></div>
    </div>
</body>
</html>
```

Replaces welcome message with HTML for toolbar and personal folder

Once you've done this for both applications, we can move on to creating the CSS stylesheets that will manage the layout and styling of the toolbar and personal folder.

ADDING THE CSS FOR THE TOOLBAR AND PERSONAL FOLDER

Styling desktop applications is no different than styling web pages. CSS can be embedded inside the HTML for a page, but it's better to put it into a separate file so that you can see all the CSS styling in one place, as well as keep the index.html file readable.

Start by creating a file in the application called app.css at the same folder level as the index.html file. Next, add the CSS in the following listing to the app.css file.

Listing 2.4 Adding the toolbar and personal folder CSS to the app.css file

```
body {
    padding: 0;
    margin: 0;
    font-family: 'Helvetica','Arial','sans';
}

#toolbar {
    position: absolute;
    background: red;
    width: 100%;
    padding: 1em;
}

#current-folder {
    float: left;
    color: white;
    background: rgba(0,0,0,0.2);
    padding: 0.5em 1em;
    min-width: 10em;
    border-radius: 0.2em;
}
```

Now, you need to make sure that the app.css file will be loaded by the index.html file. In the index.html file, add a line to the index.html file so that it reads like the following listing.

Listing 2.5 Adding the app.css link tag to the index.html file

```
<html>
  <head>
    <title>Lorikeet</title>
    <link rel="stylesheet" href="app.css" />
  </head>
```

Links tag that loads app.css file in index.html file

```
<body>
  <div id="toolbar">
      <div id="current-folder"></div>
  </div>
</body>
</html>
```

After you've saved the index.html file with this change, you can either reload the NW.js and Electron applications (if you have them open and running) or load them again from the Terminal/Command Prompt with this:

```
cd lorikeet-electron && electron .
cd lorikeet-nwjs && nw
```

Once you have reloaded the applications with the new code, you'll see that the UI is starting to take shape, as shown in figures 2.5 and 2.6.

Figure 2.5   The Lorikeet NW.js app with the toolbar and personal folder. The personal folder listing is blank, but we'll get around to making it appear soon.

Figure 2.6   The Lorikeet Electron app with the toolbar and personal folder

The toolbar and the personal folder are visible and styled, but what remains is to be able to discover what the path for the user's personal folder is and display that in the UI. This is the next step we'll take.

DISCOVERING THE USER'S PERSONAL FOLDER WITH NODE.JS

To display the path of the user's personal folder, you need a way to discover it, one that works across all OSs. On Mac OS, the user's personal folder tends to be located in the /Users/<username> folder with their username (mine is /Users/pauljensen). On Linux, the user's personal folder tends to be in the /home/<username> folder, and on Windows 10 the it's located in the C: drive under the Users/<username> folder. If only OSs operated in a common, standard fashion!

Thankfully, this is accommodated in Node.js's ecosystem on npm packages. An npm module called osenv by Isaac Schlueter (former Node.js lead maintainer and the founder of npm) has a function that discovers and returns the user's personal folder (or home folder, as it's also known). To use this, you need to install the npm module in the application. Run the following command in the Terminal or Command Prompt to install the library (make sure to do this for both versions of the Lorikeet app):

```
npm install osenv --save
```

The --save flag at the end of the command tells the npm command to add the module as a dependency in the package.json manifest file. If you open the package.json manifest file (say, in this case, for the NW.js variant of the application), you'll see the change, as shown next.

Listing 2.6 The modified package.json file

```
{
  "name": "lorikeet",
  "version": "1.0.0",            The new dependencies property,
  "main": "index.html",          with osenv listed as module
  "dependencies": {              dependency for app
    "osenv": "^0.1.3"
  }
}
```

You'll also notice that there's a new folder that appears in the application folders for both applications, a folder called node_modules. This folder contains any locally installed npm modules that are installed for the application. If you browse the node_modules folder, you'll see a folder named osenv. This is where the osenv module's code has been installed.

With the osenv module installed, you now want to load the user's personal folder and display it in the personal folder UI element in the index.html file. This demonstrates one of the unique aspects of NW.js and Electron as Node.js desktop application frameworks: you can execute Node.js code directly in the index.html file. Don't believe me? Try this. Modify the index.html file so that the code looks like the next listing.

Listing 2.7 Displaying the user's personal folder to the index.html file

```
<html>
  <head>
    <title>Lorikeet</title>               Loads osenv module via
    <link rel="stylesheet" href="app.css" />   Node.js's require function,
  </head>                                  then calls the home function
  <body>                                   on the library, and the
    <div id="toolbar">                     resulting value is written
      <div id="current-folder">            into the DOM by
        <script>                           document.write
          document.write(require('osenv').home());
        </script>
      </div>
    </div>
  </body>
</html>
```

Make sure the index.html file is changed to this in both the NW.js and Electron versions of the Lorikeet app.

After you save the files, reload the applications using the technique shown earlier:

```
cd lorikeet-electron && electron .
cd lorikeet-nwjs && nw
```

You can expect to see your personal folder listed in the personal folder UI element of the app, as shown in figures 2.7 and 2.8.

Figure 2.7   The user's personal folder displayed in the Lorikeet
NW.js app

Figure 2.7 is impressive. You can call Node.js directly in a script tag in the index.html file. How about Electron? Does it do the same? Check out figure 2.8.

Figure 2.8   The user's personal folder displayed in the Lorikeet Electron app

It does. Not only have you been able to call Node.js code inside a script tag in the index.html file, but you've been able to use a Node.js module from npm in the front-end part of your code. Plus, you've been able to use identical code across both NW.js and Electron so far, which goes to show how compatible they are, as well as why some projects have been so successful in being ported from NW.js to Electron (such as Light Table, for example).

Now that you've implemented the display of the user's personal folder in the toolbar, we should move on to implementing the next feature in the UI: the display of the user's files and folders in their personal folder.

2.3.2   *Showing the user's files and folders in the UI*

In the preceding section, we started off by creating the UI elements first and then populated the user's personal folder path in the UI element. For this feature, we'll work on getting ahold of a list of the user's files and folders first and then figure out from there how we display them in the UI of the application. For a quick reminder, figure 2.9 shows the UI element we're looking to implement.

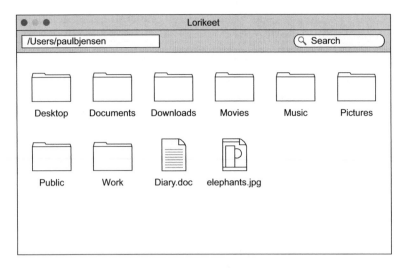

Figure 2.9   The UI element we're looking to implement next in the app

To implement this UI feature, you need to do the following:

1 Get the list of files and folders at the user's personal folder path
2 For each file/folder listing, find out if it's a file or a folder
3 Pass that list of files/folders to the UI to be rendered as files with icons

You already have a way to get at the user's personal folder path. Now what you need is a way to get ahold of the list of files and folders at that path. Luckily for you, Node.js implements a standard library for querying the computer's filesystem, called `fs`. One of the functions available to get a list of files and folders is the `readdir` function, as documented at http://mng.bz/YR5B.

For both the NW.js and Electron versions of the Lorikeet app, you'll create an app.js file. This file will contain JavaScript code that can call Node.js as well as interact with the DOM. You'll use this file to help store the code that will display the list of files for you.

First, create an app.js file at the same folder level as the index.html and app.css files. Next, you'll move the code that loads the user's personal folder path into it. Add the following code to the app.js file:

```
'use strict';

const osenv = require('osenv');

function getUsersHomeFolder() {
  return osenv.home();
}
```

After adding the code to the app.js file, the next step is to include the app.js file as a script tag in the index.html and call the `getUsersHomeFolder` method in the DOM in place of the current call to the osenv module's home function. Change the index.html file so that it looks like the next listing.

Listing 2.8   Adding the app.js file to the index.html file

```
<html>
  <head>
    <title>Lorikeet</title>
    <link rel="stylesheet" href="app.css" />
    <script src="app.js"></script>                    Includes app.js as
  </head>                                              script tag in index.html
  <body>
    <div id="toolbar">
      <div id="current-folder">
        <script>
          document.write(getUsersHomeFolder());        Calls app.js's getUsersHomeFolder
        </script>                                       function in place of direct call to
      </div>                                            Osenv module's home function
    </div>
  </body>
</html>
```

If you reload the applications, you'll see that they behave the same, which is exactly what you want. You can now start to add code to the app.js file for getting the list of the files. You'll start by requiring Node.js's filesystem module, which comes as part of Node.js's standard library, and then adding a new function called `getFilesIn-Folder` that will retrieve the files in the folder passed to it. After that, you'll create a function called `main` that will pass the user's personal folder into that function, and from the resulting list of files log the absolute paths for them out in the console.

Change the code in the app.js file so that it looks like the following.

Listing 2.9   Logging the list of files and folders in the user's personal folder

```
'use strict';

const fs = require('fs');              Node.js's fs module
const osenv = require('osenv');        loads in the app

function getUsersHomeFolder() {
  return osenv.home();
}
                                       Simple wrapper around
                                       the fs.readdir function
                                       for getting list of files
function getFilesInFolder(folderPath, cb) {
  fs.readdir(folderPath, cb);
}
                                       Function that combines user's
                                       personal folder path with
function main() {                      getting its list of files
  const folderPath = getUsersHomeFolder();
  getFilesInFolder(folderPath, (err, files) => {
    if (err) {
      return alert('Sorry, we could not load your home folder');
    }
```

Simple message to display in case of error loading folder's files

```
    files.forEach((file) => {
      console.log(`${folderPath}/${file}`);        ◁──┐  For each file in list, logs full
    });                                               │  path for file to console
  });
}

main();
```

After saving the app.js file, the next step is to see what happens when you run the code. Reload the application. In the case of Electron, if you toggle showing the developer tools for the application, you can expect to see the list of files in the Console tab, as shown in figure 2.10.

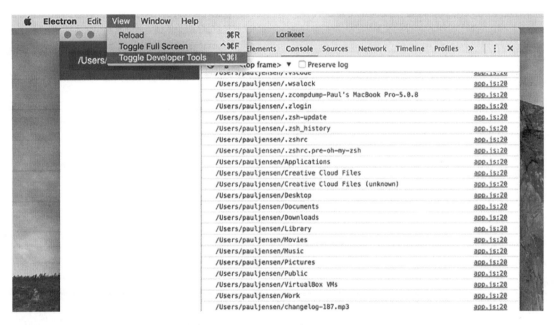

Figure 2.10 The Lorikeet Electron app showing the list of files being logged to the Console tab. To see the list of files on your computer, click View > Toggle Developer Tools.

You now know that you can get at the list of files in the user's personal folder. The next challenge is to figure out what the name and file/folder type is for each file in the list and to then display these items in the UI as a list of files and folders with icons.

Your goal is to be able to take a list of files and pass them through another function in Node.js's file system API. This will identify whether they're files or directories, as well as what their names and full file paths are. Do the following:

1 Use the `fs.stat` function method, as documented at http://mng.bz/46U5.
2 Use the async module to handle calling a series of asynchronous functions and collecting their results.
3 Pass the list of results to another function that will handle their display.

In the app.js file for both variants of the Lorikeet app, install the async module via the Terminal or Command Prompt:

```
npm install async --save
```

After installing the async module to both applications, the next step is to change the app.js code so that it will detect what the files in the user's personal folder are. Change the code to that shown next.

Listing 2.10   Changing the app.js code to detect file types

```
'use strict';

const async = require('async');
const fs = require('fs');
const osenv = require('osenv');
const path = require('path');

function getUsersHomeFolder() {
  return osenv.home();
}

function getFilesInFolder(folderPath, cb) {
  fs.readdir(folderPath, cb);
}

function inspectAndDescribeFile(filePath, cb) {
  let result = {
    file: path.basename(filePath),
    path: filePath, type: ''
  };
  fs.stat(filePath, (err, stat) => {
    if (err) {
      cb(err);
    } else {
      if (stat.isFile()) {
        result.type = 'file';
      }
      if (stat.isDirectory()) {
        result.type = 'directory';
      }
      cb(err, result);
    }
  });
}

function inspectAndDescribeFiles(folderPath, files, cb) {
  async.map(files, (file, asyncCb) => {
    let resolvedFilePath = path.resolve(folderPath, file);
    inspectAndDescribeFile(resolvedFilePath, asyncCb);
  }, cb);
}

function displayFiles(err, files) {
  if (err) {
    return alert('Sorry, we could not display your files');
  }
}
```

Includes async and path Node.js modules into app

Uses path module to get name for file

fs.stat call supplies an object you can query to find out file's type

Uses async module to call asynchronous function and collects results together

Creates displayFiles function to be end point where files will end up being displayed

```
      files.forEach((file) => { console.log(file); });
    }
    function main() {
      let folderPath = getUsersHomeFolder();
      getFilesInFolder(folderPath, (err, files) => {
        if (err) {
          return alert('Sorry, we could not load your home folder');
        }
        inspectAndDescribeFiles(folderPath, files, displayFiles);
      });
    }
    main();
```

With the app.js file saved to the computer and the applications reloaded, you'll see something like figure 2.11 in the developer tools.

Not only do you now have the application returning the list of files in the user's personal folder, but you have it in a data structure that has the filename and file type included as well. This sets you up perfectly for the next step in implementing the UI feature: displaying filenames and icons in the application's UI.

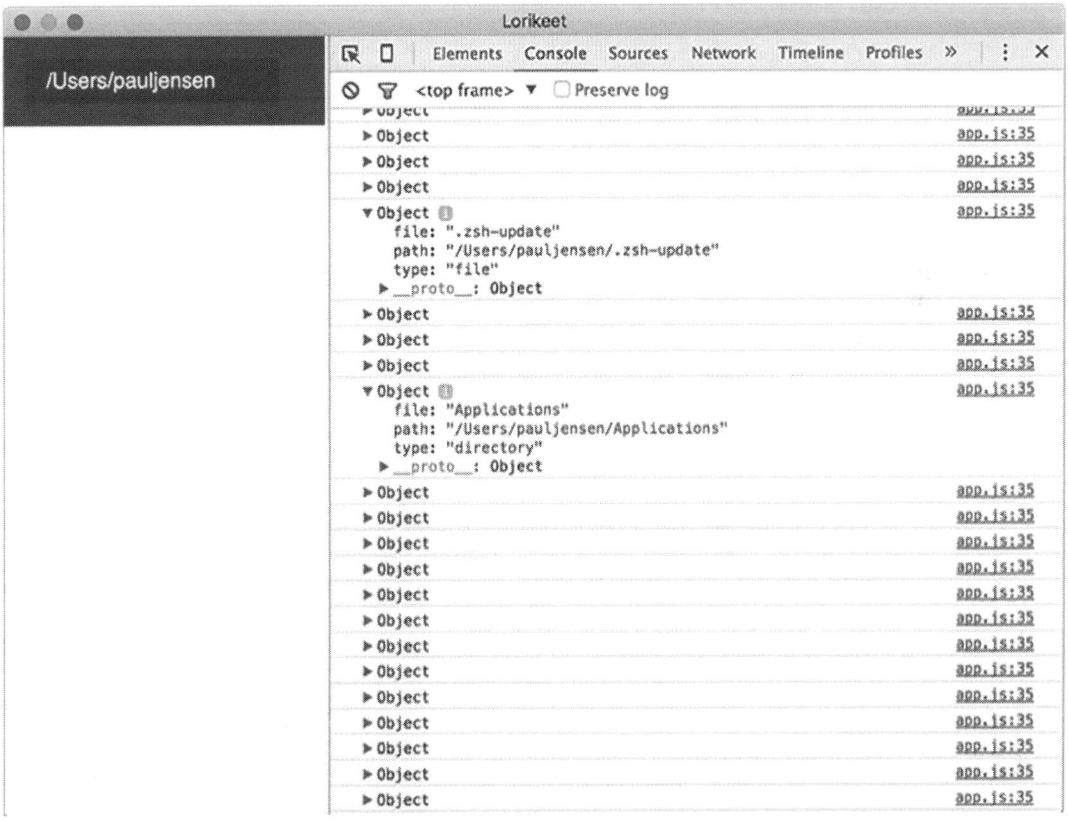

Figure 2.11 The files list in the Console tab of the Developer Tools. Notice how the first expanded object has the type `file`, and the second expanded object has the type `directory`.

VISUALLY DISPLAYING THE FILES AND FOLDERS

In the previous code for the app.js file, you created a function called `displayFiles`. You want to use this function to handle displaying the files as names and icons in the UI. Because there are many files to be rendered in the UI, you'll use an HTML template for each file and then render an instance of that template to the UI.

You'll start by adding the HTML template to the index.html file, as well as a `div` element to contain the files that are being displayed. Change the index.html file so that it looks like the following listing.

Listing 2.11   Adding the file template and main area to the index.html file

```html
<html>
  <head>
    <title>Lorikeet</title>
    <link rel="stylesheet" href="app.css" />
    <script src="app.js"></script>
  </head>
  <body>
    <template id="item-template">        ← Adds template HTML
      <div class="item">                    element to index.html
        <img class="icon" />
        <div class="filename"></div>
      </div>
    </template>
    <div id="toolbar">
      <div id="current-folder">
        <script>
          document.write(getUsersHomeFolder());
        </script>
      </div>
    </div>
      <div id="main-area"></div>         ← Adds a div element with
  </body>                                   ID "main-area" to be
</html>                                     holder for the files
```

The purpose of the template element is to hold a copy of the HTML that you'd like to render for each file, and the `div` element is where the template instances will be rendered and stored for each file that you find in the user's personal folder. You'll then add some JavaScript to the app.js file that will handle creating an instance of the template and adding it to the UI. Adjust the app.js file so that the code reads like the next listing.

Listing 2.12   Rendering the template instances in the UI via the app.js file

```javascript
'use strict';

const async = require('async');
const fs = require('fs');
const osenv = require('osenv');
const path = require('path');
```

```
function getUsersHomeFolder() {
  return osenv.home();
}

function getFilesInFolder(folderPath, cb) {
  fs.readdir(folderPath, cb);
}

function inspectAndDescribeFile(filePath, cb) {
  let result = {
file: path.basename(filePath),
path: filePath, type: ''
  };
  fs.stat(filePath, (err, stat) => {
    if (err) {
      cb(err);
    } else {
      if (stat.isFile()) {
        result.type = 'file';
      }
      if (stat.isDirectory()) {
        result.type = 'directory';
      }
      cb(err, result);
    }
  });
}

function inspectAndDescribeFiles(folderPath, files, cb) {
  async.map(files, (file, asyncCb) => {
    let resolvedFilePath = path.resolve(folderPath, file);
    inspectAndDescribeFile(resolvedFilePath, asyncCb);
  }, cb);
}

function displayFile(file) {
  const mainArea = document.getElementById('main-area');
  const template = document.querySelector('#item-template');
  let clone = document.importNode(template.content, true);
  clone.querySelector('img').src = `images/${file.type}.svg`;
  clone.querySelector('.filename').innerText = file.file;
  mainArea.appendChild(clone);
}

function displayFiles(err, files) {
  if (err) {
    return alert('Sorry, we could not display your files');
  }
  files.forEach(displayFile);
}

function main() {
  let folderPath = getUsersHomeFolder();
  getFilesInFolder(folderPath, (err, files) => {
    if (err) {
      return alert('Sorry, we could not load your home folder');
    }
```

Adds new function called displayFile that handles rendering template instance

Creates copy of template instance

Alters instance to include file's name and icon

Appends template instance to "main-area" div element

Passes files to the displayFile function in the displayFiles function

```
    inspectAndDescribeFiles(folderPath, files, displayFiles);
  });
}
main();
```

Now that HTML is being added to the app to handle the display of the files and the folders in the application, you want to make sure that the list of files and folders look styled and are displayed in a grid fashion. In the app.css file, change the CSS to match the following code.

Listing 2.13   Adding styling to the app.css file for displaying the files

```css
body {
    padding: 0;
    margin: 0;
    font-family: 'Helvetica','Arial','sans';
}

#toolbar {
    top: 0px;
    position: fixed;
    background: red;
    width: 100%;
    z-index: 2;
}

#current-folder {
    float: left;
    color: white;
    background: rgba(0,0,0,0.2);
    padding: 0.5em 1em;
    min-width: 10em;
    border-radius: 0.2em;
    margin: 1em;
}

#main-area {
    clear: both;
    margin: 2em;
    margin-top: 3em;
    z-index: 1;
}

.item {
    position: relative;
    float: left;
    padding: 1em;
    margin: 1em;
    width: 6em;
    height: 6em;
    text-align: center;
}

.item .filename {
    padding-top: 1em;
    font-size: 10pt;
}
```

This CSS will ensure that the items are displayed in a clear and grid-like fashion and that the toolbar will remain in a fixed position, visible above the files in the app as the main area `div` element is scrolled by the user.

You're almost there. All that's left to do is add the icons for the different file types to the application folder. Create a folder called images in the application folders with these commands in either the Terminal or the Command Prompt:

```
cd lorikeet-electron
mkdir images
cd ../lorikeet-nwjs
mkdir images
```

Now, you can add some images for the file and directory icons. Inside the images folder, you'll insert two images named file.svg and directory.svg. The files are sourced from the OpenClipArt.org site from these URLs:

- https://openclipart.org/detail/137155/folder-icon
- https://openclipart.org/detail/83893/file-icon

Save the files in the images folder (under the names file.svg for the file icon and directory.svg for the folder icon) and reload the application, and you should see something like figures 2.12 and 2.13.

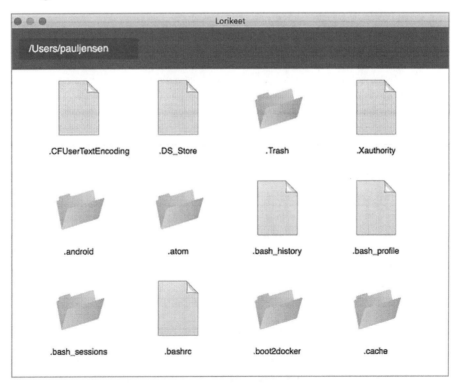

Figure 2.12　The Lorikeet NW.js app showing the files and folders. Here, you see the beginnings of what looks like a file explorer application.

The file type property of the files is used to determine whether the icon is for a file or for a directory. This helps you easily distinguish files from folders. You'll also see that the file/folder names are displayed in alphanumerical order. In figure 2.12, dotfiles and hidden folders can be seen that would otherwise be hidden by other file explorer applications. Figure 2.13 shows the Electron Lorikeet app.

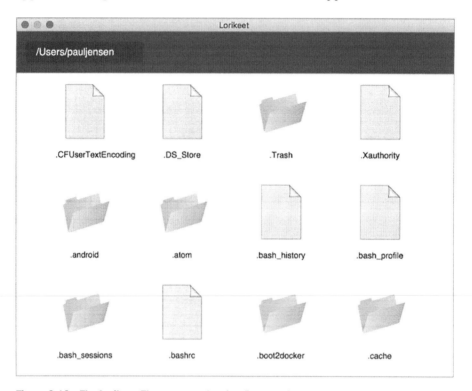

Figure 2.13   The Lorikeet Electron app showing files and folders

The Electron variant of the Lorikeet app looks almost identical to the NW.js version. All in all, the results look good, and that's the end of the exercise for this chapter.

2.4   Summary

In this chapter, you began using NW.js and Electron for building the type of application that many people use with their computers on a daily basis. You've walked through the process of creating the applications from scratch and understand how you can approach the task of building an application feature-by-feature. Here are some of the things the chapter covered:

- The best way to approach a wireframe is to tackle it one feature at a time.
- Good semantics is encouraged as a way to relate features to the underlying code that supports it.

- CSS is the prime way to style UI elements in NW.js and Electron desktop apps.
- You can use Node.js and other third-party libraries with ease in your desktop application.
- The approaches of NW.js and Electron allow for them to use almost the same code, but Electron requires a bit more code and a slightly different configuration in the package.json file.

What's been great is that in using the same code across both NW.js and Electron variants of the Lorikeet app, you've been able to see how similar the desktop application frameworks are, as well as notice the areas where they're different. This should give you the confidence that should you choose one framework for your application and find that it's not the right one for you, then it won't be too difficult to switch to using the other framework.

Another takeaway here is that you're able to use the same skills for building websites as for creating the UI for a desktop application, and that means getting up to speed quickly when building a desktop application.

In the next chapter, we'll expand on the work done here by adding the meaty parts of the application. We'll begin to explore the APIs of NW.js and Electron to add features such as browsing through folders, searching the files and folders by name, and opening files.

Building your first desktop application

Building an app is a journey of creating an initial skeleton of the app and progressively adding to the skeleton until it begins to resemble a complete product. The moment when the product comes alive with features is often, for me, the moment I get excited, and in this chapter those moments shall arrive.

In chapter 2, you began a journey of building a file explorer called Lorikeet and got to a stage where you had the UI for a working desktop application. In this chapter, you'll continue that journey and add features that will result in a file explorer app you can call a minimally viable product.

The goal is that not only will you have made the app's features by the end of the chapter, but you'll understand exactly how Electron and NW.js let you do that. The process will give you enough experience to start using those desktop app frameworks in other places as well. Chances are, your mind will open up with lots of ideas

54

for things you can do that you didn't know how to do before. Excited? Good! Get comfortable and settle in for round two.

3.1 Exploring the folders

The main ingredients for making this happen are now in place: the files and folders for a given path can now be displayed visually in the window. Next you need to build the functionality so that when the user double-clicks a folder in the main area, the app navigates to that folder and displays its contents in the main area.

3.1.1 Refactoring the code

If you look at the app.js file now, you'll notice that it's beginning to look a bit muddled, and at this point it's worth refactoring the code so that it doesn't become overwhelming and difficult to manage. Refactoring the file requires organizing the code into logical groups, as shown in figure 3.1.

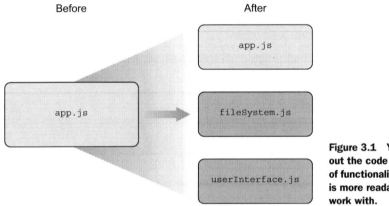

Figure 3.1 You'll start breaking out the code into logical groups of functionality so that the code is more readable and easier to work with.

In figure 3.1, the app.js file will be turned into three files. There will still be an app.js file as the main entry point for the front-end code, but there will also be two other files. The fileSystem.js file will contain code that handles interacting with the files and folders on the user's computer, and the userInterface.js file will hold functions that handle UI interactions. These are two distinct logical groups, and they will allow you to keep the code orderly.

Create two files in the Lorikeet folder at the same level as the app.js file: fileSystem.js and userInterface.js. In the fileSystem.js file, insert the code shown here.

Listing 3.1 The code for the fileSystem.js file

```
'use strict';

const async = require('async');
const fs = require('fs');
const osenv = require('osenv');
const path = require('path');
```

```
function getUsersHomeFolder() {
  return osenv.home();
}

function getFilesInFolder(folderPath, cb) {
  fs.readdir(folderPath, cb);
}

function inspectAndDescribeFile(filePath, cb) {
  let result = { file: path.basename(filePath), path: filePath, type: '' };
  fs.stat(filePath, (err, stat) => {
    if (err) {
      cb(err);
    }        else {
      if (stat.isFile()) {
        result.type = 'file';
      }
      if (stat.isDirectory()) {
        result.type = 'directory';
      }
      cb(err, result);
    }
  });
}

function inspectAndDescribeFiles(folderPath, files, cb) {
  async.map(files, (file, asyncCb) => {
    let resolvedFilePath = path.resolve(folderPath, file);
    inspectAndDescribeFile(resolvedFilePath, asyncCb);
  }, cb);
}

module.exports = {
  getUsersHomeFolder,
  getFilesInFolder,
  inspectAndDescribeFiles
};
```

The fileSystem.js file contains the `getUsersHomeFolder`, `getFilesInFolder`, `inspect-AndDescribeFile`, and `inspectAndDescribeFiles` functions from the app.js file. The extra bit of code at the bottom exposes some of the functions that need to be accessed by other files through the use of the `module.exports` function call, a CommonJS JavaScript convention for exposing public code items in libraries. This is an important factor in the way you organize and make your code usable across multiple projects.

In the userInterface.js file, insert the code shown in the following listing.

Listing 3.2 The code for the userInterface.js file

```
'use strict';

let document;

function displayFile(file) {
  const mainArea = document.getElementById('main-area');
  const template = document.querySelector('#item-template');
```

```
  let clone = document.importNode(template.content, true);
  clone.querySelector('img').src = `images/${file.type}.svg`;
  clone.querySelector('.filename').innerText = file.file;
  mainArea.appendChild(clone);
}

function displayFiles(err, files) {
  if (err) {
    return alert('Sorry, you could not display your files');
  }
  files.forEach(displayFile);
}

function bindDocument (window) {
  if (!document) {
    document = window.document;
  }
}

module.exports = { bindDocument, displayFiles };
```

> **displayFiles function is public function exposed by userInterface.js module**

Here, you expose the `bindDocument` and `displayFiles` functions in the code. The `bindDocument` function is used to pass the `window.document` context to the user-Interface.js file—otherwise, the file will not be able to access the DOM in the NW.js variant of the app (Electron is unaffected). The `displayFiles` function is used to display all the files, and because there's no need to call the `displayFile` function separate from the `displayFiles` function, you don't expose the `displayFile` function as a public API.

Now that the code that was in the app.js file has been moved into the fileSystem.js and userInterface.js files, you can replace the app.js file with the code shown here.

Listing 3.3 The code for the app.js file

```
'use strict';

const fileSystem = require('./fileSystem');
const userInterface = require('./userInterface');

function main() {
  userInterface.bindDocument(window);
  let folderPath = fileSystem.getUsersHomeFolder();
  fileSystem.getFilesInFolder(folderPath, (err, files) => {
    if (err) {
      return alert('Sorry, you could not load your home folder');
    }
    fileSystem.inspectAndDescribeFiles(folderPath, files,
      userInterface.displayFiles);
  });
}

main();
```

The app.js file is now 17 lines of code and is much more readable. Here, you can see that there are two Node.js modules included in the code (fileSystem and userInterface), and that the main function is identical to how it was in the app.js file, with the exception of calling functions from the Node.js modules instead.

The last change left is to alter the index.html file so that the function that calls the user's personal folder is calling the fileSystem file module. Change the index.html file so that it looks like the following code.

Listing 3.4   Changes for the index.html file

```
<html>
  <head>
    <title>Lorikeet</title>
    <link rel="stylesheet" href="app.css" />
    <script src="app.js"></script>
  </head>
  <body>
    <template id="item-template">
      <div class="item">
        <img class="icon" />
        <div class="filename"></div>
      </div>
    </template>
    <div id="toolbar">
      <div id="current-folder">
        <script>
          document.write(fileSystem.getUsersHomeFolder());
        </script>
      </div>
    </div>
    <div id="main-area"></div>
  </body>
</html>
```

Save the changes to the files. The refactoring is almost complete. The next feature you want to add is the ability to navigate folders by double-clicking them in the file explorer.

3.1.2   Handling double-clicks on folders

One of the common features of using a file explorer is navigating folders by double-clicking the folder icon. You'll add this functionality to the Lorikeet app.

When you double-click a folder, the UI of the app updates so that the following things happen:

- The current folder changes to that of the folder that's clicked.
- The files that were displayed in the file explorer are updated to show the files for the folder path that was clicked.
- When you click another folder, the same behavior occurs again.

You also want to make sure that double-clicking a folder behaves as you expect, and that double-clicking a file opens that file in its default application. To achieve that, you'll do the following:

- Create a function in the userInterface.js file called `displayFolderPath`, which will update the current folder path displayed in the UI.
- Add another function in the userInterface.js file called `clearView`, which will remove the files and folders that are currently displayed in the main area.
- Create a function called `loadDirectory`, which will handle querying the computer for the files and folders at a given folder path and then display the files and folders in the main area. This code is effectively moved out of the app.js file.
- Alter the `displayFile` function so that it attaches an event listener to a folder icon to trigger loading that folder.
- Change the app.js file so that it calls the `loadDirectory` function of the user-Interface.js file.
- Remove the script tag inside the `current-folder` element in the index.html file, because it's no longer needed.

In the userInterface.js file, change the code to look like the next listing.

Listing 3.5 Changing the userInterface.js file

```
'use strict';

let document;
const fileSystem = require('./fileSystem');        ⟵┘ Adds fileSystem
                                                       module to use
                                                       its APIs
function displayFolderPath(folderPath) {           ⟵┘ Adds function
  document.getElementById('current-folder').innerText = folderPath;   to display
}                                                                     current folder

function clearView() {                             ⟵┐ Clears items out
  const mainArea = document.getElementById('main-area');   of main-area div
  let firstChild = mainArea.firstChild;                    element
  while (firstChild) {
    mainArea.removeChild(firstChild);
    firstChild = mainArea.firstChild;
  }
}                                                  ┌ loadDirectory changes
function loadDirectory(folderPath) {        ⟵┘    │ current folder path and
  return function (window) {                        updates main area
    if (!document) document = window.document;
    displayFolderPath(folderPath);
    fileSystem.getFilesInFolder(folderPath, (err, files) => {
      clearView();
      if (err) {
        return alert('Sorry, you could not load your folder');
      }
      fileSystem.inspectAndDescribeFiles(folderPath, files, displayFiles);
    });
  };
}
```

```
function displayFile(file) {
  const mainArea = document.getElementById('main-area');
  const template = document.querySelector('#item-template');
  let clone = document.importNode(template.content, true);
  clone.querySelector('img').src = `images/${file.type}.svg`;

  if (file.type === 'directory') {                    ←──────  Adds double-click
    clone.querySelector('img')                                 event listener to icon
      .addEventListener('dblclick', () => {                    if it's for a directory
        loadDirectory(file.path)();
      }, false);
  }

  clone.querySelector('.filename').innerText = file.file;
  mainArea.appendChild(clone);
}

function displayFiles(err, files) {
  if (err) {
    return alert('Sorry, you could not display your files');
  }
  files.forEach(displayFile);
}

function bindDocument (window) {
  if (!document) {
    document = window.document;                           Makes sure
  }                                            loadDirectory function
}                                              is exposed as public API

module.exports = { bindDocument, displayFiles, loadDirectory };  ←──┘
```

Next, amend the app.js file so that it calls the `loadDirectory` function from the user-Interface.js file. Change the app.js file to look like the following code.

Listing 3.6 Changing the app.js file for folder clicks

```
'use strict';

const fileSystem = require('./fileSystem');
const userInterface = require('./userInterface');

function main() {
  userInterface.bindDocument(window);                    Calls userInterface.js
  let folderPath = fileSystem.getUsersHomeFolder();      file's loadDirectory
  userInterface.loadDirectory(folderPath)(window);  ←──┘ function
}
                                            Calls main function after HTML
window.onload = main;                  ←──┘ for app has loaded in window
```

One more change left to do. You can now remove the script tag from inside the current-folder div element. Change the current-folder div element in the index.html file so that it looks like this:

```
<div id="current-folder"></div>
```

With those files changed, reload the app. Now, when you double-click an app folder, you'll see that the folder path changes in the toolbar, and the files and folders on display in the main area change as well. An example of this is shown in Electron in figure 3.2.

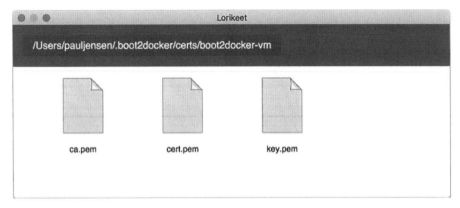

Figure 3.2 **The Lorikeet app in Electron after navigating to a list of files inside of a folder, three levels away from the starting folder path**

And figure 3.3 shows the same result in NW.js with the same file changes.

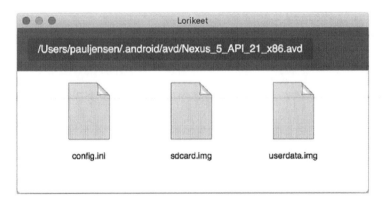

Figure 3.3 **The Lorikeet app in NW.js, navigating to a hidden folder inside of my home folder**

You can see here that you've been able to use plain vanilla JavaScript, HTML, and CSS to implement what is beginning to feel like a real desktop app. So far so good—but it's not mission complete yet. You're going to add quick search functionality to the app.

3.2   Implementing quick search

Figure 3.4 shows a preview of what you'll add next: quick search functionality.

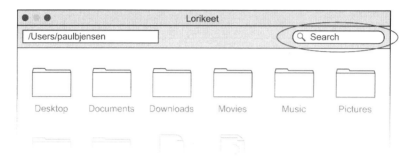

Figure 3.4   The quick search feature that you want to implement in the app

If you have a folder containing lots of files, searching through the entire list of them can be tedious. In the wireframe, the toolbar features a search field in the top right, and to implement an in-directory search feature is relatively easy. You'll need to do the following:

1 Add a search field to the top right of the toolbar.
2 Add an in-memory search library.
3 Add the list of files and folders in the current folder to the search index.
4 When the user begins searching, filter the files displayed in the main area.

3.2.1   Adding the search field in the toolbar

The first thing you need to do is add some HTML for the search field in the top toolbar. Insert the following HTML snippet into the index.html file, after the `current-folder` div element:

```
<input type="search" id="search" results="5" placeholder="Search" />
```

This adds an input tag with the type `search` and some extra attributes that give it the visual style of a search field. The next step is to add the following CSS to the app.css stylesheet:

```
#search {
  float: right;
  padding: 0.5em;
  min-width: 10em;
  border-radius: 3em;
  margin: 2em 1em;
  border: none;
  outline: none;
}
```

Once this is done, the search field appears as shown in figure 3.5.

Figure 3.5 **The search field in the top toolbar, like the wireframe in figure 3.4. Interestingly, the** `results` **attribute on an input element with the type** `search` **inserts a magnifying glass inside the text field.**

3.2.2 Adding an in-memory search library

Now that the search field exists, you need a way to perform searching on the list of files and folders with a searching library. Thankfully, you don't need to write one, as this is a common need that has already been satisfied.

lunr.js is a client-side search library, written by Oliver Nightingale (a colleague of mine when we both worked at New Bamboo, now part of Thoughtbot). It allows you to create an index for the list of the files and folders and perform searches with that index.

You can install lunr.js with npm from the command line:

```
npm install lunr --save
```

This will install lunr.js inside the node_modules folder and save it as a dependency to the package.json file. Now, you need to create a new file at the same level as the app.js file, called search.js. You can create it either on the command line with the command `touch search.js` or via your text editor. Once it exists, add the code shown in the next listing to the search.js file.

Listing 3.7 Inserting code into the search.js file

```
'use strict';

const lunr = require('lunr');          Requires lunr.js as
let index;                             dependency via npm

function resetIndex() {                resetIndex function
  index = lunr(function () {           resets search index
    this.field('file');
    this.field('type');
    this.ref('path');
  });
}

function addToIndex(file) {            Adds file to index for
  index.add(file);                     searching against
}

function find(query, cb) {            Queries index for a
  if (!index) {                        given file here
    resetIndex();
  }
```

```
    const results = index.search(query);
    cb(results);
}
module.exports = { addToIndex, find, resetIndex };
```

Exposes some functions for public API

The code implements three functions: addToIndex allows you to add files to the index, find allows you to query the index, and resetIndex resets the index when you need to view a new folder and clear the existing index. You expose these functions through module.exports so that you can load the file in app.js and access those functions.

Once you've created and saved the search.js file, you need to attach it to the search field in the UI, as well as get it to change what files are displayed in the main area.

3.2.3   *Hooking up the search functionality with the UI*

To have the search field trigger searching the file names, you need to be able to intercept the event of typing the query in the field. You can do this by adding a function to the userInterface.js file called bindSearchField, which will attach an event listener to the search field. In the userInterface.js file, add the following function to the file:

```
function bindSearchField(cb) {
  document.getElementById('search').addEventListener('keyup', cb, false);
}
```

This code will intercept any events where the user has typed in the search field, and the key on the keyboard is back up (hence, the event name keyup). You also add this function to the module.exports object at the bottom of the userInterface.js file so that you can expose it to the app.js file, as shown here:

```
module.exports = { bindDocument, displayFiles, loadDirectory, bindSearchField };
```

This function will be used to attach a function to the search field in the UI that triggers each time the user presses a key on the keyboard while typing into the search field.

Here, you'll inspect the value that exists inside the search field. If it's blank, then you don't want to filter any files. But if it has another value, then you want to filter the files that are displayed in the main area. To achieve that, you need to do the following:

- Before you load a folder path in the main area, you reset the search index.
- When a file is added to the main area, you add it to the search index.
- When the search field is empty, you make sure that all files are on show.
- When the search field has a term, you filter the display of the files based on that term.

But first, you should include the search module at the top of the dependencies list of the userInterface.js file. Change the top of the userInterface.js file so that it looks like this:

```
'use strict';
let document;
const fileSystem = require('./fileSystem');
const search = require('./search');
```

This provides you with access to the search module. Following the inclusion of the search module, the first change you want to make is to the loadDirectory function. You want it to reset the search index every time it's called so it only searches for files that are in the current folder path. Change the loadDirectory function's code to match the next listing.

Listing 3.8 Resetting the search index when calling `loadDirectory`

```
function loadDirectory(folderPath) {
  return function (window) {
    if (!document) document = window.document;
      search.resetIndex();                              Adds the call to reset
    displayFolderPath(folderPath);                      the search index
    fileSystem.getFilesInFolder(folderPath, (err, files) => {
      clearView();
      if (err) {
        return alert('Sorry, you could not load your folder');
      }
      fileSystem.inspectAndDescribeFiles(folderPath, files, displayFiles);
    });
  };
}
```

Once that's done, the next thing you want to adjust is the displayFile function below the loadDirectory function. The function will handle adding the file to the search index as well as making sure that the img element contains a reference to the file's path so that the file can be filtered visually without needing to add/remove elements from the DOM. Change the displayFile function's code to look like the following.

Listing 3.9 Adding files to the search index in the `displayFile` function

```
function displayFile(file) {
  const mainArea = document.getElementById('main-area');
  const template = document.querySelector('#item-template');       Adds file
  let clone = document.importNode(template.content, true);         to search
  search.addToIndex(file);                                         index here
  clone.querySelector('img').src = `images/${file.type}.svg`;
  clone.querySelector('img').setAttribute('data-filePath', file.path);
  if (file.type === 'directory') {
    clone.querySelector('img')
      .addEventListener('dblclick', () => {                Attaches file's path as data
        loadDirectory(file.path)                           attribute to image element
      }, false);
  }
  clone.querySelector('.filename').innerText = file.file;
  mainArea.appendChild(clone);
}
```

Next, add a function for filtering the results visually. This function uses a function to look at the file paths for the files and folders on display in the main area and check whether any of them matches with the search results for the term typed into the search field. After the `bindSearchField` function, add the function shown in the next listing to the userInterface.js file.

Listing 3.10   Adding the `filterResults` function to the userInterface.js file

```
function filterResults(results) {
  const validFilePaths = results.map((result) => { return result.ref; });
  const items = document.getElementsByClassName('item');
  for (var i = 0; i < items.length; i++) {
    let item = items[i];
    let filePath = item.getElementsByTagName('img')[0]
      .getAttribute('data-filepath');
    if (validFilePaths.indexOf(filePath) !== -1) {
      item.style = null;
    } else {
      item.style = 'display:none;';
    }
  }
}
```

Collects file paths for search results so you can compare them

Does file's path match with one of the search results?

If so, make sure file is visible

If not, hide file

You can add a small utility function to handle the case of resetting the filter. This occurs when the search field is blank. Add the following function after the `filter-Results` function that was added to the userInterface.js file:

```
function resetFilter() {
  const items = document.getElementsByClassName('item');
  for (var i = 0; i < items.length; i++) {
    items[i].style = null;
  }
}
```

Here, you use a selector to select all `div` elements that have a CSS class of `item`, and make sure they're visible by removing any custom style attributes that would have marked them as hidden. Also, you want to make sure that the `filterResults` and `resetFilter` functions are publically available via the module API. Change the `module .exports` object at the bottom of the userInterface.js file so that it looks like this:

```
module.exports = {
  bindDocument, displayFiles, loadDirectory,
  bindSearchField, filterResults, resetFilter
};
```

That's all the changes to make to the userInterface.js file for now. Next, turn your attention to the app.js file and change it so that

- It binds on the search field in the user interface.
- It passes the search field's term to the search tool lunr.
- It then passes the results from the search tool back to the UI for rendering.

Change the code in the app.js file so that it looks like the code shown next.

Listing 3.11 Integrating the search feature into the app.js file

```
'use strict';

const fileSystem = require('./fileSystem');
const userInterface = require('./userInterface');     Loads search
const search = require('./search');                   module into app.js

function main() {
  userInterface.bindDocument(window);
  let folderPath = fileSystem.getUsersHomeFolder();
  userInterface.loadDirectory(folderPath)(window);    Listens for changes to
  userInterface.bindSearchField((event) => {          search field's value
    const query = event.target.value;
    if (query === '') {                               If search field is blank,
      userInterface.resetFilter();                    resets filter in UI
    } else {
      search.find(query, userInterface.filterResults);    If search field has a
    }                                                       value, passes it to
  });                                                       search module's find
}                                                           function and filters
                                                            results in UI
window.onload = main;
```

After saving this file along with the previous files, reload the app. The app loads like before, but this time you'll find that when you type a term into the search field, the files and folders in the main area of the app are filtered to show only those that match the search term. If you then type a blank value into the search field, all the files and folders inside the current folder path are shown. Even as you double-click a folder and navigate into it to see its files and folders, the search field will work on that current folder and filter its contents, as shown in figure 3.6.

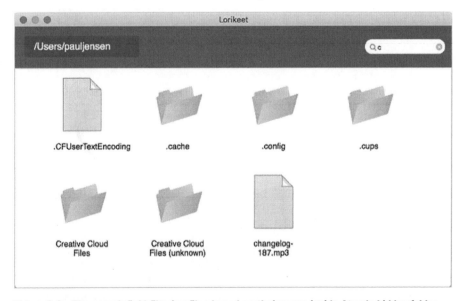

Figure 3.6   The search field filtering files based on their name inside Atom's hidden folder

With about six handcrafted files totaling no more than 281 lines of code and some npm modules, you've managed to build a file explorer. The file explorer can show the files in a folder, traverse the folders, and filter the files based on the name of the file as indicated in the original wireframe. Not bad, given the relatively small size of the code.

Next, you want to improve navigating through the app as well as getting files to open with their default application.

3.3   *Enhancing navigation in the app*

You've gotten to a stage where you can display the contents of the user's personal folder and allow them to traverse through those folders to see what other files and folders exist on their computer, as well as filter the files and folders by a search query. Now you'll help the user navigate backward as well, as there isn't currently a way to do that in the app.

To do this, you'll give the user the ability to navigate the folders via the current folder path—you'll make it a clickable path, with each folder in the path going to that folder's location on the computer.

3.3.1   *Making the current folder path clickable*

Figure 3.7 shows what you want to do.

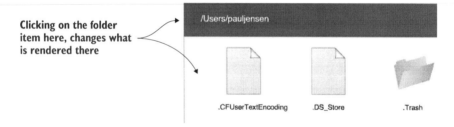

Figure 3.7   When clicking any path in the current folder path in the top toolbar, you want to display the contents of the folder in the main area.

The current folder is currently a line of text that's displayed in the UI in the toolbar, but it can be used to do so much more. In this case, you're looking to change it so that it looks the same as it looks now but allows the user to load a different folder path by clicking a folder name in the path, like clicking a link in a web page, as shown in figure 3.8.

Let's begin by looking at the code that handles the display of the current folder in the toolbar, the `displayFolderPath` function in the userInterface.js file. You'll need to modify this function so that instead of returning the current folder path, it passes the folder path to another function, which will convert that folder path into a set of

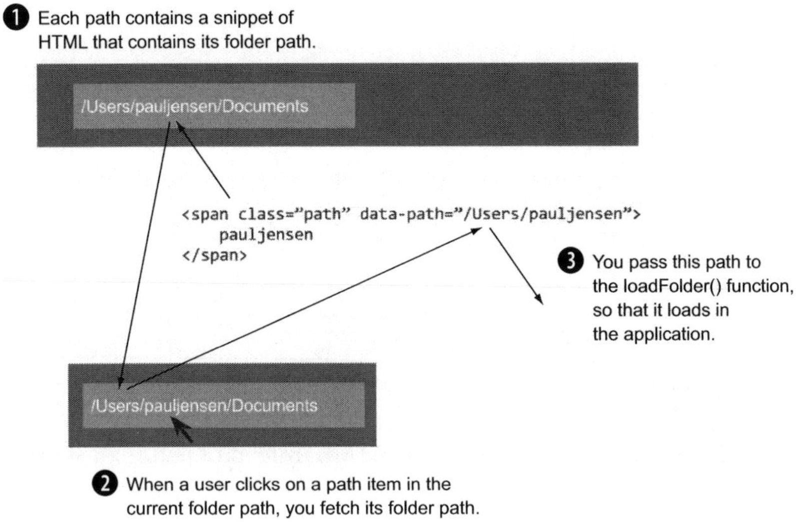

① Each path contains a snippet of HTML that contains its folder path.

/Users/pauljensen/Documents

```
<span class="path" data-path="/Users/pauljensen">
     pauljensen
</span>
```

③ You pass this path to the loadFolder() function, so that it loads in the application.

/Users/pauljensen/Documents

② When a user clicks on a path item in the current folder path, you fetch its folder path.

Figure 3.8   How clicking a path item in the current folder path will end up loading that path in the app

span HTML elements. The span tags will contain not only the name of the folder, but also a data attribute referring to the path of that folder. This is so that when the folder is selected, you can pass that folder to the loadFolder function and load the folder in the app.

Let's begin by creating a function that will receive a folder name and return the folder as a list of HTML span tags, with the path for that folder added as an attribute on the span tag. Call this function convertFolderPathIntoLinks and place it in the userInterface.js file. First, you need to add a module dependency at the top of the file (after the search module require) to load Node.js's path module:

```
const path = require('path');
```

The path module is used to return the path separator used by the operating system. In Mac OS and Linux, the path separator is a forward slash (/), but on Windows it's a backward slash (\). This will be used by the function to create the folder path for each folder as well as to display the full path for the current folder. In the convertFolder-PathIntoLinks function, the following code is used:

```
function convertFolderPathIntoLinks (folderPath) {
  const folders = folderPath.split(path.sep);
  const contents   = [];
  let pathAtFolder = '';
  folders.forEach((folder) => {
    pathAtFolder += folder + path.sep;
```

```
    contents.push(`<span class="path" data-path="${pathAtFolder.slice(0,
    -1)}">${folder}</span>`);
  });
  return contents.join(path.sep).toString();
}
```

The function takes the path for the folder and turns it into a list of folders by splitting it on the folder path separator. With this list of folders in the current folder path, you can begin to create the span tags for each one. Each span tag will have a class attribute with a value of path, a data-path attribute that contains the path for that folder, and, finally, the name of the folder as the text inside the span tag.

Once the span tags are created, the HTML is joined together and returned as a string. This HTML is then used by the displayFolderPath function. It receives the current folder path and returns the HTML to be inserted into the toolbar. As a result, you'll need to update the function to insert HTML instead of text. Adjust the display-FolderPath function to this code:

```
function displayFolderPath(folderPath) {
  document.getElementById('current-folder')
    .innerHTML = convertFolderPathIntoLinks(folderPath);
}
```

The function now uses innerHTML to insert the HTML into the current-folder element in the screen, and the convertFolderPathIntoLinks function receives the folder path passed to the displayFolderPath function and returns HTML in its place. The nice thing about this change is how you only had to change a small part of the displayFolderPath function, rather than lots of changes in multiple places. This is a desirable goal with coding: construct it so that it can be altered with ease. With this change accomplished, you now need to handle clicking a folder name in the toolbar and having the screen navigate to that folder.

In the userInterface.js file, you'll add another function that will bind on a user clicking a folder name (in this case, any span element with a class of path) and return the folder path to a callback function. The callback function can then use the folder path to pass that to the code that handles loading a folder. Add the following code to the userInterface.js file, roughly toward the bottom of the file, but before the module .exports object:

```
function bindCurrentFolderPath() {
  const load = (event) => {
    const folderPath = event.target.getAttribute('data-path');
    loadDirectory(folderPath)();
  };

  const paths = document.getElementsByClassName('path');
  for (var i = 0; i < paths.length; i++) {
    paths[i].addEventListener('click', load, false);
  }
}
```

You then want to call this function as part of the `displayFolderPath` function. Change the `displayFolderPath` function to this:

```
function displayFolderPath(folderPath) {
  document.getElementById('current-folder')
    .innerHTML = convertFolderPathIntoLinks(folderPath);
  bindCurrentFolderPath();
}
```

The userInterface.js file is easily extended to include extra functionality for handling clicks on path items in the current folder path—which is nice, because it allows you to easily alter your code without having to rewire whole swathes of the codebase.

3.3.2 *Getting the app to load at the folder path*

This simple one-line change enables the functionality to work, and the last code change you want to do before you put it into action is to make the span elements show a pointer when the cursor passes over them. Add the following code to the app.css file:

```
span.path:hover {
  opacity: 0.7;
  cursor: pointer;
}
```

With these changes saved, you can now reload the app, click through folders as normal, and then go back by clicking a folder in the current folder path. This ensures that users can navigate back to other folders, because otherwise they would be stuck. What you've done so far is replicate a feature that's common to all native file explorers across the operating systems (navigating folders via paths), but you added a twist to it so that the paths are clickable—not all file explorers do this. This shows how with Electron or NW.js you have the power to not only re-create desktop experiences using web technologies, but also combine them in ways to do new things that haven't been done in desktop apps before.

Now that you've added that feature, the next step is to handle opening files with their default application.

3.3.3 *Opening files with their default application*

So far in the app, you've focused a lot on interacting with folders, but now you need to look at how you can make the file explorer open files like images, videos, documents, and other items.

In order to implement this feature, you'll need to do the following:

- Handle clicking on a file as opposed to a folder.
- Pass the file path for that file to NW.js/Electron's way of opening external files.

We'll look at handling clicking a file first.

CLICKING A FILE

You'll probably remember from earlier on in the chapter that you detected whether the file you were rendering to the main area was a folder, and attached an event to it when it was double-clicked. You'll use the same pattern again to handle double-clicking files.

In the userInterface.js file is the displayFile function that handles displaying the individual files and folders in the main area, as well as attaching events to them. Change the function so that it looks like the following listing.

Listing 3.12 Adding file double-clicking to the displayFile function

```
function displayFile(file) {
  const mainArea = document.getElementById('main-area');
  const template = document.querySelector('#item-template');
  let clone = document.importNode(template.content, true);
  search.addToIndex(file);
  clone.querySelector('img').src = `images/${file.type}.svg`;
  clone.querySelector('img').setAttribute('data-filePath', file.path);
  if (file.type === 'directory') {
    clone.querySelector('img')
      .addEventListener('dblclick', () => {
        loadDirectory(file.path)();            Not a directory, therefore
      }, false);                               a file, so you can attach
  } else {                                     an event to it
    clone.querySelector('img')
      .addEventListener('dblclick', () => {    Calls out to new function in the
        fileSystem.openFile(file.path);        fileSystem module called openFile,
      }, false);                               which is passed the path to the file
  }
  clone.querySelector('.filename').innerText = file.file;
  mainArea.appendChild(clone);
}
```

The couple of extra lines of code allow you to listen to the file being double-clicked and attach it to a new function called openFile in the fileSystem.js module, which you'll now create.

The openFile function in the fileSystem.js module is going to call out to either Electron or NW.js's shell API. The shell API is able to open URLs, files, and folders in their default applications. To show you how compatible Electron and NW.js are as desktop app frameworks, you'll write one item of code that can be used across both frameworks without any need for modification.

In the fileSystem.js file, add the following snippet of code toward the top of the file, below the dependency declarations:

```
let shell;

if (process.versions.electron) {
  shell = require('electron').shell;
} else {
  shell = window.require('nw.gui').Shell;
}
```

This snippet of code can run on either an Electron app or an NW.js app, which means less code for you to have to write/adjust. Notice how Electron and NW.js call out to a `shell` object (though NW.js calls it via the GUI API, and with a title-cased name). If the app is running as an Electron application, it will load Electron's shell API, and if running NW.js, it will load NW.js' shell API.

With the shell API loaded for the given Node.js desktop app framework, you now call out to the shell API's method for opening files. Add the function shown in the following listing to the fileSystem.js file, right before the `module.exports` object.

Listing 3.13 Adding the openFile function to the fileSystem.js file

```
function openFile(filePath) {
  shell.openItem(filePath);          ◁──  Calls the shell API's openItem
}                                         function with the file path
```

Notice anything funny? The shell API's function name for opening files is the same across both Electron and NW.js. It's a pleasant surprise that may seem unexpected unless you know a bit about NW.js and Electron's shared history.

With this new function, all you need to do now is make sure it's available as a public API function in the fileSystem.js file. Amend the `module.exports` object so that it includes the function, as shown in the following code:

```
module.exports = {
  getUsersHomeFolder,
  getFilesInFolder,
  inspectAndDescribeFiles,
  openFile
};
```

I'd almost say you're done, but there's one more thing (to borrow a phrase from the late Steve Jobs). You want to give the app a visual indicator that the files and the folders can be clicked when the cursor is hovering over them. You can extend the last CSS rule you added earlier to the app.css file. As a reminder, it looked like this:

```
span.path:hover {
  opacity: 0.7;
  cursor: pointer;
}
```

Extend it so that it also applies to the file and folder icons in the main area:

```
span.path:hover, img:hover {
  opacity: 0.7;
  cursor: pointer;
}
```

With those changes saved, reload the app and have a go at double-clicking files in the Lorikeet app. You'll see that those files end up opening in their default applications.

Fantastic! You now have a functional file explorer that can open files, as well as explore folders and filter the view by name.

3.4 Summary

In this chapter, you built on the beginnings of a desktop app and created some rich features that make the app a usable, minimally viable product. You also had a chance to explore how you can evolve a desktop app's codebase to remain readable, and how you can organize the code for a desktop app (because there's no convention-over-configuration approach to doing this currently).

Things we've covered include the following:

- Refactoring the code by using Node.js's module functionality
- Using third-party libraries to implement search features
- Applying Electron and NW.js's shell API to handle opening files with their default applications
- Improving app navigation to make the desktop app more usable

The main thing to take away from this chapter is that with a couple-hundred lines of code and some external files, you can build an app that replicates what a native desktop app can do (and one that has relatively complex functionality). Not only that, you've been able to use third-party libraries like lunr.js to help provide this functionality, and structured the code in such a way that it can be used in web apps and allow for building apps for both the web and desktop from the same source code.

In chapter 4, you'll prepare the app for distribution: you'll hide the app developer toolbar, give the app its own icon, and build it so that it can be run as a native app on each of the operating systems.

Shipping your first desktop application

This chapter covers

- Creating an icon for the app
- Compiling the app for different OSs
- Testing the app on different platforms

In the world of software, it's easy to start a new project, but persisting with it and seeing it through to the end is not so easy. Shipping software is the big divide between those who make software that's used around the world and those who start a lot of projects but don't finish them.

In chapter 3, you fleshed out the skeleton of your desktop app until you reached the point where you could call it a minimally viable product. Now, the next step for you is to prepare the app for distribution by making it an app that users can get and run on Windows, Mac OS, and Linux.

You'll explore how to use build tools for NW.js and Electron to help build standalone executables of the Lorikeet app.

4.1   Setting up the app for distribution

Once an app is built and ready for users to get their hands on, the next step is to get the app ready for packaging and distribution. This involves a number of things:

- Getting the app to display a custom icon in place of the default app
- Creating native binaries of the app for the different OSs
- Testing those apps out on the various platforms

You'll start with creating the icons for the app.

4.1.1   Creating the app icon

For Lorikeet, you want to customize the look and feel of the app so that users can easily distinguish it from the other apps they have on their computer. Changing the app icon is a bit of a tedious process, because each OS has its own file format and approach to displaying app icons, as well as the fact that changing the app icon requires a bit of manual tinkering. You'll start by looking at the different ways that each OS implements icons and then looking at how you can create app icons for each OS.

The first step is to create an app icon as a high-resolution PNG at 512 x 512 pixels. If you feel creative and have an idea for an icon, this can be a fun exercise, but if you'd like to skip that and use one that has already been made for the app, you can download a copy of the icon I made (based on a photo of some real-life lorikeets I took in Australia) from https://github.com/paulbjensen/lorikeet/blob/master/icon.png.

Figure 4.1 shows what the icon looks like.

Figure 4.1   The icon for both versions of the Lorikeet app

Once you have this icon, you can begin the process of creating the different versions of the icon for each OS.

MAC OS

Mac OS uses the ICNS file format for app icons. This is a file format that contains versions of the app icon at the following resolutions:

- 16 px
- 32 px
- 128 px
- 256 px
- 512 px

Depending on what OS you're running on your computer (I use Mac OS), there are a number of approaches to creating an ICNS file. A quick search on the term *ICNS generator* will show some online tools as well as commercial applications that generate not only ICNS files but also icon files for Windows, iOS, and other platforms. On the Mac App Store there's a product called iConvert Icons that will convert the app icon into an ICNS file as well as a Microsoft Windows ICO file (you can also use iConvert Icons online as a free option). Alternatively, if you have a subscription to Apple's Developer Program, you can download Icon Composer for free (a tool that was originally bundled into Xcode). I'll show you the steps for creating an ICNS file using IConvert Icons (assuming you have a computer running Mac OS).

First, search for the app in the App Store, purchase it, and then open it when it's finished downloading. You should see the screen shown in figure 4.2.

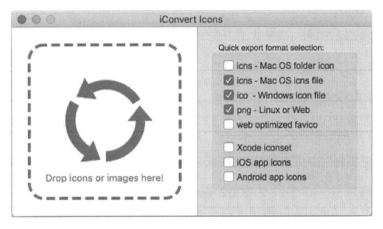

Figure 4.2   iConvert Icons, a tool for creating both ICNS and ICO icon files from an image. Notice that the iConvert Icons app has three checkboxes ticked here for the versions I want to generate.

Drag the app icon PNG image that you have into the dotted area of the app. A folder dialog box opens, asking for a place to save the generated files to. You want to save the file to the images folder of your app. Choose the folder, and you'll find that the files have been saved to that location, as shown in figure 4.3.

Now that you have the ICNS file for the app, you have a number of ways to make it the icon for your app, but you'll need to build the app before you can do that. For now, you'll keep the ICNS for use later.

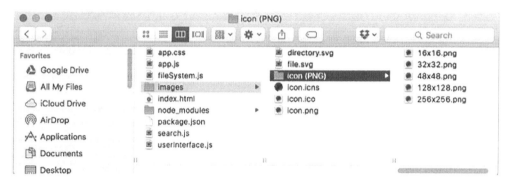

Figure 4.3   The app icon files that were generated by iConvert Icons

WINDOWS

Microsoft Windows uses the ICO file format for its icons, which is also the file format used for website icons that are displayed in web browsers. If you're already using iConvert Icons, you can use that program for the ICO file.

Alternatively, a quick search on Google shows a number of results, the top-ranking being a website called icoconverter.com. If you choose to use that website, make sure to check the checkboxes for all of the icon resolutions, because different versions of Windows use a range of icon resolutions. Once you've uploaded your app icon and saved a copy of it to your computer, it will be ready for when you build the app.

LINUX

Although there are many different distributions of Linux, the freedesktop.org organization has created a standard for handling icons across the different graphical desktop environments that are used on Linux (such as Gnome, KDE, and Xfce). It's known as the desktop entry specification, and can be found at http://standards.freedesktop.org/desktop-entry-spec/latest.

The .desktop file is a configuration file that contains details about what the app name is, where it runs from, what icon it has, and some other configuration information. Here's an example of a .desktop file:

```
[Desktop Entry]
Encoding=UTF-8
Version=1.0
Type=Lorikeet
Terminal=false
Exec=$HOME/.lorikeet/lorikeet
Name=Lorikeet
Icon=$HOME/.lorikeet/icon.png
```

The .desktop file is saved on the user's computer with a filename—for example, lorikeet.desktop. The image file format for the icon used on Linux can be a PNG file, like the one that was originally created for the app. That said, if you want to guarantee that your app icon looks good at all resolutions, it's better to use an SVG file, which is vector-based and scales with resolution much better. Either way, you now have icon files suitable for all three OSs.

To set the icon on the app, you need to go through the process of building the app, and then you can go about setting the app icon on the different builds.

4.2 Packaging the app for distribution

Now that you've configured the app to look the way you want, you're in a position to generate native executable versions of the app, one for each OS. Both NW.js and Electron have build tools that make it easy to build the app.

You'll start by looking at how to build standalone executables of the NW.js version of the Lorikeet app. Then you'll look at how to do the same thing with Electron.

4.2.1 Using a build tool for NW.js

There are quite a few build tools for NW.js, but the one that I recommend using for this case is called nw-builder. You can install nw-builder (formerly known as node-webkit-builder) by installing it with npm via the Terminal or Command Prompt:

```
npm install nw-builder -g
```

The preceding command installs nw-builder as a global npm module and therefore makes the `nwbuild` command available to you on the command line for all your NW.js apps.

Not only can nw-builder create standalone executables of the app for each OS, you can also include the app icons you created earlier. In order to do this, you need to pass some options to the `nwbuild` command to tell it to use the icons. Navigate to a folder where you would like the app files to be generated and run the following command in Terminal or Command Prompt:

```
nwbuild . -o ./build -p win64,osx64,linux64
```

This will generate a build folder in the directory where the command was run. Inside that build folder will be another folder with the name of the app (in this case, lorikeet-nwjs), and inside that you'll have six folders, one for each of the OS builds you want to create the app for (win64, osx64, linux64). These folders contain the built app with 64-bit versions of the app on each OS. If you browse through those folders, you'll see .exe files for the Windows versions of the app, as well as an app file for the Mac OS versions.

Double-click an app to see it open on your computer, and you should see it running as a standalone app; there's no Terminal window open where it's being run from, and no external software dependencies to install before running it. If you're using Mac OS, then it should appear in your Dock. In Windows, you should see the app loaded in the taskbar at the bottom of the screen. If you're running Linux (say, Ubuntu), you should see the app open in the unity bar.

4.2.2   *Using a build tool for Electron*

A number of build tools are available for Electron, and one of them is called (you guessed it) electron-builder. It's a good tool to use for packaging Electron apps, so you'll install it in this section. In Terminal or Command Prompt, install electron-builder via npm:

```
npm install electron-builder electron --save-dev
```

You install electron-builder and electron as development dependencies for the app. After installation, you'll want to alter the package.json file so that it contains the configuration information for how to build the app.

In order to make electron-builder work, you need to check that the package.json file has the following fields (or add them if it doesn't):

- Name
- Description
- Version
- Author
- Build configuration
- Scripts for packing and distribution

That's the bare minimum required for electron-builder to make a standalone executable of the app. The following listing shows an example of how your package.json file might look.

Listing 4.1   An example of the package.json file with electron-builder config

```
{
  "name": "lorikeet",
  "version": "1.0.0",
  "main": "main.js",
  "author": "Paul Jensen <paul@anephenix.com>",
  "description": "A file explorer application",
  "dependencies": {
    "async": "^2.1.4",
    "lunr": "^0.7.2",
    "osenv": "^0.1.4"
  },
  "scripts": {
    "pack": "build",
    "dist": "build"
  },
  "devDependencies": {
    "electron": "^1.4.14",
    "electron-builder": "^11.4.4"
  },
  "build": {}
}
```

Once you have those fields filled in on the package.json file, you can look to build the standalone executables for the Electron version of the Lorikeet app. You can then run the following command via npm to start creating the standalone executables:

```
npm run pack
```

This will kick off building the Lorikeet Electron app. When the app build has finished, there'll be a new folder called dist, which will contain another folder named mac. This contains the Lorikeet app in multiple builds—a zip file and a DMG file.

Now that you have the app standalone, you can work on setting the app's icon to the one you created in the previous section.

> **CONFIGURING OPTIONS FOR ELECTRON-BUILDER** A huge range of options for configuring how electron-builder builds the various versions of your app is available. For more information, see this link: https://github.com/electron-userland/electron-builder/wiki/Options.

4.2.3 Setting the app icon on the apps

Now that you have the app and the icon files for the different OSs, you need to combine them. The best way to do that is to follow the approaches described for each OS.

MAC OS

There's a simple way to change the icon of an app in Mac OS. In the build folder containing the Mac OS version of the app, right-click the app and select Get Info. You should see a screen like figure 4.4.

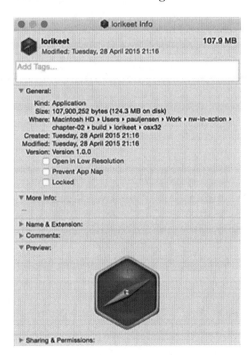

Figure 4.4   The Info window on the Lorikeet NW.js app, pre-icon change

In another Finder window, find the icon.icns file you created earlier and drag it over the icon of the app in the top left-hand corner of the Info window. You should then expect to see the Info window look like figure 4.5.

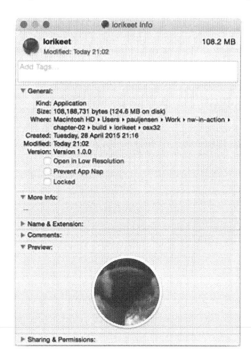

Figure 4.5   The Info window on the Lorikeet NW.js app, post-icon change

That's it! Drag and drop the icon.icns file over the app's icon in the Info window. If you double-click the app, you should see the new app icon in the Dock, in the Finder window when browsing to where the app is stored, and in the list of apps that opens when you press Command-Tab. This version of the app is now ready for distribution, and is quite the simplest and most effective way of changing the app icon for Mac versions of the app.

MICROSOFT WINDOWS

Changing the icon for Windows versions of the app is not as simple as for Mac OS, but it's not that difficult either. There are two ways you can approach this. One is to change it manually with a third-party tool, and the other is to have nw-builder do it for you. I'll document both approaches and let you use the one that works best for you.

Assuming that you have a Microsoft Windows PC available (or, alternatively, run an image of Microsoft Windows via a virtual machine), you can download a free tool called Resource Hacker (http://angusj.com/resourcehacker). Resource Hacker is a tool for modifying executable files and will allow you to replace the .ico file that's used for the app.

Once you have the Windows build of the app copied to the Windows desktop, open the lorikeet.exe file with Resource Hacker and click Action > Replace Icon in the menu bar, as shown in figure 4.6.

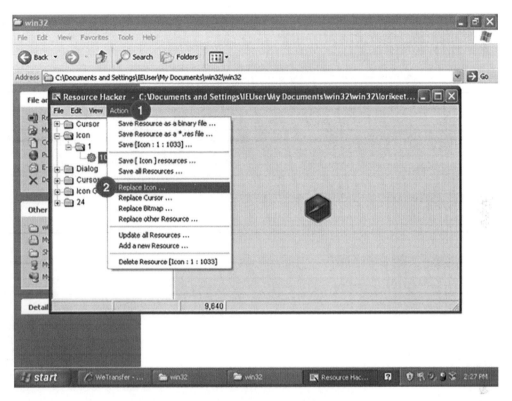

Figure 4.6   Replacing the Windows app executable icon with Resource Hacker

Select the icon.ico file that was created for the Windows app and click File > Save. Select the lorikeet.exe file to be replaced, and the Windows app should now have an updated icon. When you double-click the app icon, you should see the app running in Windows, with the icon displayed in the task bar. This approach works well with older versions of Windows, but not with the latest versions of Windows.

nw-builder can handle setting the icon for the app, but isn't always guaranteed to work across all platforms—this approach is guaranteed to work with the latest versions of Windows.

The first thing to do is to make sure that you have a copy of the app icon some-where in the app folder (it doesn't matter where exactly—it can be on the same folder level as the package.json file or nested inside an assets folder). Assuming that you've saved the file as icon.png in the same folder as the package.json file, modify the pack-age.json's `window` section so that it includes the following line:

```
"icon":"icon.png"
```

With this line in place, you tell NW.js to load the icon.png file as the icon for the title bar, and nw-builder will spot this file and use it to set the app's icon as displayed in the file explorer, as well as when the app is displayed in the task bar. After you make this change, rebuild the app using nw-builder's nwbuild command (as mentioned in the previous section), and when the app is built, you should see that the app icon has been set to that of the lorikeet-based icon, rather than the dark blue hexagon icon for NW.js.

If you now double-click on that app, you should expect to see a screen like figure 4.7.

Figure 4.7   Lorikeet NW.js running on Windows 8.1. Notice that the taskbar icon and title bar icon display the app's lorikeet-inspired icon.

This allows you to ensure that the app's visual identity is complete on Windows 8. Something to bear in mind here is that your users will likely be using different versions of Windows (there are many Windows XP users in China, for example), so depending on what versions of Windows you want/need to support for your apps, the best course of action is to establish what versions of Windows will be used, use the nwbuild option first, and then for older OSs, manually adjust the icon using Resource Hacker.

With that done, you can finally look to set up the app icon on the third OS, Linux.

Getting a blank NW.js app on Windows?

This is an issue that some NW.js users have been having with getting their apps to work on Windows (see https://github.com/nwjs/nw.js/issues/3212). It turns out that Windows has a 256-character limit on file paths. People developing Node.js apps on Windows have run into this issue due to the way that npm nests module dependencies in folders.

npm worked on resolving this issue in version 3 of the CLI by making npm install dependencies in a flat-folder structure, avoiding nested folders and thereby not running into Windows' 256-character limit.

You can install version 3 of npm by running the following command:

```
npm install npm
```

For more on this issue, and for tools to help resolve it, see the article http://engineroom.teamwork.com/dealing-with-long-paths/.

LINUX

Depending on which distribution of Linux you use (I tend to use Ubuntu), the process of setting the icon on the app built for Linux can be even simpler than the process for Mac OS. If you don't have a copy of Linux running on your computer, you can download and install VirtualBox, download Ubuntu Linux's ISO image, and then create a virtual machine that uses the ISO image. This way you can test whether your desktop apps work on other OSs without needing to have multiple computers and laptops with different OSs installed.

Once you have Linux booted and running, and assuming that you're using the Gnome desktop environment, copy either version of the Lorikeet app built for Linux and its files to a location on your computer, as well as the PNG image of the icon. Click the Files icon to open Gnome's file explorer, browse to the location of either version of the Lorikeet app, right-click the icon, and select Properties. In the Properties window that appears, click the icon in the top left, select the path to the PNG image for the icon, and then confirm. This is all it takes to change the icon for the app. Now, if you double-click the app icon, you should see the app running, and it will appear in the unity bar as well, as shown in figure 4.8.

That's all it takes to set up the app for Ubuntu Linux. You can now distribute the app as a standalone app for others to use on their computers. This means you have completed the journey of building a desktop app and shipping it.

Figure 4.8   The Lorikeet NW.js app running on Ubuntu Linux

4.3   *Testing your app on multiple OSs*

In order to ensure that your apps work on multiple OSs, you have to try them on each OS, which can be tricky if you only have one development machine.

Chances are, you might only use one OS for your development machine, and so when you need to support multiple OSs for your apps, you may ask, "Where do I start?"

If you're rich enough (or lucky enough to work somewhere with a good budget for equipment), you can purchase extra computers with the versions of Windows, Linux, and Mac OS that you want to support. But if that option isn't available, there are other options.

4.3.1   *Targeting Windows OSs*

In terms of market share, Windows is the biggest desktop OS, and there are multiple variants of Windows out there: Windows XP, Vista, 7, 8, 8.1, and 10. How do you cater to all these varieties of Windows if your development machine runs Mac OS or Linux?

The answer involves *virtual machines*. VMs allow an OS to run in an isolated environment, sharing access to hard disk, memory, and other hardware resources with the computer's main OS. They can be used to run apps in secure, isolated environments (such as infrastructure-as-a-service companies like Amazon, Linode, and DigitalOcean) as well as test apps.

In the case of virtualization software, a variety of both commercial and open source offerings are available. On the Mac, commercial options include VMware Fusion and Parallels, and for open source options, there's VirtualBox (which also works on Linux). There are some other open source virtualization tools (such as QEMU), but the three listed here are well known.

Once you've installed a virtualization tool, the next step is to purchase a copy of Windows and generate a VM for it, or use an available Windows image. Microsoft provides a range of VM images for different OS platforms to assist developers with testing websites on Internet Explorer (http://dev.modern.ie/tools/vms/mac/), and if you're happy with the terms for using the VMs, then you can do that pretty quickly.

4.3.2 *Targeting Linux OSs*

Linux is easy to test apps for—the only challenge is knowing which distributions of Linux and which versions of them to test for. VirtualBox is a popular tool for testing Linux distributions on both Mac OS and Windows PCs. Users can download ISO images for their preferred Linux distributions and easily set up a Linux distribution to test their app on.

4.3.3 *Targeting Mac OS*

Sadly, testing your apps on Mac OS is not as straightforward. Mac OS's End User License Agreement (EULA) prohibits the running of Mac OS on non-Apple hardware. That said, an internet search will reveal that some developers have managed to run Mac OS on non-Apple computers, but I can't recommend that course of action. It looks like your best (legal) bet is to purchase an Apple computer (either a MacBook laptop or a Mac mini as a cheaper option), and use that to test your app.

4.4 *Summary*

In this chapter, you've gone through the process of taking a minimally viable product and preparing it for distribution for multiple OSs. You've disabled the developer toolbar, generated a custom icon for the app, built both 32-bit and 64-bit binaries across all the OSs, and discussed practical strategies for testing the app on those different OSs. Here are some key takeaways to bear in mind:

- nw-builder and electron-builder provide the easiest ways to build your app for multiple OSs.
- You have to check that the app icons work across multiple versions of Windows, because they're not always guaranteed to work.
- If you don't have multiple computers running the different OSs that you need to target, you can use a virtualization tool like VirtualBox.
- From a legal standpoint, you need to own a Mac computer in order to test your app on Mac OS.

Well done on getting this far and going through the process of making a desktop app with NW.js and Electron. You know enough now to be able to do it again with a different app. This exercise has helped set the foundations for diving deeper into both Electron and NW.js, and lays the groundwork for better understanding the frameworks. In chapter 5, you'll explore the Node.js framework that underpins them both and see how that works.

Part 2

Diving deeper

After building a file explorer app with both NW.js and Electron, we'll take a step back and cast our eyes on the programming framework behind them: Node.js. You'll learn about its origins, how it works, and how it implements asynchronous programming. Then, we'll explore some of Node.js's key concepts such as callbacks, streams, events, and modules.

In chapter 6, we'll continue on this theme by looking at how NW.js and Electron operate under the hood. You'll see how the frameworks approach integrating Node.js with Chromium, how they handle managing state between the front-end and back-end parts of the app, and how they're structured.

By the end of this part, you should be a in a good position to put Node.js to use in your desktop app as well as other Node.js apps, and you'll understand how NW.js and Electron differ in their approaches to desktop app development.

Using Node.js within NW.js and Electron

This chapter covers

- Exploring Node.js
- Understanding the asynchronous nature of Node.js
- Managing events and streams
- Installing and using npm modules
- Packaging your apps with npm

Long before NW.js and Electron, a programming framework called Node.js was demoed by Ryan Dahl at JSConf in Berlin, showing a way to write and execute server-side JavaScript. Since that demo back in 2009, Node.js has spawned a huge ecosystem of libraries, applications, utilities, and frameworks (including NW.js and Electron). As a programming framework, it offers a different approach compared with other programming languages and their frameworks.

For those new to the world of Node.js, this chapter offers a gentle introduction to the programming framework and a chance to learn how to apply it not only when developing desktop apps, but also in other projects such as web apps. For those already familiar with Node.js, this chapter covers a lot of the ground that you might already be familiar with (the event loop, callbacks, streams, and node modules), so feel free to skip it.

One of the underrated features of both NW.js and Electron is the massive collection of packages available through Node.js's package management tool, npm, that can be used for building desktop apps. This chapter will show how you can put Node.js to use when developing your desktop apps, as well as for organizing your code.

5.1   What is Node.js?

Node.js is a programming framework created by Ryan Dahl back in 2009. It provides a way to write server-side programs with JavaScript and uses an evented architecture to handle the execution of that code. The programming framework combines V8 (a JavaScript engine) with libuv, a library that provides access to the OS libraries in an asynchronous fashion.

Because of this, JavaScript code is executed by Node.js in such a way that code executing on one line doesn't block the execution of the code on the next line. This is distinctly different from other languages where code on one line executes *after* the code on the previous line has finished executing. It's important to get familiar with how Node.js handles executing code. You'll tackle this in the next section.

5.1.1   Synchronous versus asynchronous

To clearly differentiate between synchronous and asynchronous programming, let's revisit the case of reading the contents of a folder using Node.js and compare it to how it can be done with Ruby. Ruby is a programming language with a simple syntax that works in a synchronous fashion, making it a good example to compare Node.js against. Here's an example written in Ruby:

```
files = Dir.entries '/Users/pauljensen'
puts files.length
```

This is a nice example that demonstrates the appeal of Ruby—the clean syntax. In this case, the first line executes, and then the second line executes when the first line has finished. This is known as *blocking*. If I were to insert the following between lines 1 and 3,

```
sleep 5
```

that line would cause the program to block for 5 seconds before printing out the number of files in the list. Figure 5.1 illustrates how that executes in time.

We refer to this as *synchronous programming*—each operation waits on the previous operation to complete. There may be cases where you want to start doing something else while you're waiting for the list of files to be counted, but can't because the previous line hasn't finished yet.

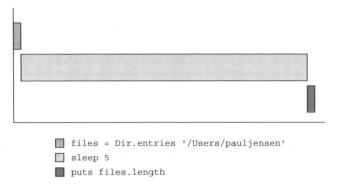

```
▢  files = Dir.entries '/Users/pauljensen'
▢  sleep 5
▢  puts files.length
```

Figure 5.1   A diagram showing how Ruby's execution of code is synchronous

The following listing shows you can do the same thing as the Ruby example in a synchronous fashion in Node.js.

Listing 5.1   Synchronous files count in Node.js

```
const fs = require('fs');
const files = fs.readdirSync('/Users/pauljensen');
console.log(files.length);
```

⟵ **Gets the list of files in the directory**

⟵ **Counts how many files there are**

Though this isn't as elegant as the Ruby code example, it does exactly the same thing. Notice that the call to the file system API's readdirSync function has the word Sync attached to the end of it. This is to make clear that the function operates in a synchronous fashion. You would still have the issue of blocking code that delays the execution of other code until it has completed its operation.

What is needed is a way to fire off an operation, let it go off and do what it's doing, and then when it's ready to return some data, send that data to another function, or a *callback*, as it's commonly referred to in Node.js. The next listing shows an example of the same task using asynchronous Node.js.

Listing 5.2   Asynchronous files count in Node.js

```
const fs = require('fs');
fs.readdir('/Users/pauljensen', (err, files) => {
if (err) { return err; }
console.log(files.length);
});
```

⟵ **Gets list of files in directory**

⟵ **If there's an error, returns the error**

⟵ **Counts how many files there are**

You can see that the code to log out the number of files in the folder is inside a function (the callback). This function will execute the moment the `readdir` function has either returned an error (as the `err` object) or the list of files. Figure 5.2 shows an alternative way to visualize it.

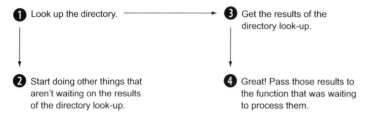

Figure 5.2   Asynchronous programming's flow of execution

Any code that's placed after the callback function on the next line will execute immediately. For example, you can place a simple line to log out a message after the callback, such as this:

```
const fs = require('fs');
fs.readdir('/Users/pauljensen', (err, files) => {
if (err) { return err.message; }
    console.log(files.length);
});
console.log('hi');
```

When you run this with Node.js, you should see the following result in Terminal or Command Prompt:

```
hi
56
```

You'll notice that the `console.log` statement executed before the file count did, even though it was placed after it in the code. This is one of the aspects of asynchronous programming that newcomers to Node.js initially struggle to get their head around. The best way to illustrate it is with a diagram like figure 5.3.

If you've worked with Gantt charts in project management, figure 5.3 might be familiar to you. Whereas synchronous execution mirrors the typical waterfall flow of a sub-optimal project plan, asynchronous execution mirrors the flow of a project where multiple tasks can run in parallel, and the project completes faster as a result. It's important to keep this in mind when working with Node.js. It's one of the bigger concepts to digest when you first start working with it—otherwise, the code will execute in an order different from what you expect, and that can lead to confusion and loss of time.

Figure 5.3 **Comparison of the ways in which synchronous and asynchronous differ in the time order of executing code.**

5.1.2 *Streams as first-class citizens*

Another aspect of Node.js is the way that it encourages you to use *streams* as a method of handling data within your apps. This has the benefit of allowing you to handle transmitting and processing large amounts of data without requiring large amounts of memory. Cases where you would want to do this include uploading large files to Amazon S3 or reading a big JSON file containing addresses and filtering the data to return only a subset that's then written to a file. When developing any kind of app, it's important to ensure that it's efficient in its memory usage—otherwise, it will slow down the computer it's running on and eventually stop working, as illustrated in figure 5.4.

In figure 5.4, you can see how loading entire files into memory can become problematic. Now, you might say that there's little chance you'll be loading a file that's bigger than the amount of RAM on a server, but when a server's amount of *free* RAM is used up over time, a small file bigger than the amount of free RAM can end up being the straw that breaks the camel's back.

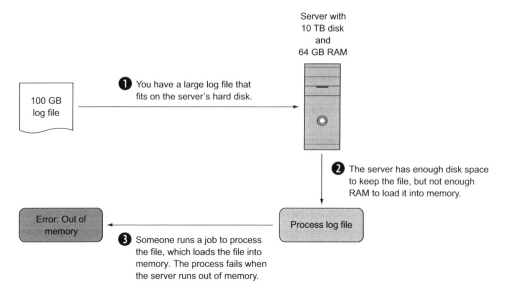

Figure 5.4   How loading a large file for processing creates pitfalls if the file is larger than total RAM available or the amount of memory free in the server

What can you do about this? You can use streams to load the file, a bit at a time, as you can see by looking at the following example of using streams in Node.js.

Let's say you have a text document that you want to scan the contents of for a particular term, but it's large, and loading all of it in memory isn't ideal. What you would like to do is load the text document in chunks and scan each chunk for the term. If the term is found, you record that the term is in the text document—otherwise, you conclude that you have yet to find the term in the text document. This is a live search of a text document, where the contents of the text document are not indexed.

Find a book you like that's available online—I'll pick Frank Herbert's *Dune* (a great book). Let's take a phrase from the end of the book, in this case, *history will call you wives*. You want to scan the book for this term, but you don't want to load the whole book's contents into memory in order to find it. Instead, you'll load it chunk by chunk until you come across the term and can verify that it appears in the book. (You can get a copy of the book from http://mng.bz/9sOS.)

You can use Node's file system API to help you read the contents of the file as a stream with the following code.

Listing 5.3   Streaming a book's contents

```
'use strict';                                              Creates readable
const fs = require('fs');                                  stream of book file
const filePath = '/Users/pauljensen/Desktop/Frank-Herbert-Dune.rtfd/TXT.rtf';
const fileReader = fs.createReadStream(filePath, {encoding:'utf8'});
let termFound  = false;
```

```
fileReader.on('data', (data) => {
  if (data.match(/history will call you wives/) !== null) {
    termFound = true;
  }
});

fileReader.on('end', (err) => {
  if (err) { return err; }
  console.log('term found:',termFound);
});
```

For each chunk of data . . .

. . . checks if there's a match for that term

After reading file, reports errors or whether term was found

You create a readable stream for a rich text file, and tell it to expect the contents of the file to be encoded in UTF-8. Then, you attach a callback function to the data event so that every time a piece of data is read from the file, you check whether the term is contained in that piece of data. If it is, you set the `termFound` variable to `true`—otherwise, it remains set to `false`.

When the readable stream has finished reading the contents of the file, it will emit an end event, to which you attach a callback function where you either return an error object or log whether the term was found.

If you run the example code along with the text of the book in your terminal, you can expect to see the following result in your terminal:

```
$> node findTerm.js
=> term found: true
```

What you've achieved here is a way to read a Rich Text Format (RTF) document and find a term within. But you could have done the same thing with less code by using the file system API's `readFile` function, with the code shown next.

Listing 5.4 Term finding with Node.js's `fs.readFile` function

```
'use strict';

const fs = require('fs');
const filePath = '/Users/pauljensen/Desktop/Frank-Herbert-Dune.rtfd/TXT.rtf';
let termFound = false;

fs.readFile(filePath, {encoding: 'utf8'}, (err, data) => {
  if (err) { return err; }
  if (data.match(/history will call you wives/) !== null) {
    termFound = true;
  }
  console.log('term found:',termFound);
});
```

Loads file's contents in full

Checks for error and returns if that's the case

Checks whether term is found

Reports back if term is found

This example achieves the same result but only requires one callback function rather than two callbacks for the readable stream version. So, why would you use streams over the simpler `fs.readFile` method?

The answer is speed. Streaming the contents of a file with `fs.createReadStream` completes faster than attempting to read the contents of a file with `fs.readFile`. You can try this out by using Node's `process.hrtime` function to measure the time it takes for the process to complete. Adjust the previous examples so they include the following line at the top of each file:

```
const startTime = process.hrtime();
```

Then, include the following lines after the console.log statement printing whether the term was found:

```
const diff = process.hrtime(startTime);
console.log('benchmark took %d nanoseconds', diff[0] * 1e9 + diff[1]);
```

Here, calling the `process.hrtime` function without any arguments records a timestamp, which you store as the `startTime` variable. After creating this variable, you compare it to a later time, after the code has finished reading the contents of the Rich Text Format document and printed out whether the term was found. By passing the `startTime` variable into the `process.hrtime` function, you get back the difference between now and that `startTime` as a tuple of seconds and nanoseconds. You then print the time difference using `console.log`, allowing you to see how long it took to read the contents of the document with both approaches.

Your results may vary, but in running them on my laptop (a 13-inch mid-2014 MacBook Pro with 16 GB RAM and a 3 GHz processor), I get the results shown in table 5.1.

Table 5.1   Streaming saves time

API function	Time taken
`fs.readFile`	62.61 milliseconds
`fs.createReadStream`	21.59 milliseconds

You can see that in this test run, the streaming function is almost three times as fast as the `fs.fileRead` function (usually, for reliable metrics you would do lots of test runs and measure the standard deviation and variance between each function's results, but that's beyond the scope of this book). This result varies only slightly between multiple test runs.

Structuring your code to make use of streams will allow for it to execute faster and be more efficient with memory. You can see this for yourself by tracking the memory usage of both approaches using Node's `process.memoryUsage` function in the code examples. In the code examples, after they have finished reading the data of the document, insert the following line of code:

```
console.log(process.memoryUsage());
```

When you add this line to both the streaming-read and full-read examples and then run them, you should see this output for the full `fs.readFile` example:

```
{ rss: 36184064, heapTotal: 20658336, heapUsed: 16310280 }
```

And for the streaming file example:

```
{ rss: 18276352, heapTotal: 6163968, heapUsed: 2869000 }
```

What's noticeable already is that the memory usage numbers are smaller in the streaming file code than in the full `readFile` code (49% smaller RSS, 70% smaller `heapTotal`, and 82% smaller `heapUsed`). Not only are streams faster, they're more memory efficient, too.

5.1.3 Events

Another kind of API interface that Node.js exposes to developers is the event pattern. Those who have used jQuery or `addEventListener` in browser-based JavaScript will be familiar with this pattern, and the `fs.createReadStream` example discussed in the last few pages also exposes an events API interface where functions can be executed when a chunk of data is read, when the file has finished streaming, or when an error occurs reading the file.

This fits with the way that Node.js's code is executed: it makes use of the *event loop*. This involves executing non-blocking code when an event is triggered, meaning that other events can occur at the same time. In various programming languages such as Ruby and Python, there's a way to run code in an asynchronous fashion within an event loop, but this requires using libraries that are structured to execute non-blocking code, such as EventMachine for Ruby, and Twisted for Python. With Node.js, there's no external library to load and execute—the programming framework has a built-in event loop that it automatically begins executing when it starts.

Not only do various API functions in Node.js expose an events interface, but Node.js also provides a library for creating your own event interfaces using the EventEmitter module. Here's an example of using the EventEmitter module to greet someone with a message when the `welcome` event is emitted:

```
'use strict';

const greeter = new events.EventEmitter();

greeter.on('welcome', function () {
    console.log('hello');
});

greeter.emit('welcome');
```

An event emitter instance called `greeter` is created, and you create an event on it with the name `'welcome'`, which when emitted will log `'hello'`. You then emit the event 'welcome' on the greeter object. If you run the code in your Node.js REPL, you can see that the message "hello" is printed in the Terminal.

As you work through NW.js's and Electron's APIs, you'll see the event pattern in use and get a chance to work with it as you go through the examples in the book.

5.1.4   Modules

Structuring code into reusable libraries is an important part of any programming language's ecosystem, and a good package system goes a long way toward helping developers be productive. In Node.js, groups of functions are organized into modules, and these modules can be easily created and reused in other places.

Node.js uses a module format called CommonJS. The CommonJS spec in brief is a standard for creating nonbrowser JavaScript libraries that can work with each other, but has also been applied to browser-based JavaScript libraries as well.

Let's work through an example of creating a module in order to get a better feel for it.

CREATING PUBLIC API METHODS WITH MODULE.EXPORTS

To make functions, objects, and other values publicly available in a JavaScript file, the developer has to use either one of two specific expressions: exports or module .exports. Say you have a function for performing some business logic in your file, and you want to be able to load the file and call the following function:

```
function applyDiscount (discountCode, amount) {
  let discountCodes = {
    summer20: (amt) => {
      return amt * 0.8;
    },
    bigone: (amt) => {
      if (amt > 10000) {
        return amt - 10000;
      } else {
        return amt;
      }
    }
  };

  if (discountCodes[discountCode]) {
    return discountCodes[discountCode](amount);
  } else {
    return amount;
  }
}
```

If you want to make this a publicly available function on the file, you can do that like so:

```
exports.applyDiscount = applyDiscount;
```

Or like this:

```
module.exports = {
  applyDiscount: applyDiscount
};
```

Or if the file has only one function that you want to call, you could export the function like this:

```
module.exports = applyDiscount;
```

These methods don't have to expose only functions or objects; they can be used to export any kind of value in JavaScript. This allows you to organize your code as you like and make it easily reusable. The next stage is to be able to load libraries together, via the `require` method.

LOADING LIBRARIES VIA REQUIRE

Once you have a file that has publicly available functions or values, you can then include it in other files by use of the `require` function. For example, say you turned the bit of business logic for applying discounts into a file called discount.js. You could include that file in another place, say at the same location as the discount.js file in the app's folder, like this:

```
const discount = require('./discount');
```

You would now have the file's exported functions or objects loaded and attached to the discount variable in your file. You can then call the `applyDiscount` function in your file like so:

```
discount.applyDiscount('summer20', 4999);
```

This allows you to structure your code into small, reusable libraries that are easy to understand and easy to use elsewhere. This is a key philosophy of Node.js—to use and combine lots of little modules when developing rather than create large files that are difficult to read through and understand.

   The `require` function isn't used only to load local files; it can be used to load modules, as well. The Node.js API contains a set of modules that can be loaded explicitly by using a `require` function that's passed either the name of a module or the relative file path to the module, like this example:

```
const os = require('os');
```

That code loads Node's OS module. Node.js provides a number of modules in its core, and you can load them without having to install them. A few of the modules are loaded as global objects in Node.js's namespace, and the rest have to be loaded via the `require` function. The list of modules that Node.js provides by default can be viewed at https://nodejs.org/api.

Apart from Node.js's core modules, there's also the ability to install and use modules via npm (which stands for Node Package Manager). npm is a free central repository that lets you publish and download modules to use in your apps. You can search for and find modules via https://npmjs.com and then install them (for example, request) via this command on the Terminal:

```
npm install request
```

This will download a copy of the request module (a library used to make HTTP requests), and place it in a folder called node_modules. Then you'll be able to load that module within your code as a locally installed module as you would with Node's main modules, like this:

```
const request = require('request');
```

This will load the request module that's located in the node_modules folder. If you open that folder, you'll see the folder for the request module there. The `require` function in Node.js is designed to work so that if you pass the name of a module, it will look up the modules that are either available in Node.js' core, or installed globally, or installed locally in the node_modules folder.

You can also install npm modules globally, meaning that they're not installed in the app's node_modules folder but instead in a folder where they're available to any Node.js process that loads via `require`. Examples of npm modules installed globally tend to be build tools like Grunt and Bower. To install them globally, append a -g argument to the npm `install` command, like this:

```
npm install -g grunt-cli
```

The reason for installing grunt-cli globally in this case is so you only have to install it once, not once per app you use it with. Also, npm modules can have binary commands, and installing an npm module globally allows you to run that binary command without having to install the npm package each time. The same can be said for installing NW.js and Electron as global npm modules.

This is something of a quick overview of what Node.js offers from a developer's perspective. Given that we've been discussing installing third-party modules, we'll look at the mechanism behind installing third-party modules—the package manager known as npm.

5.2   *Node Package Manager (npm)*

Node Package Manager (or npm) is the tool used by Node.js developers to handle installing libraries. It's built into Node.js by default and has proven to be a popular tool, maintaining a central repository of over 400,000 packages to date. It allows developers to download modules for use in their apps as well as publish modules for others to use.

5.2.1   *Finding packages for your app*

Visit npmjs.com, and you'll be able to find out more information about npm and what it does, besides finding modules that may be of interest, such as webpack and Type-Script. You can search for packages by typing in a term that matches the name, description, or keywords used for those modules. Alternatively, you can click the most popular packages and see whether they're of use to you.

Once you've found a package you want to use in your app (or experiment with), you can install it via the command line like so:

```
npm install lodash
```

You'll now have the lodash module installed inside the node_modules folder in the current directory that your command-line terminal is in, and you'll be able to use it in your code like this:

```
const _ = require('underscore');
```

Now, any places in your code where require('lodash') is called will have the module already loaded, and reuse it from require's module cache, rather than go through the process of loading the module from scratch.

5.2.2   *Tracking installed modules with package.json*

After a while, you'll be using a bunch of modules in your app, and you'll want to keep a record of what they are, as well as which version of them you're using. You'll need a manifest file. npm uses a manifest file called package.json as the way to describe an npm module, as well as what module dependencies it has. In the previous example, you installed the lodash module but did not append its information to a package.json file.

Create a package.json file to track your dependencies. You can start that process by running this command in your terminal:

```
npm init
```

This triggers the process of creating a package.json file by asking a bunch of questions in the command line and populating the package.json file's contents as a result. By the end of the question process, you should see a package.json file that resembles this:

```
{
  "name": "pkgjson",
  "version": "1.0.0",
  "description": "My testbed for playing with npm",
  "main": "index.js",
  "scripts": {
    "test": "echo \"Error: no test specified\" && exit 1"
  },
  "author": "",
  "license": "ISC"
}
```

This creates a package.json file that can store configuration information for your app and that also contains information about the module, what file it should load when required as a dependency, any script commands it has, and what software license it has.

Now that you've got a package.json file to work with, you can track your module dependencies. Run the following command in your terminal:

```
npm install lodash --save
```

Not only will it install the lodash module, it will also add the following configuration information to the package.json file:

```
"dependencies": {
  "lodash": "^4.15.0"
}
```

The name and version of the module are now stored in the package.json file, meaning that you can track your app's modules and versions.

Now, if you use version control for your app (like Git) and want to allow other developers to set up the app quickly on their computer, they'll be able to install all of the app's module dependencies by running the following command at the same working directory as the package.json file:

```
npm install
```

When passed no arguments, `npm install` will look for the package.json file and install all the module dependencies that are listed in the file.

INSTALLING DEVELOPMENT-ONLY DEPENDENCIES

There are some module dependencies that you want to use only for development purposes and not as part of the app, such as testing libraries like Mocha and Karma. You can install these modules as development dependencies using the following command from your terminal:

```
npm install mocha --save-dev
```

This will install the Mocha module into the node_modules folder and will add the following JSON to the package.json file:

```
"devDependencies": {
  "mocha": "^3.0.2"
}
```

Being able to separate dependencies required for the app to run from dependencies used to test and build the app helps developers ship smaller binaries of the app.

5.2.3 *Packaging your modules and apps with npm*

One of the major factors in collaborating successfully on an npm module is how easy it is for other developers to install and get running on their local development machine. Packaging your modules and apps so that they install and run seamlessly from one machine to another is key to this.

CONTROLLING DEPENDENCY VERSIONS IN PACKAGE.JSON

When it comes to installing an app that has Node.js modules, there's first a question of what to track in version control. There are two things that can be done: either the developer has the Node.js modules and all their files checked into version control, or they check the package.json file into version control (which will track what dependencies the app has) and exclude the node_modules folder from being tracked by version control.

Developers tend to go for the latter approach for two reasons. The first is that there are fewer files to track in version control (making it easier to use the version control tool to look through only the app files). The second is for compatibility with multiple OSs. There are some Node.js modules that use extensions written in C++, and for those Node.js modules to be installed, they need to be compiled on the developer's machine. If the Node.js module is compiled on Mac OS and then checked into version control, and then someone else wants to use it but on a different computer (Linux or Windows), then the Node.js module will fail to work because it has been compiled to work against a different OS.

My personal preference is to not only track the package.json file of your app, but also lock down the version of the dependencies in that package.json file. To explain: When a Node.js module is added to the package.json file via `npm install`, you'll notice that the dependency listing in the package.json will show a caret character (^) before the version number of the module. The ^ indicates to npm that when installing that dependency, it can install a more up-to-date version, so long as it's compatible with the major version specified in the package.json file. As an example, say you install a version of CoffeeScript for use in your app:

```
npm install coffee-script --save
```

If you look at the package.json file, you'll see something like this:

```
"dependencies": {
  "coffee-script":"^1.10.1"
}
```

Notice the ^ preceding the version 1.10.1 of CoffeeScript. You've installed version 1.10.1 of CoffeeScript, but let's say a couple months later someone downloads a copy of the app's code from GitHub and runs `npm install` to download the dependencies. If CoffeeScript 1.11.0 comes out, or even 1.10.2, those will be downloaded instead of 1.10.1. The caret character indicates that you can install a more up-to-date version of the dependency, so long as the changes are only at patch level (the number of the version after the second dot, indicating a bug fix or change that doesn't affect existing functionality) or minor level (the number after the first dot in the version number, indicating a small change to the module which shouldn't cause breaking changes to your app). If CoffeeScript 2.0.0 is out, it won't install that version because that's a major-level change (indicating new features/changed API and therefore likely to cause breaking changes to your app).

The idea behind this approach is to allow developers to pull in fixes and non-breaking updates to their dependencies without having to manually update those numbers in the package.json file. This can work as long as the developers of Node.js modules follow the principles of semantic versioning, as well as take care not to introduce bugs during those updates. From a DevOps perspective, this can provide room for production errors to creep in (hence, the need for a comprehensive testing strategy, which I'll cover later in the book). You want control over the version of the dependencies.

How do you lock down the versions of the dependencies? There are two ways you can do this. The first is to remove any ^ or ~ characters from the front of the version numbers of the dependencies listed in the package.json file. If you don't want to do that manually, the alternative approach is to use `npm shrinkwrap`.

npm's `shrinkwrap` command will lock down the version of dependencies that are installed with the module. Running `npm shrinkwrap` in the same working directory as the package.json file will produce a file called npm-shrinkwrap.json, a JSON file that has configuration information to specify exactly what version of the module should be installed, which looks like this:

```
{
  "name": "pkgjson",
  "version": "1.0.0",
  "dependencies": {
    "underscore": {
      "version": "1.8.3",
      "from": "underscore@",
      "resolved": "https://registry.npmjs.org/underscore/-/underscore-1.8.3.tgz"
    }
  }
}
```

This file helps npm know exactly what versions of the software should be installed for the module.

Based on my experience working with Node.js since 2010, my suggestion is to use the approach of keeping dependencies in the package.json file up to date, keep the node_modules folder out of version control, and, when needed, use `npm shrinkwrap` to lock down the dependencies in use.

PUBLISHING APPLICATIONS AND MODULES TO NPM

Once you've created a module or an app and begun tracking its dependencies, you may want to make it available for others to download and use. You can do that through npm. You'll need to create a free account with npm (unless you have one already) by going to npmjs.com and clicking the signup link. Fill in your details, and once you've set up your account, in your command-line terminal, run the following command:

```
npm login
```

Once you've logged in, you'll be able to publish modules from the command line up to npm. Say you've created a module that you want to be able to install via npm. In the same working directory as the package.json for the module, run the following command:

```
npm publish
```

That will push a copy of the module up to npm, and you'll then be able to install it via `npm install`. You'll also be able to publish updates to your package using this command, and incrementing the version number of the module in the package.json file.

5.3   *Summary*

This chapter presented a broad introduction to Node.js. Now you have a better understanding of what it's like to use as a programming framework, and you'll be able to start implementing it in your apps. Things that you'll want to take away from this chapter include the following:

- Node.js uses asynchronous programming. Make sure to structure your code to use callbacks and streams when interacting with Node.js' APIs and modules.
- Streams are an effective way to read/write data without using much memory.
- Some of the browsers' APIs overlap with Node.js's APIs. Note when you use them because they will have subtle differences.
- Use npm modules to install libraries that will help you build app features faster.
- You can publish modules to npm to share your libraries with the community.

In chapter 6, we'll turn our attention back to NW.js and Electron and take a look at how they operate under the hood, so you can understand how they work differently.

Exploring NW.js and Electron's internals

This chapter covers

- Understanding how NW.js and Electron combine Node.js and Chromium
- Developing with Electron's multi-process approach
- Building with NW.js's shared-context approach
- Sharing state by passing messages

Although NW.js and Electron consist of the same software components, and Cheng Zhao has influenced the development of both, the two frameworks have evolved different approaches to how they function under the hood. Analyzing how they operate internally will help you understand what's going on when you're running an app and demystify the software.

In this chapter, we'll look at how NW.js and Electron function internally. We'll take a look at NW.js first to see how it combines Node.js with Chromium (because that was the first Node.js desktop app framework) and then explore how Electron took a different approach to combining those software components. Following that, we'll look at the frameworks' different approaches to context and state. I'll then elaborate a bit on Electron's use of message passing to transmit data as state between the processes in a desktop app.

We'll also look at some resources for further reading. The goal is that you'll be in a good position to understand how the two frameworks differ in their internal architecture and the implications this has on building desktop apps with them.

6.1   How does NW.js work under the hood?

From a developer's view, NW.js is a combination of a programming framework (Node.js) with Chromium's browser engine through their common use of V8. V8 is a JavaScript engine created by Google for its web browser, Google Chrome. It's written in C++ and was designed with the goal of speeding up the execution of JavaScript in the web browser.

When Node.js was released in 2009, a year after Google Chrome, it combined a multiplatform support library called libuv with the V8 engine and provided a way to write asynchronous server-side programs in JavaScript. Because both Node.js and Chromium use V8 to execute their JavaScript, it provided a way to combine the two pieces of software, which Roger Wang came to understand and figure out. Figure 6.1 shows how those components are combined.

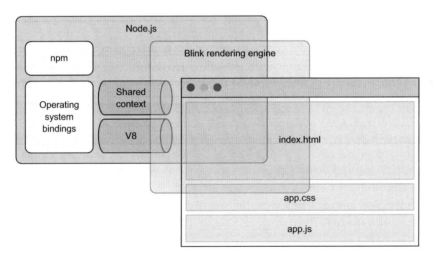

Figure 6.1   Overview of NW.js's component architecture in relation to loading an app

Looking at figure 6.1, you can see that Node.js is used in the back end to handle working with the OS, and that Blink (Chromium's rendering engine) is used to handle rendering the front-end part of the app, the bit that users see. Between them, both Node.js and Blink use V8 as the component that handles executing JavaScript, and it's this bit that's crucial in getting Node.js and Chromium to work together. There are three things necessary for Node.js and Chromium to work together:

- Make Node.js and Chromium use the same instance of V8
- Integrate the main event loop
- Bridge the JavaScript context between Node and Chromium

NW.js and its forked dependencies

NW.js, a combination of Node.js and the WebKit browser engine, used to be known as node-webkit. Recently, both components were forked: Google created a fork of WebKit called Blink, and in October 2014 a fork of Node.js called IO.js emerged. They were created for different reasons, but as projects that received more regular updates and features, NW.js opted to switch to using them.

As node-webkit no longer used Node.js and WebKit (but IO.js and Blink instead), it was suggested that the project should be renamed; hence, the project was renamed to NW.js.

In May 2015, the IO.js project agreed to work with the Node.js foundation to merge IO.js back into Node.js. NW.js has switched back to using Node.js since.

6.1.1   *Using the same instance of V8*

Both Node.js and Chromium use V8 to handle executing JavaScript. Getting them to work together requires that a couple of things happen in order. The first thing NW.js does is load Node.js and Chromium so that both of them have their JavaScript contexts loaded in the V8 engine. Node's JavaScript context will expose global objects and functions such as `module`, `process`, and `require`, to name a few. Chromium's JavaScript context will expose global objects and functions like `window`, `document`, and `console`. This is illustrated in figure 6.2 and involves some overlap because both Node and Chromium have a `console` object.

When this is done, the JavaScript context for Node.js can be copied into the JavaScript context for Chromium.

Although that sounds quite easy, the reality is that there's a bit more glue involved for Node.js and Chromium to work together—the main event loop used by both has to be integrated.

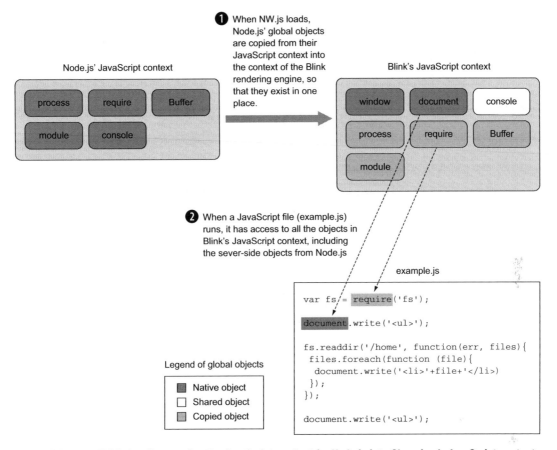

❶ When NW.js loads, Node.js' global objects are copied from their JavaScript context into the context of the Blink rendering engine, so that they exist in one place.

❷ When a JavaScript file (example.js) runs, it has access to all the objects in Blink's JavaScript context, including the sever-side objects from Node.js

Node.js' JavaScript context

Blink's JavaScript context

example.js

```
var fs = require('fs');

document.write('<ul>');

fs.readdir('/home', function(err, files){
  files.foreach(function (file){
    document.write('<li>'+file+'</li>)
  });
});

document.write('<ul>');
```

Legend of global objects

- ■ Native object
- □ Shared object
- ▨ Copied object

Figure 6.2 How NW.js handles copying the JavaScript context for Node.js into Chromium's JavaScript context

6.1.2 Integrating the main event loop

As discussed in section 5.1.3, Node.js uses the event loop programming pattern to handle executing code in a non-blocking, asynchronous fashion. Chromium also uses the event loop pattern to handle the asynchronous execution of its code.

But Node.js and Chromium use different software libraries (Node.js uses libuv, and Chromium uses its own custom C++ libraries, known as `MessageLoop` and `Message-Pump`). To get Node.js and Chromium to work together, their event loops have to be integrated, as illustrated in figure 6.3.

When the JavaScript context for Node.js is copied into Chromium's JavaScript context, Chromium's event loop is adjusted to use a custom version of the `MessagePump` class, built on top of libuv, and in this way, they're able to work together.

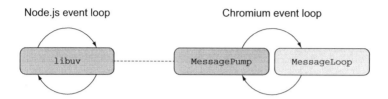

Figure 6.3   NW.js integrates the event loops of Node.js and Chromium by making Chromium use a custom version of `MessagePump`, **built on top of** `libuv`.

6.1.3   *Bridging the JavaScript context between Node and Chromium*

The next step to completing the integration of Node with Chromium is to integrate Node's `start` function with Chromium's rendering process. Node.js kicks off with a `start` function that handles executing code. To get Node.js to work with Chromium, the `start` function has to be split into parts so that it can execute in line with Chromium's rendering process. This is a bit of custom code within NW.js that's used to monkey-patch the `start` function in Node.

Once this is done, Node is able to work inside of Chromium. This is how NW.js is able to make Node.js operate in the same place as the front-end code that's handled by Chromium.

That rounds up a bit about how NW.js operates under the hood. In the next section, we'll explore the different approach taken by Electron.

6.2   *How does Electron work under the hood?*

Electron's approach shares some similarities in terms of the components used to provide the desktop framework, but differs in how it combines them. It's best to start by looking at the components that make up Electron. To see an up-to-date source code directory, take a look at http://mng.bz/ZQ2J.

Figure 6.4 shows a representation of that architecture at a less-detailed level. Electron's architecture emphasizes a clean separation between the Chromium source code and the app. The benefits of this are that it makes it easier to upgrade the Chromium component, and it also means that compiling Electron from the source code becomes that much simpler.

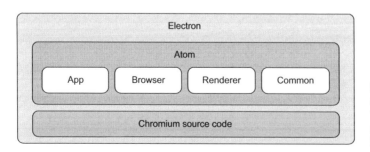

Figure 6.4   Electron's source code architecture. This diagram shows the main blocks of components that make up Electron.

The Atom component is the C++ source code for the shell. It has four distinct parts (covered in section 6.2.2). Finally, there's Chromium's source code, which the Atom shell uses to combine Chromium with Node.js.

How does Electron manage to combine Chromium with Node.js if it doesn't rely on patching Chrome to combine the event loops for Chromium and Node.js?

6.2.1 *Introducing libchromiumcontent*

Electron uses a single shared library called libchromiumcontent to load Chromium's content module, which includes Blink and V8. Chromium's content module is responsible for rendering a page in a sandboxed browser. You can find this library on GitHub at https://github.com/electron/libchromiumcontent.

You use the Chromium content module to handle rendering web pages for the app windows. This way, there's a defined API for handling the interaction between the Chromium component and the rest of Electron's components.

6.2.2 *Electron's components*

Electron's code components are organized inside Electron's Atom folder into these sections:

- App
- Browser
- Renderer
- Common

We'll look at what each of those folders contains in a bit more detail.

APP
The App folder is a collection of files written in C++11 and Objective-C++ that handles code that needs to load at the start of Electron, such as loading Node.js, loading Chromium's content module, and accessing libuv.

BROWSER
The Browser folder contains files that handle interacting with the front-end part of the app, such as initializing the JavaScript engine, interacting with the UI, and binding modules that are specific to each OS.

RENDERER
The Renderer folder contains files for code that runs in Electron's renderer processes. In Electron, each app window runs as a separate process, because Google Chrome runs each tab as a separate process, so that if a tab loads a heavy web page and becomes unresponsive, that tab can be isolated and closed without killing the browser and the rest of the tabs with it.

Later in this book, we'll look at how Electron handles running code in a main process, and how app windows have their own renderer processes that run separately.

COMMON

The Common folder contains utility code that's used by both the main and renderer processes for running the app. It also includes code that handles integrating the messaging for Node.js' event loop into Chromium's event loop.

Now you have an idea of how Electron's architecture is organized. In the next section, we'll look at how Electron handles rendering app windows in a process that's separate from the main app process.

6.2.3   *How Electron handles running the app*

Electron handles running apps differently than NW.js. In NW.js, the back-end and front-end parts of the desktop app share state by having the Node.js and Chromium event loops integrated and by having the JavaScript context copied from Node.js into Chromium. One of the consequences of this approach is that the app windows of an NW.js app end up sharing the same reference to the JavaScript state.

With Electron, any sharing of state from the back-end part of the app to the front-end part and vice versa has to go through the ipcMain and ipcRenderer modules. This way, the JavaScript contexts of the main process and the renderer process are kept separate, but data can be transmitted between the processes in an explicit fashion.

The ipcMain and ipcRenderer modules are event emitters that handle interprocess communication between the back end of the app (ipcMain), and the front-end app windows (ipcRenderer), as shown in figure 6.5.

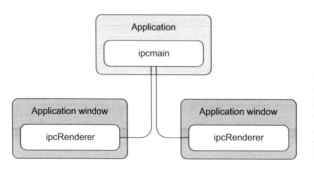

Figure 6.5   **How Electron passes state via messaging to and from the app windows. In Electron, each app window has its own JavaScript state, and communicating state to and from the main app process happens via interprocess communication.**

This way, you have greater control over what state exists in each app window as well as how the main app interacts with the app windows.

Regardless of which desktop framework you choose to build your app with, keep in mind how you want data to be accessed and altered within your app. Depending on what your app does, you may find that one framework is better suited to your needs than the other, and in cases where you're working with those desktop app frameworks already, you'll want to keep in mind how NW.js and Electron handle JavaScript contexts.

Now let's take a closer look at how Electron and NW.js make use of Node.js.

6.3 How does Node.js work with NW.js and Electron?

Node.js interacts with the hybrid desktop environments of NW.js and Electron similarly to server-side apps. But to understand the few differences, we'll look at the way Node.js is integrated into NW.js.

6.3.1 Where Node.js fits into NW.js

NW.js's architecture consists of a number of components, Node.js being one of them. NW.js uses Node.js to access the computer's file system and other resources that would otherwise not be available due to web browser security. It also provides a way to access a large number of libraries through npm (figure 6.6).

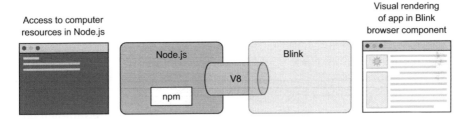

Figure 6.6   How Node.js is used within NW.js for desktop apps

NW.js makes Node.js available through the context of the embedded web browser, which means you can script JavaScript files that access both Node.js's API and API methods related to the browser's JavaScript namespace—such as the `WebSocket` class, for example. In earlier examples in the book, you've written code that has accessed Node.js's file system API in the same file that also accesses the DOM in the screen.

This is possible through the way that NW.js has merged the JavaScript namespaces of Node.js and the Blink rendering engine, as well as merged the main event loops of both, allowing them to operate and interact in a shared context.

6.3.2 Drawbacks of using Node.js in NW.js

Because of how NW.js merges the JavaScript contexts of the Blink rendering engine and Node.js, you should be aware of some of the consequences that come with this approach. I'll describe what those things are and how you can handle them so that they don't trip you up.

THE NODE.JS CONTEXT IS ACCESSIBLE TO ALL WINDOWS

I've talked about Node.js and Blink sharing the same JavaScript context, but how does that work in the context of an NW.js app where there are multiple windows?

In Blink, each window has its own JavaScript context, because each window loads a web page with its own JavaScript files and DOM. The code in one window will operate in the context of that window only, and not have its context leak into another window—otherwise, this would cause issues with maintaining state in the windows as well as security issues. You should expect the state that exists in one window to be isolated to that window and not leak.

That said, NW.js introduces a way to share state between windows via the way that Node.js's namespace is loaded into the namespace of Blink to create a shared JavaScript context. Even though each window has its own JavaScript namespace, they all share the same Node.js instance and its namespace. This means there's a way to share state between windows through code that operates on Node.js's namespace properties (such as the API methods), including via the `require` function that's used to load libraries. Should you need to share data between windows in your desktop app, you'll be able to do this by attaching data to the *global* object in your code.

COMMON API METHODS IN CHROMIUM AND NODE.JS

You may know that both Node.js and Blink have API methods with the same name and that work in the same way (for example, `console`, `setTimeout`, `encodeURIComponent`). How are these handled? In some cases, Blink's implementation is used, and in other cases, Node.js's implementation is used. NW.js opts to use Blink's implementation of `console`, and for `setTimeout`, the implementation used depends on whether the file is loaded from a Node.js module or from the desktop app. This is worth keeping in mind when you're using those functions, because although they're consistent in their implementations of inputs and outputs, there might be a slight difference in speed of execution.

6.3.3   *How Node.js is used within Electron*

Electron uses Node.js along with Chromium, but rather than combining the event loops of Node.js and Chromium together, Electron uses Node.js's `node_bindings` feature. This way, the Chromium and Node.js components can be updated easily without the need for custom modification of the source code and subsequent compiling.

Electron handles the JavaScript contexts of Node.js and Chromium by keeping the back-end code's JavaScript state separate from that of the front-end app window's state. This isolation of the JavaScript state is one of the ways Electron is different from NW.js. That said, Node.js modules can be referenced and used from the front-end code as well, with the caveat that those Node.js modules are operating in a separate process to the back end. This is why data sharing between the back end and app windows is handled via inter-process communication, or *message passing*.

If you're interested in learning more about this approach, check out this site from GitHub's Jessica Lord: http://jlord.us/essential-electron/#stay-in-touch.

6.4   *Summary*

In this chapter, we've exposed some differences between NW.js and Electron by exploring how their software components work under the hood. Some of the key takeaways from the chapter include the following:

- In NW.js, Node.js and Blink share JavaScript contexts, which you can use for sharing data between multiple windows.
- This sharing of JavaScript state means that multiple app windows for the same NW.js app can share the same state.
- NW.js uses a compiled version of Chromium with custom bindings, whereas Electron uses an API in Chromium to integrate Node.js with Chromium.
- Electron has separate JavaScript contexts between the front end and the back end.
- When you want to share state between the front end and back end in Electron apps, you need to use message passing via the ipcMain and ipcRenderer APIs.

In the next chapter, we'll look at how to use the various APIs of NW.js and Electron to build desktop apps—specifically, at the way in which you can craft an app's look and feel. It will be more visual, and hopefully more fun.

Part 3

Mastering Node.js desktop application development

Many APIs are available in desktop application frameworks to help provide features like accessing the webcam and clipboard, opening and saving files to the hard disk, and more. This part explores the various ways in which NW.js and Electron allow you to add a number of features to your desktop apps.

Chapters 7, 8, and 9 look at ways to control the look and feel of your desktop apps, from controlling the window dimensions and full-screen behavior, through to creating menus and making tray apps.

Chapter 10 explores how to implement drag-and-drop functionality in your apps through HTML5 APIs, and chapter 11 shows you how to integrate webcam functionality for taking photos from your computer's webcam and saving them to disk.

Chapters 12 and 13 deal with different ways you can store and access app data and how to access data in the OS clipboard.

Toward the end of this part of the book, we'll look at using keyboard shortcuts to implement controls for a game, and how to integrate a real-time Twitter feed into a desktop notifications app.

Controlling how your
desktop app is displayed
7

This chapter covers

- Controlling the application window
- Setting the application window's dimensions
- Making applications run in full-screen mode
- Creating kiosk applications

When you build a desktop app, one of the first considerations is how the user will interact with it. Will it be a windowed app that can operate at the same time as other apps, a publicly accessible terminal in a bank, or an immersive experience that will consume all of the user's attention, like a game?

A desktop app can take many forms. It can operate in a window that can be maximized and minimized as needed, or run in full-screen mode, like a video game. In this chapter, we'll explore options for controlling the way the app is displayed to the user, and I'll show you some methods that will come in handy when you're building apps.

7.1 Window sizes and modes

User interfaces come in a range of different dimensions; traditional IM apps like AIM or MSN Messenger (if you're old enough to remember them) tended to have a long portrait window listing many contacts that users would want to chat with. Over time, apps like Slack and Gitter have approached the world of IM with a different window size, much in the style of a forum, and to accommodate longer messages and images (there's a tendency in Slack communities to use a lot of animated GIFs). Window sizes for apps need to provide the best possible UX, so it's important to be able to make them fit the dimension required for the UI. Figure 7.1 shows an example.

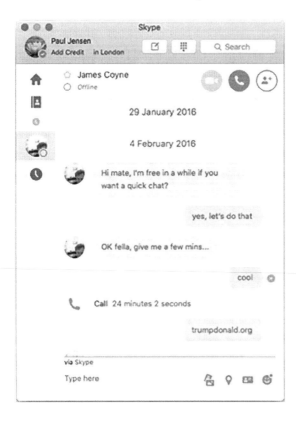

Figure 7.1 **Skype in action. Notice the tall style of the UI, accommodating mainly chat messages.**

In NW.js and Electron, there are multiple ways to configure the window. We'll take a look at how you can configure an app window's width and height in NW.js.

7.1.1 *Configuring window dimensions for an NW.js app*

NW.js allows you to configure the window's width and height via the package.json file. In the GitHub repository for this book, the chapter-07 folder holds a copy of the example NW.js app called window-resizing-nwjs. The code for it looks like this:

```
<html>
  <head>
    <title>Window sizing NW.js</title>
  </head>
```

```
  <body>
    <h1>Hello World</h1>
  </body>
</html>
```

This is a pretty basic HTML file, containing an h1 element inside the body tag with the words *Hello World*, much like the Hello World examples shown earlier in this book. If you want to add window dimensions to the app, you can adjust them to work by using this for the package.json file:

```
{
  "name" : "window-sizing-nwjs",
  "version" : "1.0.0",
  "main" : "index.html",
  "window" : {
    "width" : 300,
    "height" : 200
  }
}
```

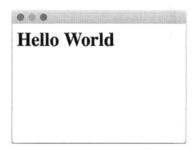

The window's width and height are specified in pixels. This allows you to make sure that when the app opens, its width and height are set at those dimensions. This is one way you can control the window's width and height. Figure 7.2 shows an example of what the changes look like.

This demonstrates how you can control the app window's initial width and height in NW.js. How do you do the same with Electron?

Figure 7.2   An app with window properties applied. You can see here that the app is small.

7.1.2 *Configuring window dimensions for an Electron app*

Electron's ability to configure window dimensions is similar to that of NW.js, but the approach is different. Where NW.js allows you to specify the configuration in the package.json manifest file, Electron requires that you configure window dimensions at the point in which the app window is initialized.

In the book's GitHub repository, you'll find an Electron app inside the chapter-07 folder called window-sizing-electron. Here's what the code for that app looks like:

```
{
  "name"    : "window-sizing-electron",
  "version" : "1.0.0",
  "main"    : "main.js"
}
```

And then there's the accompanying index.html file that you'll display:

```
<html>
  <head>
    <title>Window sizing Electron</title>
```

```
    </head>
    <body>
      <h1>Hello from Electron</h1>
    </body>
</html>
```

Finally, the place where the magic happens: the main.js file, shown next.

Listing 7.1   The main.js for the Electron window sizing app

```
'use strict';

const electron = require('electron');
const app = electron.app;
const BrowserWindow = electron.BrowserWindow;

let mainWindow = null;

app.on('window-all-closed', () => {
  if (process.platform !== 'darwin') app.quit();
});

app.on('ready', () => {
  mainWindow = new BrowserWindow({ width: 400, height: 200 });
  mainWindow.loadURL(`file://${__dirname}/index.html`);
  mainWindow.on('closed', () => { mainWindow = null; });
});
```

Where the width and height of the window are set

Now, you can run the app with `electron .` from the Terminal or Command Prompt, and you should see the app pop up looking like figure 7.3.

Figure 7.3   The Electron app running with a dimension of 400-pixel width and 200-pixel height. Notice that the app looks like it's running in an extreme landscape mode.

Electron's approach means you have fine-grained control over the dimensions of each app window. For more details on all the attributes you can pass into the creation of a BrowserWindow object instance, see http://electron.atom.io/docs/api/browser-window/.

That covers adjusting the size of the app window at loading time. Now, we'll look into how to get greater control over those window dimensions for the app.

7.1.3   *Constraining dimensions of window width and height in NW.js*

If you want to prevent the users of your apps from changing the width and height of your desktop app (and causing the UI to look skewed and weird), you can pass the options listed in table 7.1.

Table 7.1 Options to restrict window resizing

Property	Description
max_width	Sets the maximum width of the window
max_height	Sets the maximum height of the window
min_width	Sets the minimum width of the window
min_height	Sets the minimum height of the window

Here's how it would look in the package.json file:

```
"window": {
  "max_width": 1024,
  "min_width": 800,
  "max_height": 768,
  "min_height": 600
}
```

Figure 7.4 shows what dimensions are affected in the app window.

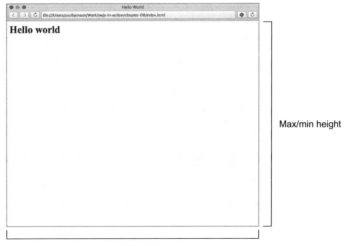

Figure 7.4 The window dimensions affected by the max/min width and max/min height

In the example JSON payload, you constrain the width of the window so that it can't be greater than 1024 pixels or less than 800 pixels. You also constrain the height of the window to be no greater than 768 pixels and no less than 600 pixels. Being able to constrain the window width and height (even when the user attempts to resize them) gives you greater control over making sure the look and feel of the app fits with the intended design.

This is good when you know what window dimensions you want to constrain to when the app loads. But what if you want the app window's width and height to be set to dynamic values, such as an app displaying an image (where the window's width and height match the dimensions of the image)?

The good news is that there's a way to do that with NW.js's window API. Say you have an image on your computer with dimensions of 900 x 550 pixels, and you want to size the window to match. You can set the width and height of the window to 900 pixels wide and 550 pixels high with the code shown in the following listing.

Listing 7.2   Dynamically resizing the app window

```
const gui = require('nw.gui');          References GUI
const win = gui.Window.get();           API in NW.js

win.width = 1024;      Sets width and height    Uses GUI API to select
win.height = 768;      of window dynamically    current app window
```

Being able to resize the window programmatically lets you make the app window match the dimensions of the content inside it and therefore give a better experience to the user.

You can also use the same API to control where the window is rendered on the screen. The GUI API in NW.js allows you to position the window at a set of coordinates relative to the screen. The next listing shows an example of doing this programmatically with NW.js.

Listing 7.3   Positioning the window relative to the screen

```
const gui = require('nw.gui');
const win = gui.Window.get();       Sets horizontal coordinate
win.x = 400;                        of app window
win.y = 500;       Sets vertical coordinate
                   of app window
```

This code affords you the ability to determine exactly where on the screen the app window will be positioned, which is good in the case of utility applications and the like.

We'll now take a look at how Electron handles constraining app windows.

7.1.4   *Constraining dimensions of window width and height in Electron*

The settings for constraining the dimensions of app windows in Electron are defined on the `BrowserWindow` instance. You'll remember from earlier in the chapter that to create an app window, you have to initialize an instance of the `BrowserWindow` class in the code.

Listing 7.4 Initializing a `BrowserWindow` instance in Electron

```
'use strict';

const electron = require('electron');
const app = electron.app;
const BrowserWindow = electron.BrowserWindow;

let mainWindow = null;

app.on('window-all-closed', () => {
  if (process.platform !== 'darwin') app.quit();
});

app.on('ready', () => {
  mainWindow = new BrowserWindow({ width: 400, height: 200 });
  mainWindow.loadURL(`file://${__dirname}/index.html`);
  mainWindow.on('closed', () => { mainWindow = null; });
});
```

Passes options to BrowserWindow instance

The `mainWindow` variable is an instance of the `BrowserWindow` class of Electron and is passed an object containing the width and height for the window. Here, you can set the maximum and minimum width and height properties for the app window. Say, for example, you want to make sure that the app cannot be resized below 300 px wide and 150 px high, and cannot be resized beyond 600 px wide and 450 px high—you can pass these options into the BrowserWindow instance:

```
mainWindow = new BrowserWindow({
  width: 400, height: 200,
  minWidth: 300, minHeight: 150,
  maxWidth: 600, maxHeight: 450
});
```

Table 7.2 shows the properties to change for the window width and height.

Table 7.2 Properties for changing window width and height

Property	Description
maxWidth	Sets the maximum width of the window
maxHeight	Sets the maximum height of the window
minWidth	Sets the minimum width of the window
minHeight	Sets the minimum height of the window

The approach taken by Electron is nice because it lets you define individual settings for each app window that your app creates, and you can configure all of those settings in one place in the code, rather than look for them in separate places in the code. It's simpler than in NW.js, and where NW.js uses snake case (as in `max_width`) property names, Electron uses camel case (as in `maxWidth`) property names, JavaScript-style.

By default, Electron renders the app in the middle of the screen. If you want to position the app window in a specific area of the screen, you can control this by passing x and y coordinates to the initialization of the `BrowserWindow`, like this:

```
mainWindow = new BrowserWindow({
  width: 400, height: 800,
  x: 10, y: 10
});
```

The position of the window is set to begin at 10 pixels from the left (x) and 10 pixels from the top (y), and so it offers you the ability to control where you position the app window on the screen.

Having explored window sizing and positioning, we'll now look at how to configure the app to run as a frameless application, or even in full-screen mode.

7.2   *Frameless windows and full-screen apps*

When you visit a train station and look at the display of train times and announcements, chances are the display is powered by a desktop app running in full-screen mode. Touch-screen monitors such as ATM machines also run desktop apps that are designed to prevent users from exiting the app, known as *kiosk apps*. Computer games also exhibit the same behavior, so the need for building apps that hide the underlying OS is a common one.

Electron and NW.js allow developers to tailor their apps so that they run in full-screen mode (for video playback and games), as well as frameless (for media players and other utilities) and kiosk (for information kiosks and point-of-sale applications). We'll take a look at how NW.js enables this and then look at Electron's approach for comparison.

7.2.1   *Full-screen applications in NW.js*

Video games are a prime example of apps that run in full-screen mode when they first boot up. Recent versions of Mac OS have enabled apps to operate easily in full-screen mode, and NW.js takes advantage of this feature in two ways: via configuration options in the package.json manifest file, or dynamically via the JavaScript API. The following code is an example of enabling your desktop app to run in full-screen mode when it launches via the package.json file:

```
{
  "window": {
    "fullscreen": true
  }
}
```

If you put the following JSON into the package.json file of an NW.js desktop app and then run the app, you can expect to see the app go straight into full-screen mode upon launch, where the title bar is not visible and the contents of the app take up the entire screen.

Alternatively, if you want to prevent users from being able to make an app enter full-screen mode, you can set the value to `false`.

As mentioned earlier, it's possible to make the app go full-screen programmatically via NW.js's native UI API, as follows:

```
const gui = require('nw.gui');
const window = gui.Window.get();
window.enterFullscreen();
```

Say you have a dead-simple NW.js app (such as a Hello World example), and you want a screen click to trigger full-screen mode. The app has some simple HTML for the home page, as shown next.

Listing 7.5 Example of programmatically triggering full-screen mode

```
<html>
  <head>
    <title>Full-screen app programmatic NW.js</title>
    <script>
      'use strict';

      const gui = require('nw.gui');          // Loads NW's UI library
      const win = gui.Window.get();           // Gets ahold of the app window

      function goFullScreen () {              // Creates function that will
        win.enterFullscreen();                // put app in full-screen mode
      }
    </script>
  </head>
  <body>
    <h1>Full-screen app example</h1>
    <button onclick="goFullScreen();">Go full screen</button>   // Clicking button calls goFullScreen function, putting app window in full-screen mode
  </body>
</html>
```

Insert that into the main index.html file for the app and run the app from the command line with nw. You should see a screen like figure 7.5.

Figure 7.5 App with a button that turns on full-screen mode when clicked

Click the Go Full Screen button and you should see the app go to full-screen. So how did that happen? Going through the HTML, you can see some embedded JavaScript that called out to NW.js's GUI API, fetched the current window, and told it to enter full-screen mode. You wrapped the call to enter full-screen mode in a function called goFullScreen, which the button element in the page triggered when clicked.

This is all good, but what if you're already in full-screen mode and want to leave that mode? NW.js accommodates this as well. You can modify the existing code so that it can call the API function leaveFullscreen, but the trick here is to track what the current state of the window is (whether it's already in full-screen mode). You can find out what the mode of the app window is with an API call called isFullscreen.

You'll modify the previous example so that when the button is clicked and the app window enters full-screen mode, the button will change its text to "Exit Full Screen" and leave full-screen mode. Replace the HTML in the index.html file with this code:

```
<html>
  <head>
    <title>Full-screen app example</title>
    <script>
      'use strict';
      const gui = require('nw.gui');
      const win = gui.Window.get();

      function toggleFullScreen () {
        const button = document.getElementById('fullscreen');
        if (win.isFullscreen) {
          win.leaveFullscreen();
          button.innerText = 'Go full screen';
        } else {
          win.enterFullscreen();
          button.innerText = 'Exit full screen';
        }
      }

    </script>
  </head>
  <body>
    <h1>Full-screen app example</h1>
    <button id="fullscreen" onclick="toggleFullScreen();">Go full
      screen</button>
  </body>
</html>
```

This replaces the goFullScreen function with a toggleFullScreen function that makes an API call to determine whether the app window is in full-screen mode. The API call returns either true (it is in full-screen mode) or false. The function is called when the user clicks the button. When the user first clicks it, the function will enter into full-screen mode (because the app isn't initially in full-screen mode). It will also change the text on the button to read "Exit Full Screen" to reflect the fact that the app is in full-screen mode. When the user clicks the button a second time, because the app window is in full-screen mode, you'll leave that mode, and alter the text of the button to read "Go Full Screen." This behavior allows the user to toggle full-screen mode in a simple and easy-to-understand fashion.

After you've changed the HTML and reloaded the app from the command line, click the Go Full Screen button. Not only should the app window enter full-screen mode, the button should now display "Exit Full Screen," as shown in figure 7.6.

Fullscreen app example

Exit full screen

Figure 7.6 Example app in full-screen mode. Notice that the button text has changed to allow the user to exit full-screen mode.

Being able to enter and exit full-screen mode in desktop apps can be handy, particularly when it comes to video playback. In fact, due to a bug that existed with supporting full-screen playback of videos in NW.js apps (see issue #55 on the GitHub repository), we (at Axisto Media) managed to work around the issue for our British Medical Journal (BMJ) app by accessing the shadow DOM of the video element and toggling the full-screen mode when the user clicked the Play/Pause button.

Full-screen mode enables users to take full advantage of the screen when using the app and display it in such a way as to eliminate the distractions of other windows in the background.

Now that you've seen how this is done in NW.js, we'll take a look at how Electron handles supporting full-screen applications.

7.2.2   *Full-screen applications in Electron*

Electron also offers configuration for full-screen mode. When creating a new `Browser-Window` instance, you can set options to configure for full-screen mode. To make an Electron app run in full-screen mode when it's started, pass the following configuration option when creating the `BrowserWindow` instance:

```
mainWindow = new BrowserWindow({fullscreen: true});
```

When the app runs, it will go straight into full-screen mode. This is a good option for an app that plays videos or games.

But what if you don't want people to have this option? How do you disable it? Simple: you pass the `fullscreenable` property with a value of `false` when initializing the `BrowserWindow` instance, as demonstrated in the following code:

```
mainWindow = new BrowserWindow({fullscreenable: false});
```

This configuration option means that the user will not be able to make the app enter full-screen mode from the title bar. This can be useful in cases where you want to maintain the dimensions of an app's user interface, such as with a small utility application.

If you want to be able to trigger this functionality programmatically, you'll need to call a function on the `mainWindow` instance after it's initialized. I'll re-create the example that I made for NW.js, using Electron instead, so you can compare the two.

Listing 7.6 Code for the main.js file for the full-screen Electron example

```
'use strict';

const electron = require('electron');
const app = electron.app;
const BrowserWindow = electron.BrowserWindow;

let mainWindow = null;

app.on('window-all-closed', () => {
  if (process.platform !== 'darwin') app.quit();
});

app.on('ready', () => {
  mainWindow = new BrowserWindow();
  mainWindow.loadURL(`file://${__dirname}/index.html`);
  mainWindow.on('closed', () => { mainWindow = null; });
});
```

Here, you see that the app code is pretty much standard. Next, you'll create the index.html file that has the button for toggling between full-screen mode and window mode.

Listing 7.7 The index.html file for the full-screen Electron example

```
<html>
  <head>
    <title>Fullscreen app programmatic Electron</title>
  </head>
    <script src="app.js"></script>
  <body>
    <h1>Hello from Electron</h1>
    <button id="fullscreen" onclick="toggleFullScreen();">
      Go full screen
    </button>
  </body>
</html>
```

Loads client-side code as separate JavaScript file

Calls function in the app.js file called toggleFullScreen to do the toggling

As in the NW.js variant of the code, the app has a button that is used to trigger toggling between full-screen mode and window mode. The only difference here is that you load a separate app.js file that has the client-side code for toggling. Finally, you add a standard package.json file as from the previous Electron example, and then the code for the app.js file shown next.

Listing 7.8   The app.js file for the full-screen Electron example

**Uses remote API to get current
window page is being rendered in**

**Uses remote API to interact
with main process from
renderer process**

```
const remote = require('electron').remote;

function toggleFullScreen() {
  const button = document.getElementById('fullscreen');
  const win = remote.getCurrentWindow();
  if (win.isFullScreen()) {
    win.setFullScreen(false);
    button.innerText = 'Go full screen';
  } else {
    win.setFullScreen(true);
    button.innerText = 'Exit full screen';
  }
}
```

**Calls BrowserWindow
instance's isFullScreen
function to check if window
is in full-screen mode**

**If so, switches to window
mode by calling the
instance's setFullScreen
function with false**

**If not, switches to
full-screen mode**

This is a good example of the difference in approaches between NW.js and Electron. Electron handles how the front-end calls to the back-end of the app by providing an API called remote. This allows the renderer process (front end) to send messages to the main process (back end), so that you can do things like get ahold of the Browser-Window instance and interact with it. You can then call various functions on the BrowserWindow instance to inspect its current settings (such as whether it's running in full-screen mode) and use that to determine whether to make it render in full-screen mode or windowed mode.

What other functions can I call on the BrowserWindow instance?

This book touches on some (but not all) of the functions that can be called on the BrowserWindow instance. There's a wide range of configuration options for the BrowserWindow class in Electron, like being able to make the title bar styling different in Mac OS X (such as what Hyper, Kitematic, and WebTorrent use).

For more about these configuration options and functions that can be called on initialized BrowserWindow instances, check out http://electron.atom.io/docs/api/browser-window/.

This demonstrates how to toggle between full-screen mode and window mode in Electron. Next, we'll look at how to make more-radical changes to your app UI, in the form of frameless apps.

7.2.3   Frameless apps

Although being able to make your apps go full-screen at the click of a button is fun, it may not be suited for your app's purposes. Some apps, including media players, onscreen widgets, and other utility apps, run without displaying any of the app window around them, and instead display a unique UI. An example of this is the music player VOX on Mac OS X, shown in figure 7.7. Notice that the UI is custom, and there is no Mac OS X UI visible (no title bar, no traffic-light buttons, only a simple X to close the window).

Figure 7.7   **VOX music player in Mac OS X, playing a song. Notice the distinct lack of Mac OS X's UI elements and title bar.**

CREATING FRAMELESS APPS IN NW.JS

These apps are known as *frameless apps*, and you can create them in NW.js as well. Alter the package.json manifest file so that the window section contains a property called `frame`, with the value set to `false`, as in this code sample:

```
{
"name" : "frameless-transparent-app-nwjs",
"version" : "1.0.0",
"main" : "index.html",
"window" : {
  "frame" : false
}
}
```

You can modify the package.json further to allow for transparency behind the app's screen, so that you can use rounded corners and create interesting interfaces. Changing the package.json to use this:

```
"window" : {
  "frame" : false,
  "transparent": true,
  "width": 300,
  "height": 150
}
```

You now have the basis for creating an app that's similar in style to the interface style presented in the VOX app if you adjust the index.html file to look like the next listing.

Listing 7.9   Creating a frameless app with styled rounded corners

```
<html>
  <head>
    <title>Transparent NW.js app - you won't see this title</title>
```

```
    <style rel="stylesheet">
      html {
        border-radius: 25px;
        }
      body{
        background: #333;
                          color: white;
        font-family: 'Signika';
      }
      p {
        padding: 1em;
        text-align: center;
        text-shadow: 1px 1px 1px rgba(0,0,0,0.25);
      }
    </style>
  </head>
  <body>
    <p>Frameless app example</p>
  </body>
</html>
```

If you run the example via the command line, you'll see the app on your desktop, as shown in figure 7.8.

Figure 7.8   A frameless app running on the desktop. The app style mimics an exaggerated version of the rounded-corner UI on VOX, to demonstrate how the app can have a transparent background.

Although this offers the chance to create some snazzy custom UIs for your desktop apps, bear in mind some caveats to using this approach. The first is that after disabling the window frame, you need to provide buttons for closing/minimizing the app window (alternatively, you can allow the user to close the app from the main toolbar of the OS).

It's important to note that frameless apps aren't draggable by default. This is because they have no UI element set (such as the title bar) that allows them to be dragged. That said, there's a way to enable them to be dragged. The key is to use a custom CSS property on the HTML for the screen, known as -webkit-app-region.

For HTML elements that you want to make draggable (such as the body tag for example), apply the following CSS:

```
-webkit-app-region: drag;
```

If you append this CSS property to the body tag in the embedded CSS stylesheet from the previous example and reload the app, you'll see that it can now be dragged across the screen. I'd like to be able to say that's all there is to it, but unfortunately that's not the case. Applying this CSS property to the body tag makes all HTML elements within the app an area that will drag the app, including the text that says "Frameless app example." Try selecting the text—you cannot. The entire contents of the DOM under the body tag are also draggable, which might not be the behavior that you want for that part of the app. How do you resolve this?

The answer depends on what the nature of the HTML element needs to do. If the HTML element in question is a clickable element, like a button or a drop-down field, then you'll want to give those HTML elements the -webkit-app-region property with a value of no-drag, like this:

```
button, select {
  -webkit-app-region: no-drag;
}
```

This will enable you to be able to click buttons without the draggable behavior kicking in. Alternatively, if the HTML elements in question are elements that you want to be able to select snippets of for copying and pasting into other documents and apps (such as p tags and img tags), then you can make them selectable by the -webkit-user-select property alongside the -webkit-app-region CSS property with a value of no-drag:

```
p, img {
  -webkit-user-select: all;
  -webkit-app-region: no-drag;
}
```

You'll need to do this on all the HTML elements that you want to be selectable, as well as all UI elements that need to be clickable. It can be a bit of a pig, but it ultimately means that you can have a completely custom look to your UI and make your app stand out from the rest.

The final version of the index.html file should look like the following.

Listing 7.10   The index.html file for the transparent frameless app

```
<html>
  <head>
    <title>Transparent NW.js app - you won't see this title</title>
    <style rel="stylesheet">
      html {
        border-radius: 25px;
        -webkit-app-region: drag;
      }

      body {
        background: #333;
```

```
      color: white;
      font-family: 'Signika';
    }

  p {
    padding: 1em;
    text-align: center;
    text-shadow: 1px 1px 1px rgba(0,0,0,0.25);
  }

    button, select {
      -webkit-app-region: no-drag;
    }

    p, img {
      -webkit-user-select: all;
      -webkit-app-region: no-drag;
    }
  </style>
 </head>
 <body>
   <p>Frameless app example</p>
 </body>
</html>
```

Now you can drag the app around the screen and see the background behind the rounded corners. That gives you an idea of how you can approach creating transparent apps in NW.js. Now we'll look at how the same can be done with Electron.

CREATING FRAMELESS APPS WITH ELECTRON

As demonstrated earlier in the chapter, Electron handles configuring app windows via the initialization of the `BrowserWindow` instance. You can make the app frameless or transparent by passing a property to the initialization of the `BrowserWindow` at runtime. The following code is an example of how to configure a frameless app in Electron:

```
mainWindow = new BrowserWindow({ frame: false });
```

The app will now run in frameless mode, and you'll see something like figure 7.9.

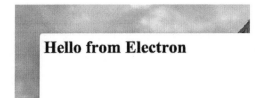

Figure 7.9 An Electron app running in frameless mode. Notice how the content of the app is positioned so closely to the top and left of the app? The app's corners are rounded by default as part of Mac OS X.

If you want to try this example for yourself, you can give it a spin in the chapter-07 folder of the GitHub repository at https://github.com/paulbjensen/cross-platform-desktop-applications, under the app example frameless-app-electron.

Electron also allows you to make app windows transparent by passing the `transparent` property in the following example:

```
mainWindow = new BrowserWindow({ transparent: true });
```

Figure 7.10 shows what a transparent Electron app looks like.

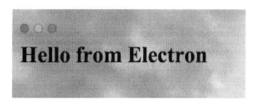

Figure 7.10   **A transparent app in Electron. Notice how the background is completely transparent, but you can see the title bar buttons as well as the app's text.**

Transparency in Electron is a great feature as long as it doesn't complicate the UX. For small utility applications, this can be a useful attribute, but that depends on what the app is doing and whom it is for.

Some apps can run in environments where the user isn't necessarily trusted with complete access to the computer, such as in public terminals with touchscreen interfaces. In the next section, we'll look at implementing kiosk applications.

7.2.4   *Kiosk mode applications*

Sometimes you get the chance to build an app that will be used by lots of people, but with a catch—the app is public, such as the information area of a museum, or maybe a bank, and needs to be able to run in a mode where the user can't quit the app and start messing around with the computer (not a prospect anyone wants to entertain). Apps like these need to restrict access to the underlying OS, as though they're running at kiosks (which, in some cases, they are).

Kiosk mode in both NW.js and Electron is a locked-down mode where access to the underlying OS is difficult—in fact, being able to quit the app has to be manually added by the developer (otherwise, they have to physically reboot the computer to regain access to it).

CREATING KIOSK-MODE APPS IN NW.JS

To enable your app to run in kiosk mode, you'll need to modify your package.json manifest file so that it has a property of `kiosk` with the value set to `true`, as in the following example:

```
{
  "window": {
    "kiosk":true
  }
}
```

You can go ahead and give this a try in one of the example apps, *but* (and it is a *big but*) *make sure that nothing is left unsaved before you do.*

This is because you might have to reboot your computer in order to regain access to it. In kiosk mode, the app automatically enters full-screen mode, but without the title bar. The only way you can exit the app is by pressing Alt-Tab or Ctrl-Alt-Del on the keyboard—otherwise, you're stuck inside the app with no way out of it.

Say you need to build a kiosk app for someone, but you also need to be able to exit the program (in case there's an issue with the OS). How do you do that?

The answer is to implement some kind of keyboard shortcut or button that when clicked or typed calls an API function on the app window called `leaveKioskMode`. Like the full-screen API functions, kiosk mode has equivalent API functions for entering/leaving kiosk mode, as well as for detecting whether the app window is in kiosk mode.

Imagine that you have an app that will run at a display kiosk and you want to provide a way for the IT systems administrator to get access to the computer's OS without having to resort to rebooting the computer (in particular, if access to the computer's power supply and reboot button is physically obscured). You decide to add a button called `exit` to the app window to help the administrator get back to the OS.

Make sure that the package.json file looks like this:

```json
{
  "name"      : "kiosk-mode-example-app",
  "version"   : 1.0,
  "main"      : "index.html",
  "window"    : {
    "kiosk"   : true
  }
}
```

And the index.html file should look like the following.

Listing 7.11   Kiosk app's index.html file, with an essential toggle button

```html
<html>
  <head>
    <title>Kiosk mode NW.js app example</title>
    <script>
      'use strict';

      const gui = require('nw.gui');          Creates function to tell
      const win = gui.Window.get();           app window to get out
                                              of kiosk mode
      function exit () {
        win.leaveKioskMode();
      }

    </script>
  </head>
  <body>                                      Clicking button calls
    <h1>Kiosk mode app</h1>                   function to get out of
    <button onclick="exit();">Exit</button>   kiosk mode
  </body>
</html>
```

You'll notice you use the same pattern you used for the first full-screen mode app example (click a button, exit mode). This is so you can easily demonstrate the functionality of being able to leave kiosk mode from the app. If you now run the app, you should expect to see something like figure 7.11.

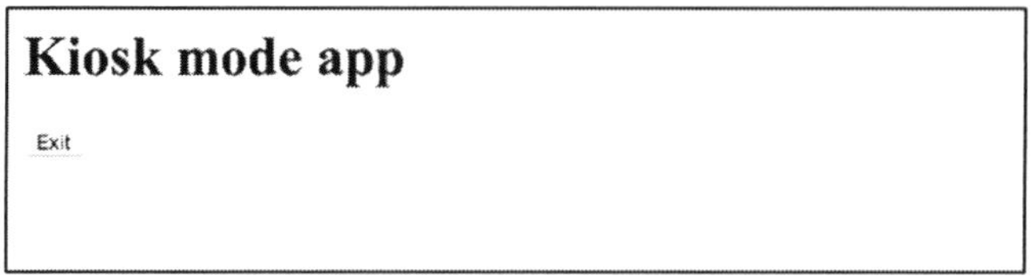

Kiosk mode app

Exit

Figure 7.11 An app running in kiosk mode. The app runs across the entire screen, and access to the OS is obscured.

Click the Exit button, and the app will leave kiosk mode and switch back to a normal window layout.

> **ARE ALL KEYBOARD SHORTCUTS BLOCKED BY KIOSK MODE?** No, NW.js still allows users to quit apps using the global keyboard shortcuts (for example, Alt-F4 on Windows). The reason it allows this is because virus detection software will block apps that attempt to override access to these global keyboard shortcuts.

This shows how you can create kiosk apps with NW.js. For Electron, the process for creating kiosk mode apps is dead simple.

CREATING KIOSK APPS WITH ELECTRON

Electron is able to make apps run in kiosk mode by passing one attribute to the initialization of the BrowserWindow instance called (can you guess?) kiosk. Here's an example:

```
mainWindow = new BrowserWindow({ kiosk: true });
```

With the browser window configured this way, the app is able to run in full-screen mode, and the only way to quite the app is via the keyboard shortcut (Command-Q on Mac OS X, Alt-F4 on Windows/Linux).

But if you want to provide some form of programmatic access to kiosk mode and be able to toggle it via a button, you can do that in precisely the same fashion as you would with toggling the full-screen app example.

You can try the app from the source code in the kiosk-app-programmatic-electron folder in the chapter-07 folder of the book's GitHub repository. The app is a pretty standard setup, but with distinct differences in the index.html and app.js files. The following listing shows what the index.html file looks like.

Listing 7.12 The index.html file for the programmatic kiosk mode Electron app

```
<html>
  <head>
    <title>Programmatic Kiosk app Electron</title>
  </head>
```

```
    <script src="app.js"></script>
  <body>
    <h1>Hello from Electron</h1>
    <button id="kiosk" onclick="toggleKiosk();">Enter kiosk</button>    ◁──┐
  </body>                                                                    |
</html>                                              **Clicking button triggers**
                                                **entering or exiting kiosk mode**
```

When the kiosk button is clicked, you expect it to call a function called `toggleKiosk`. This is a function that is defined in the app.js file, shown next.

Listing 7.13   The app.js file for the programmatic kiosk mode Electron app

```
const remote = require('electron').remote;          **Defines toggleKiosk**
                                                    **function that's called**
function toggleKiosk() {                         ◁  **when button is clicked**
  const button = document.getElementById('kiosk');
  const win = remote.getCurrentWindow();              **Detects if app is**
  if (win.isKiosk()) {                            ◁   **running in kiosk mode**
    win.setKiosk(false);                     ◁──┐
    button.innerText = 'Enter kiosk mode';       **If so, triggers exiting kiosk mode**
  } else {                                        **and updating button text**
    win.setKiosk(true);                       ◁
    button.innerText = 'Exit kiosk mode';        **If not, triggers entering kiosk**
  }                                              **mode and updating button text**
}
```

When running, the app is able to enter kiosk mode when the button is first clicked, and then is able to exit it when it has been put into kiosk mode. This allows you to create buttons for easily closing the app—say, if it's running at a computer that doesn't have keyboard access.

Kiosk mode is useful for apps that are used by members of the public, and where access to the underlying OS needs to be obscured. That said, as mentioned earlier, there are still ways to be able to escape from kiosk mode, so it's not a complete guarantee of protection from those who know their way around, but at least it will keep the majority from messing around with computers in public areas.

7.3   Summary

In this chapter, we've looked at different ways in which you can craft your app's display, depending on what the app needs to do for the user. Some quick takeaways:

- You can create windowed apps with specific width and height dimensions.
- You can restrict those dimensions so that the app's display stays fixed.
- It's easy to run your app in full-screen mode for videos and gaming.
- Alternatively, you can remove the app window and run it as a frameless app.
- Be careful with frameless apps because they come with some UI quirks you'll need to handle around dragging, click events, and text selection.
- Kiosk-mode apps are useful for ATMs and apps running in public areas.

The first thing to think about with crafting your app is whether the app needs to operate within a fixed or dynamic window, or even if it needs a window at all. Then, you can configure the window options in the package.json manifest file to make the app window constrained to specific dimensions, or expand to take up the full screen. Also, remember that depending on whether your app is window-based or even a kiosk-mode app, the ability to navigate is important, so make sure you can exit a kiosk app from somewhere within the app's UI.

In chapter 8, we'll look at implementing tray applications with NW.js and Electron.

Creating tray applications

This chapter covers

- Building tray-based applications
- Displaying application windows from the tray menu
- Adding menu items to the tray menu

Some apps aren't as beefy as others and focus on doing something specific and doing it well. They also focus on being accessible to the user without having to switch windows or switch focus from the current app that's in front of them. As a result, app functionality is made available from the tray bar of the OS, which is located at the bottom of the Windows GUI, at the top of the screen on a Mac, and—depending on what flavor of distribution and graphical desktop environment you use—either the top or bottom on Linux (Gnome tends to be at the top, and KDE tends to be at the bottom).

Tray apps tend to be utility apps like timers, music controls, and instant messaging. They use menus and changing icons to communicate the status of the app. In this chapter, we'll look at how you can use NW.js's UI API to make tray apps by creating a small utility tray app with a dropdown menu. We'll then replicate this example with Electron to compare its tray app functionality.

8.1 *Creating a simple tray app with NW.js*

You'll build something small and simple, as shown in figure 8.1.

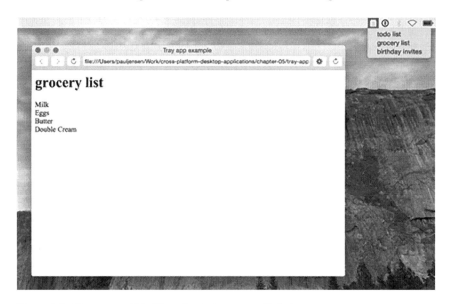

Figure 8.1   The app you'll build: a simple tray app with lists

Let's say you have a simple Hello World NW.js app, and you'd like to give it a tray icon to access it from the OS's main bar. Figure 8.2 shows what you want to create in the menu bar.

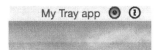

Figure 8.2   Your tray app displaying in the tray area of the OS's main bar

You can do that by changing index.html to contain the following embedded JavaScript:

```html
<html>
  <head>
    <title>tray app example</title>
    <script>
      const gui = require('nw.gui');
      const tray = new gui.Tray({title: 'My tray app'});
    </script>
  </head>
  <body>
    <h1>Hello world</h1>
  </body>
</html>
```

In this code, you extend the example Hello World app with some embedded Java-Script, and in that script are two lines of interest: the first is the one that loads NW.js's UI API, and the second is the one that creates a new tray, with the title "My tray app." If you run this app from the command line, you should see the usual Hello World example app, but you'll also see this item appear in your OS's main bar, as shown in figure 8.2.

> **SHOULD YOU USE TEXT LABELS FOR TRAY APPS?**   If you want to support Mac OS X only, then that's fine, but on Windows and Linux, tray apps display icons only. Your safest option is to go with using icons only for your tray apps.

You'll see that the text label you gave the tray app is displayed in the tray area. You'll also notice some other tray apps running there (VOX and 1Password), which choose not to display labels, only icons. If you want to display an icon as well (because it uses less space in the tray area), you can do that too with NW.js. Assume that you have a simple .png icon that you'd like to use (in this case, I've created a simple note-taking icon with Pixelmator, at a resolution of 32 x 32 pixels). Save it in the same folder where the index.html file is kept and alter the JavaScript line that creates the tray app to this:

```
const tray = new gui.Tray({icon: 'icon@2x.png'});
```

After making those changes, you'll need to rerun NW.js from the command line, and you should see the tray app icon look like figure 8.3.

Figure 8.3   The tray app displaying a custom icon created with Pixelmator

This gives you a nice icon that fits with the pattern of tray apps on Mac OS X, but you'll probably notice one oddity: the app icon's colors are in grayscale. That's something that NW.js does, but Electron renders the icon in color.

8.1.1   Adding menus to your tray icon

If you click on your tray app icon now, it doesn't do anything. You want to use the tray app as a way to execute other commands and interact with your app. Menus provide a way for tray apps to display a list of contents or trigger other actions. You want a solution that shows a menu listing the notes when the icon is clicked, as in figure 8.4.

Figure 8.4   The notes tray app displaying a list of notes

You can extend your simple tray app by adding a menu that lists a number of pre-defined notes. Clicking one of the notes loads the contents of that note in the app window. Let's start by creating some sample note content to put at the start of the embedded JavaScript:

```
const notes = [
  {
    title: 'todo list',
    contents: 'grocery shopping\npick up kids\nsend birthday party invites'},
  {
    title: 'grocery list',
    contents: 'Milk\nEggs\nButter\nDouble Cream'},
  {
    title: 'birthday invites',
    contents: 'Dave\nSue\nSally\nJohn and Joanna\nChris and Georgina\nElliot'
  }
];
```

Now that you have content, you can add the titles of the notes to a new menu as menu items, and attach that new menu to the tray:

```
const menu = new gui.Menu();
notes.forEach((note) => {
  menu.append(new gui.MenuItem({label: note.title}));
}

tray.menu = menu;
```

Here, you initialize a new `Menu` object and then loop through the list of notes, displaying their titles in the menu. After that, the menu is attached to the tray. Run NW.js on the app's code from the command line, and you should see a result like the one shown in figure 8.4.

So far, so good, but there's a bit more to do. You haven't yet got the tray menu items to interact with the app window, and you'd like to make the tray app work in such a way that when a note is clicked from the menu, the contents of that note are loaded into the app window.

To do this, you'll need to do the following:

- Change the HTML in the screen to have placeholders for the title and contents of a note.
- Create a function to insert the title and contents of a note into the HTML.
- Alter the `menuItem` objects to trigger this function when they're clicked.

Start by modifying the body tag's inner HTML. Change it to this:

```
<body>
  <h1 id="title"></h1>
  <div id="contents"></div>
</body>
```

The h1 tag will contain the title of the note (hence, the id attribute with a value of "title"), and the div tag will contain the contents of the note (again, with the id attribute of "contents"). Next, at the top of the embedded JavaScript, create a function that will insert the title and contents of a note into the page:

```
function displayNote (note) {
  document.getElementById('title').innerText = note.title;
  document.getElementById('contents').innerText = note.contents;
}
```

This function inserts the title and contents of the note object passed to it into the HTML elements on the page. Once you have this function, you'll modify the menu-Item objects so they call the displayNote function with the note object when clicked.

To do that, though, you need to move some of that code into a new function, because you shouldn't make functions within a loop (otherwise, you get some unexpected behavior with the variable that's passed to the function). Create a new function called appendNoteToMenu and define it after the initialization of the menu object:

```
function appendNoteToMenu (note) {
  const menuItem = new gui.MenuItem({
    label: note.title,
    click: () => { displayNote(note); }
  });
  menu.append(menuItem);
}
```

The function receives the note object and generates a MenuItem object. It sets the label of the menu item to the note's title and defines a function to execute when the menu item is clicked. The function calls displayNote with the note object, so that when the menu item is clicked, the note's title and contents are displayed in the app window. Finally, the menu item is added to the menu object.

Before the menu is added to the tray, modify the bit of code that loops through the notes to call the appendNoteToMenu function, like so:

```
notes.map(appendNoteToMenu);
```

You're almost there. Next, make sure the app displays the first note in the list and give it a bit of styling to make it more genuine.

When the HTML for the app has loaded, you'll be able to trigger displaying the first note that's available. Add the following JavaScript toward the end of the script tag:

```
document.addEventListener('DOMContentLoaded', () => {
  displayNote(notes[0]);
});
```

When the app loads, as shown in figure 8.5, you should see that the first note is displayed in the app window.

Figure 8.5   The notes app displaying the first note in the list

Before you call this app done, add a link in the index.html file to a CSS stylesheet called app.css so you can make the notes app look a bit more like a note, as shown next.

Listing 8.1   Adding the CSS link to the index.html file

```html
<html>
  <head>
    <title>tray app example</title>
    <link href="app.css" rel="stylesheet">        Adds the link for
    <script>                                       an app.css file
      'use strict';
```

Next, add an app.css file with the following CSS:

```css
body {
  background: #E2D53C;
  color: #292929;
  font-family: 'Comic Sans', 'Comic Sans MS';
  font-size: 14pt;
  font-style: italic;
}
```

With the styling change in place, the notes app should now look like figure 8.6.

Figure 8.6   The notes app with CSS styling applied

If you run the app with NW.js from the command line, when you click a note title in the tray app's menu, you can expect the note's title and contents to display in the app window.

> **IS THERE A COPY OF THIS APP'S FULL SOURCE CODE?**   Yes, you can grab the code example tray App NW.js from this GitHub Repository: https://github.com/paulbjensen/cross-platform-desktop-applications

Now that you've created a tray app with NW.js, let's see how you go about replicating the example with Electron.

8.2 Creating a tray app with Electron

Electron's modular approach to creating apps lends itself well to creating tray apps. The API is similar to the one provided by NW.js, and this section shows how to re-create the tray app from the previous section, but with Electron's API.

8.2.1 Building the initial app skeleton

The bare-minimum set of files needed for a tray app follows:

- main.js for the app's code
- A PNG image for the app icon
- A package.json file for the app's configuration

When creating a tray app in Electron, you don't need an index.html file, but you want to show the content of the notes in the list, so you'll have a file for that, as well as an app.js file for the app's front-end code.

You'll start by writing the app's package.json. Make a folder called tray-app-electron and insert a file named package.json with the following code:

```
{
  "name"    : "tray-app-electron",
  "version" : "1.0.0",
  "main"    : "main.js"
}
```

Now, create the index.html file where the contents of the notes will be displayed. Create an index.html file and insert the following HTML into it:

```
<html>
  <head>
    <title>tray app Electron</title>
    <link href="app.css" rel="stylesheet">
    <script src="app.js"></script>
  </head>
  <body>
    <h1 id="title"></h1>
    <div id="contents"></div>
  </body>
</html>
```

The index.html applies the same HTML structure as the NW.js example, except that where NW.js has inline JavaScript, you move the front-end JavaScript into the app.js file. This is because Electron keeps the front-end JavaScript separate from the back-end JavaScript and requires using inter-process communication to transmit data from the app's back end to the browser window, as you'll see later in the example.

The app.css file is identical to the app.css file that you used in the NW.js tray app, so I won't repeat it here, and the same goes for the app icon. The main meat of the app is in the main.js file (back end) and the app.js file (front end). We'll look at the main.js file first.

Create a file called main.js and insert the following code.

Listing 8.2 The main.js file for the Electron tray app

```
'use strict';

const electron = require('electron');
const app = electron.app;
const Menu = electron.Menu;                                    Requires Electron's
const tray = electron.Tray;                                    Menu API
const BrowserWindow = electron.BrowserWindow;
                                                               Loads its tray API
let appIcon = null;
let mainWindow = null;                 Creates a null appIcon
                                       variable so tray app doesn't
const notes = [                        get garbage collected
  {
    title: 'todo list',
    contents: 'grocery shopping\npick up kids\nsend birthday party invites'
  },
  {
    title: 'grocery list',
    contents: 'Milk\nEggs\nButter\nDouble Cream'
  },
  {
    title: 'birthday invites',
    contents: 'Dave\nSue\nSally\nJohn and Joanna\nChris and Georgina\nElliot'
  }
];

function displayNote (note) {
  mainWindow.webContents.send('displayNote', note);     Uses Electron's
}                                                       WebContents API to send
                                                        data to browser window to
function addNoteToMenu (note) {                         display note's contents
  return {
    label: note.title,
    type: 'normal',
    click: () => { displayNote(note); }                          Creates context
  };                                                              menu for tray
}                                                                 app, looping
                                                                  through notes to
                                    Creates tray                  add menu items
app.on('ready', () => {             app with icon
  appIcon = new Tray('icon@2x.png');
  let contextMenu = Menu.buildFromTemplate(notes.map(addNoteToMenu));
  appIcon.setToolTip('Notes app');
  appIcon.setContextMenu(contextMenu);                    Binds context
                                                          menu to tray app
  mainWindow = new BrowserWindow({ width: 800, height: 600 });
  mainWindow.loadURL(`file://${__dirname}/index.html`);
```

Sets a
tooltip on
tray app

```
mainWindow.webContents.on('dom-ready', () => {
  displayNote(notes[0]);
});
});
```

◁— **When app window is loaded, defaults to displaying first note**

Now, the back-end code will create the tray app, its menu, and a `BrowserWindow` instance to display a note's contents. This will allow the app to load up with the first note. The app.js file handles when a note is clicked in the menu. The app.js file will use Electron's `ipcRenderer` module to handle receiving the `displayNote` event and the note passed from the main process to the renderer process, so you can update the HTML inside the `BrowserWindow` process.

In the app.js file, insert the code shown next.

Listing 8.3   The app.js file for the Electron tray example

```
function displayNote(event, note) {
  document.getElementById('title').innerText = note.title;
  document.getElementById('contents').innerText = note.contents;
}

const ipc = require('electron').ipcRenderer;
ipc.on('displayNote', displayNote);
```

◁— **displayNote function inserts contents of note into HTML**

◁— **Electron's ipcRenderer module listens for events being triggered by back-end process**

Upon menu item click or when app loads, ipcRenderer module intercepts event and note; then passes them to displayNote

Electron's `ipcRenderer` module is able to send and receive data to/from Electron's main process. In the context of the tray app, the back-end process passes data to the browser window via the web contents API, so the `displayNote` event and the note are passed from the back end to the front end, and `ipcRenderer` listens on that event. When the event is triggered, `ipcRenderer` will pick up the note and pass it to the function that handles inserting the note into the HTML. Figure 8.7 shows what the app looks like.

Figure 8.7   The Electron notes app. Notice how Electron renders the app icon in color by default.

In this section, you've been able to use your knowledge of menus to build tray apps that users can access easily—usually utility apps like chat apps, password managers, and to-do list apps. You've seen how to configure the icon for the app as well as attach a menu to it when it's clicked.

8.3   *Summary*

In this chapter, we've looked at different ways to create tray apps in NW.js and Electron. Tray apps are neat little utilities. When creating them, make sure to check how they work across all OSs, because there will be variation (Mac OS X lets you use labels with them, for example, but Windows and Linux only show icons). Also, remember that icons need to be within a 32 x 32–pixel dimension. We also looked at how to add menu items to tray apps.

Some key takeaways:

- You can use text for the app's tray menu display, but icons are preferable due to how Windows and Linux display them.
- NW.js tray apps seem to display the tray icon in grayscale on Mac OS X, whereas Electron tray apps display in color.

In chapter 9, we'll look at ways to mimic the look and feel of the user's OS.

Creating application and context menus

This chapter covers

- Creating application window menus
- Handling Mac OS's approach to menus
- Handing Windows's/Linux's approach to menus
- Creating context menus for the content inside of the application

Menus are important for providing users with lots of feature choices. Anyone familiar with using Microsoft Office will know how much functionality is available to users from the app menu when using Word or Excel. It's one of the most effective UI patterns in widespread use today.

In this chapter, we'll look at how to create app menus for your desktop apps. You'll see how they're handled differently by Mac OS compared to Windows and Linux. We'll then look at context menus, which provide the user with options when right-clicking on elements within the app, such as being able to insert an item of content at a particular point within a document.

9.1   *Adding menus to your app*

Three kinds of menus are available for your Node.js desktop apps: app window menus, context menus, and tray menus (covered in chapter 8). App window menus appear in the top of an app window under the title bar (or in the system menu on Mac OS), and you see context menus when right-clicking an item in the app. We'll take a look at app window menus first.

9.1.1   *App window menus*

Creating an app menu bar is a bit tricky, and you must consider which OSs you're targeting.

Surprisingly, this is something that Microsoft Windows and Linux operating systems handle exactly the same way, and Mac OS is the odd one. On Windows and Linux, each app window has its own menu placed within it. For Mac OS, there's only one app menu for all the windows (displayed in the OS's menu bar, separate from the app window).

NW.js accommodates this difference in approaches by offering an API method specific to Mac OS and other methods for Windows and Linux. Electron, however, does not. It provides a single API method for creating app menus. We'll look at these APIs with examples in both frameworks to compare their approaches.

9.1.2   *Creating menus for Mac OS apps with NW.js*

A special API function is available for creating an app menu for Mac OS. To demonstrate this, let's take an example Hello World app and add a Mac OS app menu to it (this code is the mac-app-menu-nwjs app in the book's GitHub repository). You'll add the basic package.json file and then a standard index.html file with a link to an app.js file that will contain the code for the app's Mac OS menu.

> **Listing 9.1   The app.js file for the Mac app menu with NW.js**

```
'use strict';

const gui = require('nw.gui');

const mb = new gui.Menu({ type: 'menubar' });        ◁──  Creates Menu instance as menu bar
mb.createMacBuiltin('Mac app menu example');         ◁──  Transforms menu into a Mac OS menu and passes app name

gui.Window.get().menu = mb;                          ◁──  Attaches that menu to app's window
```

The app.js file in listing 9.1 embeds some JavaScript that initializes a new Menu object, creates the built-in Mac menu from it, gets the current app window, and sets its menu to be the Mac menu you generated. The end result should look like figure 9.1.

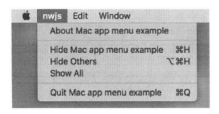

Figure 9.1   NW.js's default app menu for Mac OS apps. The menu provides some default actions such as copying/pasting content, hiding/closing windows, and finding out a bit about the app.

The built-in menu options allow the user to get up and running with a set of commands nested under the Edit and Window menu items, listed in table 9.1.

Table 9.1   Commands for menu options

Edit menu command	What it does
Undo	Reverts the last action
Redo	Restores the last action that was undone
Cut	Copies content and removes it from its current location
Copy	Copies selected content
Paste	Puts copied content in a given location
Delete	Removes selected content from a location
Select All	Selects all content
Window menu command	**What it does**
Minimize	Shrinks the window and animates its location in the task bar
Close Window	Closes the window
Bring All to Front	Makes all the windows for the app appear above other windows

These are pretty standard commands that you'll find across apps with any kind of comprehensive functionality.

Let's take a look at how Electron handles making Mac OS menus compared to NW.js.

9.1.3   *Creating menus for Mac OS apps with Electron*

The logical composition of menus and menu items is the same when you're creating menus in Electron apps, but the API functions to create and combine them are named differently. To illustrate this, we'll walk through an example app with a menu in Electron. The code for this is also in the book's GitHub repository under the app name mac-app-menu-electron.

When you download the app, you'll find a typical Electron app example, and the part of the code we're interested in is in the app.js file. When defining an app menu in Electron, you need to add it to an app window, and therefore this needs to be done in the code for the render process that handles the app window. Let's now walk through the code for defining an app menu in Electron.

Listing 9.2   Creating an app menu in Electron

```
'use strict';

const electron = require('electron');
const Menu    = electron.remote.Menu;
const name    = electron.remote.app.getName();

const template = [{
  label: '',
  submenu: [
    {
      label: 'About ' + name,
      role: 'about'
    },
    {
      type: 'separator'
    },
    {
      label: 'Quit',
      accelerator: 'Command+Q',
      click: electron.remote.app.quit
    }
  ]
}];

const menu = Menu.buildFromTemplate(template);
Menu.setAppMenu(menu);
```

LoadMenu module via remote API

App name also loaded via remote

Submenu items defined as array

Defines template array to contain menu items

Leaves label blank— app's name overridden on Mac OS

Menu item can have types that do default actions (displaying About dialog)

Menu items can have other types (separators between menu items)

Passes keyboard shortcut as string via accelerator property

Defines custom actions when menu item is clicked on click property

Uses buildFromTemplate function to create app menu

Sets app's menu from template

This code will result in an app that has a simple set of actions that can be performed as illustrated in figure 9.2.

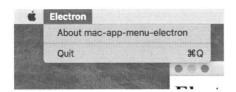

Figure 9.2   Electron rendering the menu items for Mac OS apps. Note the process name is displayed as the app menu's label name, with an About menu item, a separator, and the Quit menu item, with the keyboard shortcut displayed to the right.

This example is basic, and you may want to have more options available, such as Edit and Window menus that have typical actions like resizing windows and copy-and-paste actions. If you want full control over those actions, you can copy the example provided by Electron at http://electron.atom.io/docs/api/menu/ into your app. Or you can avoid copying lines of code into your app by using an npm module called electron-default-menu, available from www.npmjs.com/package/electron-default-menu. To show the menu library in action, you'll alter the app's code to use it in place of the template variable. First, you need to install the module in the app's code via npm:

```
npm install electron-default-menu --save
```

After installing the npm module, change the contents of the app.js file to the code shown next.

Listing 9.3 Using `electron-default-menu` in the app.js file

```
'use strict';

const electron = require('electron');
const defaultMenu = require('electron-default-menu');     ⟵┐  Requires npm
const Menu    = electron.remote.Menu;                          module to use later

const menu = Menu.buildFromTemplate(defaultMenu());       ⟵┐  Calls it in place of
Menu.setAppMenu(menu);                                         template code to
                                                               provide default menu
```

Now, reload the app, and you'll see a full app menu, as shown in figure 9.3.

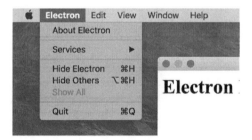

Figure 9.3 The Electron app with menu items for Edit, View, and Window options

The electron-default-menu module provides the app window with more actions and provides a base for adding other menu items. The `defaultMenu()` function returns an array, so adding/removing menu items can be done via pop, push, shift, and unshift functions on the menu variable. For a full list of functions available on the array, see http://mng.bz/cS21.

> **HOW DO I CHANGE THE APP MENU'S FIRST ITEM NAME?** On Mac OS, the app menu's first item is set to the app's name, regardless of what value is set in the code. This is because Mac OS gets that name from the app's Info.plist file. If you want to change the first menu item's label, you'll need to edit this file in the built version of your app. For more information, see http://mng.bz/12r1.

Now that we've covered how to handle Mac menus in your desktop apps, we'll turn our attention to how to handle them in Windows and Linux.

9.1.4   *Creating menus for Windows and Linux apps*

Because Windows and Linux handle menus differently than Mac OS, NW.js provides different API methods for creating menus, so you'll go through the same example (Hello World) with those methods. First, you'll create an app with NW.js.

BUILDING WINDOWS/LINUX APP MENUS WITH NW.JS

Let's say you have an app that needs a menu bar, with one menu item (File), and for nested menu items, you have the following commands: Say Hello and Quit the App. Figure 9.4 shows the app you want to create.

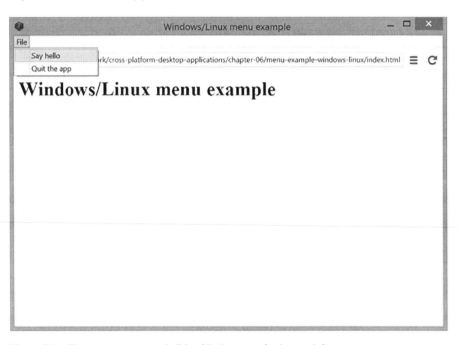

Figure 9.4   The app you want to build, with the menu in the top left

The Say Hello menu item shows an alert dialog with the message "Hello World" inside it, and the Quit the App menu item closes the app. First, let's focus on creating the menu bar and implementing the File menu item.

CREATING THE MENU BAR

Let's say you start with the following index.html content:

```
<html>
  <head>
    <title>Windows/Linux menu app example for NW.js</title>
  </head>
  <body>
    <h1>Windows/Linux menu example</h1>
  </body>
</html>
```

This initial page contains no code for the menu yet, so you'll start by adding a `script` tag in the head section of the HTML (after the `title` tag):

```
<script>
  'use strict';
</script>
```

Next, inside the `script` tag you'll load the GUI library:

```
<script>
  'use strict';

  const gui       = require('nw.gui');
  const menuBar   = new gui.Menu({type:'menubar'});
</script>
```

You load NW.js's GUI library so that you can begin to create the menu. On the following line, you create a menu bar, where menu items will be placed in the app window. You have to do this before you can begin to create any menu items, which is what follows next. On the following line inside the `script` tag, you initialize the File menu item:

```
<script>
  'use strict';

  const gui       = require('nw.gui');
  const menuBar   = new gui.Menu({type:'menubar'});
  const fileMenu  = new gui.MenuItem({label: 'File'});
</script>
```

Now that you've initialized all the objects you want to render in the app window, you need to attach the file menu to the menu bar:

```
<script>
  'use strict';

  const gui       = require('nw.gui');
  const menuBar   = new gui.Menu({type:'menubar'});
  const fileMenu  = new gui.MenuItem({label: 'File'});

  menuBar.append(fileMenu);
</script>
```

The menu bar has an `append` function that allows you to add menu items to it, and you use this to add the File menu item. Now, you can attach the menu bar to the app window, like so:

```
<script>
  'use strict';

  const gui       = require('nw.gui');
  const menuBar   = new gui.Menu({type:'menubar'});
  const fileMenu  = new gui.MenuItem({label: 'File'});

  menuBar.append(fileMenu);
  gui.Window.get().menu = menuBar;
</script>
```

The `gui.Window.get()` function call selects the current app window, and calling `.menu` on it allows you to attach the menu bar to it. You can take a look at the example (make sure that there's an accompanying package.json manifest file to support loading the example with NW.js) by running `nw` on the folder in the command line. You should see something like figure 9.5.

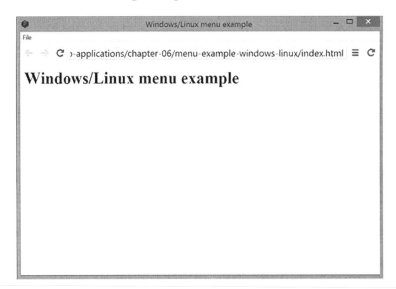

Figure 9.5   The app window shows a menu bar at the top with the File menu item.

Great! So far, you know how to create menu items in the main menu for an app window. But if you click the File menu item, nothing happens. You need to attach a menu to the File menu item with options to say hello and to quit the app.

SUBMENUS

Continuing with the existing code that you've written, you'll do the following:

- Initialize some menu items for the Say Hello and Quit the App actions.
- Create a menu to attach those menu items to.
- Attach that menu to the File menu item.

The important thing to bear in mind is that menu items always attach to menus, and a menu can be nested under a menu item, creating a submenu. You'll see this as you add the two actions to the File menu item.

Let's start by creating the menu items. In the `script` tag, add two lines for the menu items, below the initialization of the `fileMenu` menu.

Listing 9.4   Creating submenu items for the File menu item

```
<script>
  'use strict';
  const gui      = require('nw.gui');
```

```
  const menuBar    = new gui.Menu({type:'menubar'});
const fileMenu  = new gui.MenuItem({label: 'File'});

  const sayHelloMenuItem = new gui.MenuItem({label: 'Say hello'});
const quitAppMenuItem = new gui.MenuItem({label: 'Quit the app'});
  menuBar.append(fileMenu);
  gui.Window.get().menu = menuBar;
</script>
```

You've created two new menu items: sayHelloMenuItem and quitAppMenuItem. You now need to initialize a menu to attach these menu items to. We'll call this menu fileMenuSubMenu (not exactly the most inventive name, but at least it's descriptive) and initialize it after the newly created menu items. Then, you'll attach the menu items to the File menu. Adjust the code to look like the following listing.

Listing 9.5 Attaching the action menu items to the submenu

```
<script>
  'use strict';
  const gui         = require('nw.gui');
  const menuBar     = new gui.Menu({type:'menubar'});
  const fileMenu    = new gui.MenuItem({label: 'File'});

  const sayHelloMenuItem = new gui.MenuItem({label: 'Say hello'});
  const quitAppMenuItem = new gui.MenuItem({label: 'Quit the app'});

  const fileMenuSubMenu = new gui.Menu();
  fileMenuSubMenu.append(sayHelloMenuItem);
  fileMenuSubMenu.append(quitAppMenuItem);

  menuBar.append(fileMenu);
  gui.Window.get().menu = menuBar;
</script>
```

Here, you create a new menu and attach the menu items for the actions to it. You're almost there. The next bit is to bind that menu onto the File menu item. In NW.js, menu items have a submenu property, and setting this attaches a menu onto a menu item, creating a submenu. Add another line after appending the two menu items and before appending the fileMenu to the menuBar, as shown next.

Listing 9.6 Attaching the submenu to the file menu

```
<script>
  'use strict';

  const gui         = require('nw.gui');
  const menuBar     = new gui.Menu({type:'menubar'});
  const fileMenu    = new gui.MenuItem({label: 'File'});

  const sayHelloMenuItem  = new gui.MenuItem({label: 'Say hello'});
  const quitAppMenuItem = new gui.MenuItem({label: 'Quit the app'});

  const fileMenuSubMenu = new gui.Menu();
  fileMenuSubMenu.append(sayHelloMenuItem);
  fileMenuSubMenu.append(quitAppMenuItem);
```

```
fileMenu.submenu = fileMenuSubMenu;

menuBar.append(fileMenu);
gui.Window.get().menu = menuBar;
</script>
```

By setting the `submenu` property on the `fileMenu` object to the `fileMenuSubMenu`, you create a submenu for the File menu item. Save the file, run `nw` on the app folder from the command line, and when you click the File menu item, you should now see the two action items appear, like in figure 9.6.

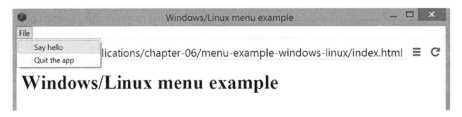

Figure 9.6   The File menu item now has a submenu, with the actions that you want to perform on the app.

Now you're beginning to see something like the finished product—nested menu items that will allow you to trigger actions when you click them. The final bit that remains is to trigger actions when you click them. This is an easy thing to do in NW.js. When specifying the menu items and their labels, you can also provide functions to call when the menu items are clicked. In this case, you can add two simple functions to the `sayHelloMenuItem` and `quitAppMenuItem` objects in your code; adjust the code to look like this:

```
const sayHelloMenuItem = new gui.MenuItem(
  {
    label: 'Say hello',
    click: () => { alert('Hello'); }
  }
);

const quitAppMenuItem = new gui.MenuItem(
  {
    label: 'Quit the app',
    click: () => { process.exit(0); }
  }
);
```

When initializing the menu item objects, you set the `click` attribute on them with functions that you want to execute when they're clicked. In this case, clicking the Say Hello menu item will trigger an alert dialog with the word "Hello," and clicking the Quit the App menu item will call Node.js's `process.exit` function to terminate the app.

Save the code and reload the app from the command line. When you click the File menu and then click Say Hello, you should see the dialog box. Once you've dismissed the dialog, click the Quit the App menu item, and the program will close.

If you run the app on OpenSUSE Linux (Tumbleweed edition), you'll see something akin to figure 9.7.

Figure 9.7   The Windows/Linux menu app example for NW.js running on OpenSUSE Tumbleweed edition

Now that you've created the app using NW.js, let's take a look at what's involved in creating the same app with Electron.

CREATING THE MENU APP WITH ELECTRON

Electron's approach to creating app menus is simpler, in my opinion, because you can pass an object with submenus as arrays, rather than having to call multiple API methods to append menus. You'll replicate the app you created for the NW.js app example using Electron's APIs, and notice the difference in approaches.

I've created an app for this called windows-linux-menu-app-electron in the book's GitHub repository. You can download the app from there and give it a spin. I'll talk you through the interesting bits of the code.

The code for the app is similar to that for the NW.js variant, but the difference here is that you add an app.js file to hold the browser window code for the app, where you'll define the custom code for the menu.

Let's take a look at that app.js file where all the interesting stuff happens.

Listing 9.7   The app.js file for the Windows/Linux app menu with Electron

```
'use strict';

const electron = require('electron');          Requires Menu API via
const Menu   = electron.remote.Menu;           Electron's remote API

const sayHello = () => { alert('Hello'); };

const quitTheApp = () => { electron.remote.app.quit(); };

const template = [
  {
    label: 'File',
    submenu: [                      Generates menu
      {                             template with submenu
        label: 'Say Hello',         items as an array
        click: sayHello
      },
```

```
      {
        label: 'Quit the app',
        click: quitTheApp
      }
    ]
  }
];
const menu = Menu.buildFromTemplate(template);
Menu.setAppMenu(menu);
```

Generates menu for that item; attaches it to app

You can see that Electron offers a simpler API when it comes to creating menus with submenu items. When you run the app on Windows 10, you see figure 9.8.

Figure 9.8   The Electron Menu app running on Windows 10. Note that it's almost identical to the NW.js example, bar the app icon.

Now you know how to create app menus, but suppose you want your app to have different menus for the various OSs (so as to follow their UX conventions). How do you cater for that?

9.1.5   *Choosing which menu to render based on the OS*

Now that you have different code for handling menus for both Mac and Windows/Linux, the next step is to be able to load different versions of the menu specific to the OS that the app is running on. For example, say you have two functions that wrap loading the menus for the different OSs, one called loadMenuForMacOS and another called loadMenuForWindowsAndLinux, and you need to make sure that loadMenuForMacOS runs only on a Mac—otherwise, loadMenuForWindowsAndLinux executes instead. This can be done using Node.js's OS API, with the following code:

```
const os = require('os');

function loadMenuForWindowsAndLinux () {}
function loadMenuForMacOS () {}

if (os.platform() === 'darwin') {
  loadMenuForMacOS;
} else {
  loadMenuForWindowsAndLinux;
}
```

This checks if the OS's platform name is 'darwin' (which is what Mac OS calls itself technically). If it is, you load the menu for Mac OS—otherwise, you load the menu for Windows and Linux. This is how you can ensure that the menus work for both Windows/Linux and Mac OS in their respective formats. Hopefully, one day you won't need to do this kind of workaround, but for now this is how it's done.

9.2   Context menus

Sometimes you want to be able to interact with content in
the app window and perform a number of actions relevant
to that content. For example, when you right-click a piece
of selected text in a word processor, you'll see options to
cut/copy the content, to check the spelling of the content,
and even to search for the content on a search engine.

Electron and NW.js's menu APIs can be used to create
context pop-up menus that are triggered when clicking
content inside of the app window, such as in figure 9.9.

**Figure 9.9   A context menu
displayed in Microsoft Word
2016 for Mac**

9.2.1   Creating the context menu app with NW.js

To explore how the API works across both frameworks,
I've built a simple WYSIWYG HTML editor named Cirrus
(see figure 9.10). The editor lets you create HTML pages
by typing text into the editor window, and it then gener-
ates HTML for you. The feature you'll add to Cirrus is the ability to right-click a piece
of content inside the WYSIWYG editor and display a relevant context menu that will
allow commands to be performed on that content. We'll walk through the NW.js
example first, and then the Electron example afterward for comparison.

First, download a copy of the Cirrus NW.js app from the book's GitHub repository.
Now, take a good look around the code in the app.js file to get familiar with it, and

Figure 9.10   Cirrus, a simple WYSIWYG HTML editor

then look at how you can use context menus to insert multimedia content such as images and videos. Figure 9.11 shows what you want to achieve.

Figure 9.11   A wireframe of the context menu you want to create

From the wireframe, you need to do the following:

1   Create a menu with two items, insert an image, and insert a video.
2   Create a way to bind the menu on appearing when a right-click is made on the content in the design view.
3   Create functions for the menu items of inserting an image and inserting a video.
4   Create a way to insert HTML into a specific cursor position in the content in the design view.

You'll start by creating an empty JavaScript file called designMenu.js in the cirrus folder. This will hold the code for the context menu shown in the wireframe in figure 9.11. Then you'll add a single line of HTML to the index.html file to allow you to select an image to insert into the page, as well as load the designMenu.js file in the app.js file.

In the designMenu.js file, add the code (bit by bit) shown here.

Listing 9.8   Creating insert image/video context menus, part 1

```
'use strict';

let x;
let y;
let document;

function insertContent (content) {
  const range = document.caretRangeFromPoint(x, y);
  if (range) {
    range.insertNode(content);
  }
}
```

> Uses these variables to store coordinates where context menu was clicked

> Adds function that inserts text content at the place where context menu was raised

This allows you to handle tracking where the context menu is clicked and then insert some text content into that point in the page. The following listing continues the process.

Listing 9.9 Creating insert image/video context menus, part 2

```
function openImageFileDialog (cb) {
  const inputField = document.querySelector('#imageFileSelector');
  inputField.addEventListener('change', () => {
    const filePath = this.value;
    cb(filePath);
  });
  inputField.click();
}

function insertImage () {
  openImageFileDialog((filePath) => {
    if (filePath !== '') {
      const newImageNode = document.createElement('img');
      newImageNode.src = filePath;
      insertContent(newImageNode);
    }
  });
}
```

Function to handle opening file dialog menu for selecting an image

Function to trigger opening image file dialog; then inserts image into the HTML page as image element

You now have the bits for inserting an image from the context menu when the user right-clicks in the HTML page, as shown in the next listing.

Listing 9.10 Creating insert image/video context menus, part 3

```
function parseYoutubeVideo (youtubeURL) {
  if (youtubeURL.indexOf('youtube.com/watch?v=') > -1) {
    return youtubeURL.split('watch?v=')[1];
  } else if (youtubeURL.match('https://youtu.be/') !== null) {
    return youtubeURL.split('https://youtu.be/')[1];
  } else if (youtubeURL.match('<iframe') !== null) {
    return youtubeURL.split('youtube.com/embed/')[1].split('"')[0];
  } else {
    alert('Unable to find a YouTube video id in the url');
    return false;
  }
}

function insertVideo () {
  const youtubeURL = prompt('Please insert a YouTube url');
  if (youtubeURL) {
    const videoId = parseYoutubeVideo(youtubeURL);

    if (videoId) {
      const newIframeNode = document.createElement('iframe');
      newIframeNode.width = 854;
      newIframeNode.height = 480;
      newIframeNode.src = `https://www.youtube.com/embed/${videoId}`;
      newIframeNode.frameborder = 0;
      newIframeNode.allowfullscreen = true;
      insertContent(newIframeNode);
    }
  }
}
```

Function looks after getting YouTube video URL, handling different YouTube share formats

When inserting video, user sees dialog asking for YouTube URL, which is passed into parser to handle different share formats

iframe element to load the YouTube video is constructed and inserted into HTML page

You've added the functions for inserting a YouTube video into the HTML page. Now all that's left to do is hook up those functions to the context menu interface, which you now need to construct, as in the following listing.

Listing 9.11 Creating insert image/video context menus, part 4

```
function initialize (window, gui) {                              Creates function to
  if (!document) document = window.document;                     load everything;
  const menu = new gui.Menu();                                   passed NW.js's
                                                                 window and GUI
  menu.append(                                                   library as arguments
    new gui.MenuItem({                         With NW.js GUI,
      label: 'Insert image',                   creates menu instance
      click: insertImage                       for context menu
    })
  );
  menu.append(                                 Adds menu item for
    new gui.MenuItem({                         inserting an image
      label: 'Insert video',
      click: insertVideo
    })                                         Adds another menu item
  );                                           for inserting a video

  document.querySelector('#designArea')                         Attaches that menu to
    .addEventListener('contextmenu', (event) => {               app's design area so that
      event.preventDefault();                                   right-clicking inside it loads
      x = event.x;                                              that context menu
      y = event.y;
      menu.popup(event.x, event.y);
      return false;
    });
}
                                               Exports the
module.exports = initialize;                   module
```

Next, in the index.html file, add the following line of code (in bold) after the opening body tag:

```
</head>
  <body>
    <input type="file" accept="image/*" id="imageFileSelector" class="hidden"/>
```

Finally, add the following line of code for loading the designMenu.js file in the dependencies section of the app.js file:

```
const designMenu = require('./designMenu');
```

At the end of the `initialize` function in the app.js file, add the line of code to load the `designMenu` code:

```
designMenu(window, gui);
```

You should have the same code as is in the `addContextMenu` branch of the app's code repository on GitHub. If you give the app a spin, open an HTML file to start editing, and right-click inside the content when on the design tab, you should see the context menu shown in figure 9.12.

Figure 9.12   The context menu on display in the Cirrus WYSIWYG HTML editor

If you click Insert Image, you'll get a File dialog for selecting an image to insert into the page, and if you click Insert Video, you'll see a prompt dialog asking for a YouTube URL for a video to embed in the page.

9.2.2   *How do context menus work with NW.js?*

Setting up a context menu uses a similar API to the one for setting up app window menus, with one difference—you don't have to pass any options when initializing the menu instance, as shown here:

```
const menu = new gui.Menu();
```

With the menu object initialized, you can add menu items for the Insert Image and Insert Video options to the menu object:

```
menu.append(
  new gui.MenuItem({
    label: 'Insert image',
    click: insertImage
  })
);
menu.append(
  new gui.MenuItem({
    label: 'Insert video',
    click: insertVideo
  })
);
```

At this stage, clicking either menu item will trigger commands for picking an image file or a YouTube video to embed in the page. You can ignore the specifics of how those work for now and focus on how the menu appears where the user right-clicks the content inside the app.

In NW.js's API, the menu object instance has a pop-up function that when passed the x and y coordinates on the app, will bring up the menu at that location on the app, as shown in figure 9.13.

```
menu.popup(20,40);
```

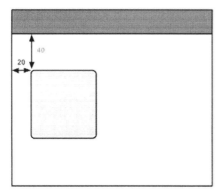

Figure 9.13   The menu.popup function allows you to control the exact placement of the context menu within the app.

To bind this function with the location the user right-clicks in the app window, you need a way to track the coordinates of the user's right-click. There's a way to do this with browser-specific JavaScript, as illustrated in the following code:

```
document.querySelector('#designArea')
  .addEventListener('contextmenu', (event) => {
    event.preventDefault();
    menu.popup(event.x, event.y);
    return false;
  });
```

Here, you look for the div element where the WYSIWYG part of the page is displayed that can be edited, and attach an event listener on it for whenever a user right-clicks anywhere inside the div element (the event is named contextmenu). When this event occurs, you prevent the default behavior from occurring and instead call the menu's pop-up command with the coordinates where the right-click occurred.

9.2.3   Giving menu items icons

You'll notice from the context menu in the Cirrus app that the options aren't easy to distinguish between—they have similarly named labels. You can use icons to help make them more distinct. In NW.js, you have the ability to add icons to menu items, which is an easy way to identify them.

The menu items created for the Insert Image and Insert Video commands can be modified to look like this:

```
menu.append(
  new gui.MenuItem({
    icon: 'picture.png',
    label: 'Insert image',
    click: insertImage
  })
);
menu.append(
  new gui.MenuItem({
    icon: 'youtube.png',
    label: 'Insert video',
    click: insertVideo
  })
);
```

You add an `icon` attribute to the `MenuItem`'s options, with images that have been generated from the Font Awesome library. You can use these icons in the app (they exist in the icons branch on the Cirrus app's GitHub repository), and when you load the app and right-click a loaded page in design view, you should see something like figure 9.14.

Figure 9.14 The context menu, with icons displayed next to the menu item commands

In the last couple of pages, you've created a WYSIWYG app from scratch and added features for inserting images or videos via context menu items. Now we'll take a quick look at how you'd do the same thing using Electron.

9.2.4 *Creating a context menu with Electron*

Rather than build the entire app from scratch, you can download a copy of the code for the app Cirrus Electron from the book's GitHub repository. We'll walk through the bit concerning the context menu so that you can grasp how Electron handles implementing that.

The app is built, and you want to add a context menu for displaying options to insert an image or video. The context menu has two items: Open, for opening an HTML file to edit, and Save, for saving the updates to that file back on the computer. These actions involve reading data from a file on the user's computer, as well as saving data to those files back onto the user's computer. The part of the app that the user sees is the UI, which runs in the render process, and the part that reads and writes data to the hard disk runs in the main process. You need to use Electron's inter-process communication APIs (ipcMain and ipcRenderer) to transmit file paths and content from the front end (renderer) to the back end (main), as well as transmit content and file save state changes from the back end (main) to the front end (renderer).

If you've downloaded a copy of the app's code from GitHub, take a look at the app.js file inside the cirrus-electron folder. At the top of the app.js file, you declare the dependencies for the app, as shown here.

Listing 9.12   The app dependencies for the Cirrus-electron's front-end code

```
const electron      = require('electron');
const Menu          = electron.remote.Menu;            ◁──┐  Loads menu API from
const MenuItem      = electron.remote.MenuItem;          │  renderer process via
const ipc           = electron.ipcRenderer;         ◁─┐  │  remote API
const dialog        = electron.remote.dialog;    ◁─┐  │  │
const designMenu    = require('./designMenu');     │  │
let currentFile;                                   │  │  Calls ipcRenderer API
let content;                                       │     so you can pass data
let tabWas;               Accesses Dialog API for        to main process
let done;                 File Opening dialog,
                          again via remote API
```

Anytime you want to access an API that's in the main process, you can do it via Electron's remote API. In this case, you want to access the menu and dialog APIs for the app. Because you're going to be asking the main process to read files and save content to files as well, you call Electron's ipcRenderer module to allow you to pass messages to the app's main process.

Figure 9.15 shows a diagram to demonstrate what you're trying to achieve. This figure illustrates the flow of IPC events from the renderer process (where the front end exists) to the main process (where the back end exists). This is used when you select an index.html file from the Open File dialog and want to load the contents of that file

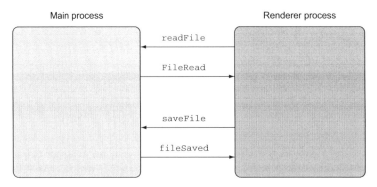

Figure 9.15   The IPC events in the app for communicating when to read a file and when to save it

into the editor. It's also used when you want to save the contents in the editor back to the file.

To demonstrate this in action, let's take a look at the bit of code in the app.js file that handles when you want to open a file, on line 26, shown next.

Listing 9.13 The code for opening files from the UI on Cirrus Electron

```
function openFile (cb) {
  dialog.showOpenDialog((files) => {        ◁──┐  Calls dialog API to
    ipc.send('readFile', files);            ◁──┤  load dialog for
    if (files) currentFile = files[0];         │  opening an HTML file
    if (cb && typeof cb === 'function') cb();  ┐
  });                                          │  Pass list of files
}                                              │  to main process
```

A list of files is passed to the main process, which is then intercepted in code that exists in the main.js file, and is shown next.

Listing 9.14 The code for opening files from the back end on Cirrus Electron

```
'use strict';

const electron = require('electron');
const fs = require('fs');
const app = electron.app;                          ┐  Includes Electron's
const BrowserWindow = electron.BrowserWindow;      │  IPC API for main
const ipc = electron.ipcMain;              ◁───────┘  process
let mainWindow = null;

app.on('window-all-closed', () => {
  if (process.platform !== 'darwin') app.quit();
});
                                                       readFile function
app.on('ready', () => {                                reads contents of a
  mainWindow = new BrowserWindow();                    given file
  mainWindow.loadURL(`file://${__dirname}/index.html`);
  mainWindow.on('closed', () => { mainWindow = null; });
});
                                                       Chooses first filePath
function readFile (event, files) {         ◁──────┐    in list of files—you
  if (files) {                                    │    can work only with
    const filePath = files[0];            ◁───────┘    one at a time
    fs.readFile(filePath, 'utf8', (err, data) => {
      event.sender.send('fileRead', err, data);  ◁─┐  Once contents are read, sends
    });                                             │  it back to renderer process
  }
};

function saveFile (event, currentFile, content) {  ◁─┐  Defines saveFile function
  fs.writeFile(currentFile, content, (err) => {        │  that saves contents to a file
    event.sender.send('fileSaved', err);       ◁──┐  Sends result back to
  });                                              │  renderer process
}

ipc.on('readFile', readFile);          ◁──┐  Listens for readFile and saveFile
ipc.on('saveFile', saveFile);              │  events emitted via IPC
```

This code wraps filesystem API methods and attaches them to event listeners that are provided by the IPC module, thus bridging the separate JavaScript contexts of the main process (back end) and the renderer process (front end). To complete the walk-through, we'll look next at what happens on the front end in the app.js file when a file is read or saved.

In the app.js file, you use the same pattern of listening on events in the IPC module to intercept when a file is read ('fileRead') or saved ('fileSaved'). You then trigger actions when those events are emitted. The next listing shows the code that handles this.

Listing 9.15 Handling `fileRead` and `fileSave` IPC events on the front end

```
ipc.on('fileRead', (event, err, data) => {        ◁─┐  When fileRead event is
  loadMenu(true);                                      emitted, loads UI for editor
  if (err) throw(err);                                 with that file's contents
  if (!done) bindClickingOnTabs();
  hideSelectFileButton();
  setContent(data);
  showViewMode('design');                                    Reports on whether
});                                                       ┌─ save succeeded or not
ipc.on('fileSaved', (event, err) => {             ◁──────┘
  if (err) return alert('There was an error saving the file');
  alert('File Saved');
});
```

This code demonstrates that you can send data from the front end to the back end and back, as long as the front-end code is set up to listen on events that are emitted by the back end.

With all this in place, you're able to display the UI for the editor with a file loaded and allow users to insert images or videos by right-clicking the HTML file in design mode.

9.2.5 *Adding the context menu with Electron*

The code for the context menu is similar to the NW.js example, but differs in a few places. The following is a snippet of the code from the designMenu.js file:

```
function initialize () {
  const menu = new Menu();
  menu.append(new MenuItem({label: 'Insert image', click: insertImage }));
  menu.append(new MenuItem({label: 'Insert video', click: insertVideo }));
  document.querySelector('#designArea')
  .addEventListener('contextmenu', function (event) {
    event.preventDefault();
    x = event.x;
    y = event.y;
    menu.popup(event.x, event.y);
    return false;
  });
}
```

You can see that Electron offers a similar API for appending menu items to a menu. The process is also identical in the way that the menu is able to appear.

> **HOW DOES ELECTRON HANDLE CALLING PROMPT()?** Electron doesn't support the `prompt()` browser call, which shows a dialog with a text field. Cheng Zhao has said that because the feature would require a lot of work to implement and because the feature is rarely used, he won't implement it. In order to support using the prompt in Electron, you can use the dialog's npm module, available at www.npmjs.com/package/dialogs.

9.3 *Summary*

This chapter covered how to implement app window menus and context menus with NW.js and Electron. Some key takeaways from the chapter include the following:

- There are different API methods for handling the different ways that Windows/ Linux and Mac handle app menus. The best strategy is to use OS detection to support both approaches.
- To implement context menus, you'll want to override the app's `contextmenu` DOM event.
- When you want app window menu items to manipulate contents in the browser window, use Electron's IPC APIs to facilitate transmitting the data.

Important aspects to consider when you're constructing menus for your app is whether the menu needs to be unique for each window of the app, as well as whether the app will be used on Macs. Mac OS has a single menu that applies to all app windows, and this needs to be taken into account.

In chapter 10, we'll continue on the theme of the UI by looking at implementing drag-and-drop functionality, as well as how to make the app look like it's native to the user's OS.

Dragging and dropping files and crafting the UI

This chapter covers

- Configuring drag-and-drop functionality
- Mimicking the native look and feel of the user's OS

The UI of an app is one of the most important things to get right, as it's the first thing people see when using your app. People can and will judge whether to use an app based purely on how the UI looks. But it's not only about the UI; you also have to think about the user experience.

When drag-and-drop was introduced to computer users way back in the twentieth century, it helped to make computers friendlier. It's become a key behavior that spans across most computing devices today, including small-form devices like phones and tablets. It's therefore appropriate to show you how to implement drag-and-drop functionality in your desktop apps.

We'll also look at how to style the UI to mimic the look and feel of the user's OS.

10.1 Dragging and dropping files onto the app

Most users of computers are familiar with organizing their files by dragging and dropping them between file explorer windows and the desktop. In recent years, the introduction of the file API in web browsers has meant that this functionality has

176

found its way into web apps as well, typically with forms requiring files to be uploaded to the web app. This is useful in cases like converting a file into another format, such as the app Gifrocket (which uses NW.js). Gifrocket generates an animated GIF from a video, and the interface for kicking off the process is to drag-and-drop the video file onto the screen of the app, as shown in figure 10.1.

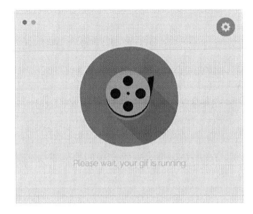

Figure 10.1   Gifrocket in action: convert a video to an animated GIF by dragging a video file to the app and dropping it in the middle of the app screen.

10.1.1 Dragging and dropping files to an app with NW.js

Say you have a feature in an app that requires processing a file (or set of files), and you'd like to make use of NW.js's drag-and-drop file support. How do you do that?

A good example is an icon generator. You want to take a large-scale image and convert it into lots of different sizes to generate an app icon that works on Mac OS. Brilliant—after all, it's a common need for building cross-platform desktop apps. You have the app at a stage where it will take an image and display that image at various icon sizes. Now you want to enable the UI to receive an image file via dragging the file to the app and dropping it onto the app screen. This exercise explores how you can add drag-and-drop functionality to an existing app.

To save time, I've built a rough prototype app called Iconic, which you can get from the book's GitHub repository at http://mng.bz/jKmw. Grab a copy of the code, and I'll show you how to add the drag-and-drop functionality.

Notice what the app looks like when it starts (see figure 10.2).

Figure 10.2   Iconic: the initial screen suggests dropping an image file onto the screen area, which you will implement support for.

The app is code complete, so we'll walk through the code and see the interesting bits that relate to adding drag-and-drop support to an app.

In the app.js file, there's an important snippet of code you use to capture any attempts to drag-and-drop a file onto the screen area:

```
function stopDefaultEvent (event) {
  event.preventDefault();
  return false;
}

window.ondragover = stopDefaultEvent;
window.ondrop = stopDefaultEvent;
```

The default behavior of a web browser when a file is dragged and dropped onto a page area is to load that file in the browser. That's not what you want to happen here, though. Instead you want to prevent that from happening by calling the preventDefault function on the event. You then bind this on the ondragover and ondrop events.

Next, you need to get the path of the file that's dropped onto the screen area and pass that to another function, displayImageInIconSet, which will load it into various img elements on the page. Getting that file path involves the following:

1 Intercept the drop event on the initial app screen.
2 Hide the initial screen.
3 Show the screen that displays the icons at different sizes.

Create a function called interceptDroppedFile that has the following code:

```
function interceptDroppedFile () {
  const interceptArea = window.document.querySelector('#load-icon-holder');
  interceptArea.ondrop = function (event) {
    event.preventDefault();
    if (event.dataTransfer.files.length !== 1) {
      window.alert('you have dragged too many files into the app. Drag just 1
      file');
    } else {
      interceptArea.style.display = 'none';
      displayIconsSet();
      const file = event.dataTransfer.files[0];
      displayImageInIconSet(file.path);
    }
    return false;
  };
}
```

A couple of things are happening in this function. For a start, you need to get ahold of the div that shows the content of the initial app screen and attach a function to the ondrop event that will execute whenever a file is dropped onto it. You do a sanity check to make sure the user hasn't dragged more than one file onto the area (because a user can drag multiple files). If they haven't, you hide the intercept area, display the screen that shows the icons, and pass the path of the dragged file to the `display-ImageInIconSet` function so that it then is rendered in the screen. You also need to add in a function for displaying that screen above the function you inserted:

```
function displayIconsSet () {
  const iconsArea = window.document.querySelector('#icons');
  iconsArea.style.display = 'block';
}
```

And you want to ensure that the initial screen stretches the entire width and height of the app, with the following code in the app.css file:

```
#load-icon-holder {
  padding-top: 10px;
  text-align: center;
  top: 0px;
  left: 0px;
  bottom: 0px;
  right: 0px;
  width: 100%;
}
```

If all goes according to plan with all the changes saved, when you drag an image file (such as the example.png file in the images folder) into the app's initial screen, you should see something like figure 10.3.

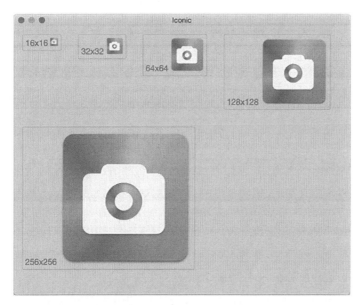

Figure 10.3 The Iconic app rendering an app icon at different size dimensions

This demonstrates how easy it is to add drag-and-drop functionality into an existing app—and what kind of potential app UIs you can build with it.

Is Electron any different in its approach? Let's find out.

10.1.2 Implementing drag-and-drop with Electron

If you take a look at the iconic-electron app in the book's GitHub repository, you'll see that the only differences in the code are in the way the app starts up. The app.js file and index.html files are identical to the ones in the iconic-nwjs variant of the app. This is fantastic, because both apps are using the HTML5 file API for web browsers to provide this functionality, and it demonstrates how easy it is to reuse web APIs when building desktop apps. Figure 10.4 shows what the app looks like running on Windows 10 with Electron.

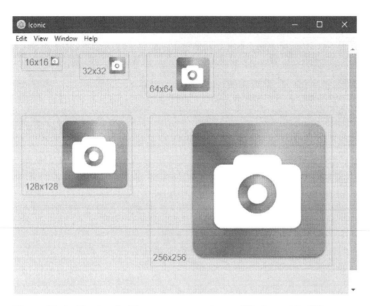

Figure 10.4   The Iconic Electron app running on Windows 10: different Node.js desktop application framework, different OS, but the same app functionality.

This also highlights one of the great aspects of developing desktop apps with NW.js or Electron: the fact that you can reuse code written for websites and apps to build desktop apps, saving time when you add drag-and-drop to your desktop apps.

Now that we've covered how drag-and-drop functionality can be added to desktop apps, we'll turn our focus to how you can replicate the look and feel of the user's OS in your desktop apps.

10.2 Mimicking the native look of the OS

A common concern of people creating desktop apps with Electron and NW.js is how to make their apps look exactly like a native app with the UI controls and elements matching what the OS uses.

This can be achieved by detecting the user's OS and version and using CSS stylesheets to tailor the style of your app.

10.2.1 Detecting the user's OS

If you're looking to match the UI style of an OS, you need to be able to detect which version of which OS is running, which you can do using Node.js's OS API. The snippet of code in the next listing will find out what platform is being run, and print out a log message saying what OS it detected.

Listing 10.1 JavaScript for detecting the user's OS

```
'use strict';

const os           = require('os');
const platform     = os.platform();

switch (platform) {
  case 'darwin':
    console.log('Running Mac OS');
    break;
  case 'linux':
    console.log('Running Linux');
    break;
  case 'win32':
    console.log('Running Windows');
    break;
  default:
    console.log('Could not detect OS for platform',platform);
}
```

If you copy this code and paste it into a Node.js REPL, you should see a message saying what OS your computer is running (in the case of my laptop, it's Mac OS).

10.2.2 Using OS detection in NW.js

If you're using NW.js, you can include the code in listing 10.1 in the JavaScript files loaded by the index.html file. You can use that code to load different stylesheets tailored for each OS. Say you have an app that has three different stylesheets (one for Windows, one for Mac, and one for Linux), and you want to be able to load the stylesheet that matches the OS of the user. You can do this with the code shown next.

Listing 10.2 Applying different styles for each OS

```
'use strict';

const os           = require('os');
const platform     = os.platform();

function addStylesheet (stylesheet) {
  const head = document.getElementsByTagName('head')[0];
  const link = document.createElement('link');
  link.setAttribute('rel','stylesheet');
  link.setAttribute('href',stylesheet+'.css');
  head.appendChild(link);
}
```

```
switch (platform) {
  case 'darwin':
    addStylesheet('mac');
    break;
  case 'linux':
    addStylesheet('linux');
    break;
  case win32:
    addStylesheet('windows');
    break;
  default:
    console.log('Could not detect OS for platform',platform);
}
```

That code is a slight modification of the code in listing 10.1. Here, you create a function called addStylesheet that inserts a link tag to the head element's inner HTML, and the link tag loads the stylesheet, given the name of the OS that's detected.

This example can take care of most cases, but if you need to go deeper and detect different versions of a specific OS (such as detecting which version of Windows a user is running), you can repeat the pattern but instead call os.release(). Note, though, you need to make sure to check the call on each version of the OS that you're looking to detect, because the release number is a number for technical reference, and doesn't always match the number that's printed in marketing materials (for example, calling os.release on Mac OS Mavericks will return a value of 14.3.0, which is different from the OS's reported version of 10.10.3).

10.2.3　*Using OS detection in Electron*

Although there are separate Node.js contexts for the main process and the renderer process, the funny thing is that you can still call out to Node.js modules in the app.js file, so you can use the OS API to detect the user's OS. The code for this example is in the Detect OS Electron app in the book's GitHub repository. The code for the app.js file is shown next.

Listing 10.3　The Detect OS Electron app's app.js file

```
'use strict';

function addStylesheet (stylesheet) {
  const head = document.getElementsByTagName('head')[0];
  const link = document.createElement('link');
  link.setAttribute('rel','stylesheet');
  link.setAttribute('href',stylesheet+'.css');
  head.appendChild(link);
}

function labelOS (osName) {
  document.getElementById('os-label').innerText = osName;
}
```

```
function initialize () {
  const os            = require('os');
  const platform      = os.platform();

  switch (platform) {
    case 'darwin':
      addStylesheet('mac');
      labelOS('Mac OS');
      break;
    case 'linux':
      addStylesheet('linux');
      labelOS('Linux');
      break;
    case 'win32':
      addStylesheet('windows');
      labelOS('Microsoft Windows');
      break;
    default:
      console.log('Could not detect OS for platform',platform);
  }
}

window.onload = initialize;
```

The app.js file is almost identical to the one featured in the NW.js variant. You are therefore able to detect the user's OS from the renderer process in Electron.

Now, let's look at the options available for replicating the look and feel of the user's OS in terms of CSS libraries.

10.2.4 *Using CSS to match a user's OS style*

Giving desktop apps a look and feel that matches the user's OS means making a web browser page look exactly like a native desktop app. The best way to pull that off is to use CSS stylesheets to tailor the look and feel of the app to the user's OS.

As suggested in the previous section, there's a way to detect the user's OS and version and load a stylesheet that's OS-specific. What stylesheets and tips are available?

METRO UI

With Windows 8 and the Surface tablet, Microsoft introduced a bold change to its UI with a new tile-based design called Metro. The change didn't merely redesign how the UI elements look, but also how app layouts are structured.

Sergey Pimenov, a programmer in Kiev, Ukraine, created a CSS framework called Metro UI CSS (https://metroui.org.ua) that allows developers to create HTML-based apps styled according to the guidelines of Metro (figure 10.5). Since the project was created, it has been used by JetBrains in its IDE PhpStorm.

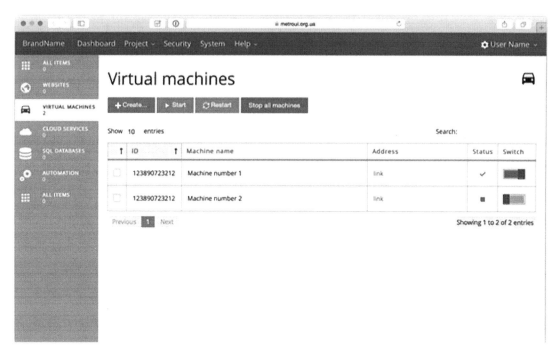

Figure 10.5   Metro UI CSS, a CSS framework for building web apps using Microsoft's Metro UI

MAC OS LION CSS UI KIT

Ville V. Vanninen, a minimalist visual designer, created a UI kit called Lion CSS UI Kit (http://sakamies.github.io/Lion-CSS-UI-Kit/) for mocking up native Mac OS apps in the browser. The purpose of the UI kit is to create authentic-looking mockups of Mac apps in the browser, as opposed to using a UI kit in graphics tools like Photoshop, Illustrator, and Sketch.

Although the UI kit passes as a Mac OS app, the entire UI is made from HTML and CSS—perfect for using with a desktop app that uses HTML, CSS, and JavaScript. That said, recent versions of Mac OS are altering the look and feel of the OS, so bear this in mind if you do consider using this CSS framework (figure 10.6).

LINUX

Unfortunately, I wasn't able to find a Linux UI CSS kit. Also, Linux has so many distributions (not to mention different graphical desktop environments with their own UIs) that to apply native UI styling with a UI kit would require a lot of effort. I recommend you avoid custom-styling the UI form elements because Chromium uses GTK as the UI toolkit, so any themes picked by the computer user will be applied to the browser's native UI elements as well.

These are CSS frameworks, but if you're looking for CSS libraries that also integrate with other JavaScript libraries and frameworks, then more options appear on the table.

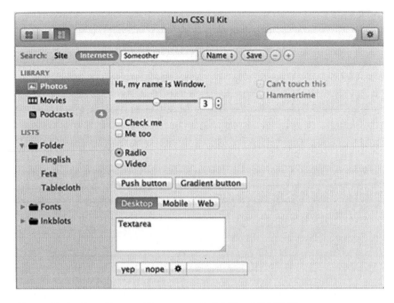

Figure 10.6   Example app UI generated with Lion UI CSS Kit

PHOTON

Photon (http://photonkit.com) is a UI framework for Electron that allows you to build apps with UIs that look identical to native Mac OS apps. The UI framework provides an extensive list of components that can be combined to create comprehensive UIs, as shown in figure 10.7.

Name	Kind	Date Modified	Author
bars.scss	Document	Oct 13, 2015	connors
base.scss	Document	Oct 13, 2015	connors
button-groups.scss	Document	Oct 13, 2015	connors
buttons.scss	Document	Oct 13, 2015	connors
docs.scss	Document	Oct 13, 2015	connors
forms.scss	Document	Oct 13, 2015	connors
grid.scss	Document	Oct 13, 2015	connors
icons.scss	Document	Oct 13, 2015	connors
images.scss	Document	Oct 13, 2015	connors
lists.scss	Document	Oct 13, 2015	connors
mixins.scss	Document	Oct 13, 2015	connors
navs.scss	Document	Oct 13, 2015	connors
normalize.scss	Document	Oct 13, 2015	connors
photon.scss	Document	Oct 13, 2015	connors
tables.scss	Document	Oct 13, 2015	connors
tabs.scss	Document	Oct 13, 2015	connors

Figure 10.7   Photon rendering what looks like Mac OS's Finder window

If you're using React for your front end and would like to use Photon with React, there's a useful wrapper library available at https://github.com/react-photonkit/react-photonkit.

REACT DESKTOP

React Desktop (http://reactdesktop.js.org) is another React-based UI library that allows you to create apps that look like either Mac OS or Windows 10, and it doesn't require you to create two sets of front-end code for the UI. Figure 10.8 shows an example of React Desktop in action.

Figure 10.8   React Desktop rendering a Windows 10 demo example

10.3   *Summary*

In this chapter, we've explored ways to use the various GUI APIs of Electron and NW.js for handling drag-and-drop. You also learned how to make desktop apps look like they have the exact same UI as the UI controls in the user's OS. Some of the main take-aways from this chapter include the following:

- Implementing drag-and-drop in Node.js desktop apps is identical to working with the HTML5 implementation in web apps, making it easy to repurpose web-based code that is designed for the same purpose.
- Users can drag multiple files into the app, so bear this in mind if you want your app to handle only one file at a time.
- Apart from the app menu and tray apps, Electron and NW.js don't provide native UI elements; you have to use OS detection and a CSS UI kit to make an app achieve a native look.
- When you detect a user's OS, remember that the release number of an app won't always match the number given to its market name.

In chapter 11, we'll look at how you can build apps that interact more closely with the OS. We'll start by looking at how to display video and images from the user's webcam into a desktop app for a photo booth app.

11

Using a webcam in your application

This chapter covers

- Accessing the webcam on your computer
- Creating still images from live video
- Saving the still images to your computer

Not many years ago, webcams were external devices that you bought to plug into your computer and used to chat with friends and family. Today, almost all laptops come with webcams and microphones built in, making it easy for people to travel and communicate with each other, as long as they have a good internet connection. Back then, the only way you could access a webcam feed was via a desktop app, or by using Adobe Flash. There wasn't an easy way to do it over a web browser.

But that changed. With the introduction of the HTML5 Media Capture API, webcams could be accessible to web pages (with good security procedures in place), and it is this capability that we'll explore in this chapter. We'll look at ways to access and use these APIs to build a photo booth app.

11.1 Photo snapping with the HTML5 Media Capture API

When using Electron or NW.js to build your desktop app, you get the benefit of Google Chrome's extensive support for HTML5 APIs, one of which is the Media

Capture API. The HTML5 Media Capture API allows you to access the microphone and video camera that are embedded in your computer, and the app you'll build will make use of this.

Selfies are powerful—look at Snapchat's IPO valuation ($22 billion as of February 2017). Build an app for selfies, people take selfies, other people view selfies, selfies spawn more selfies, network effects kick in, and suddenly you're a multibillion-dollar startup. Who knew that there was so much money in selfies?

That's why you'll build an app for selfies called Facebomb. Facebomb boils down to *open app, take photo, save photo to your computer.* Simple, usable, and straight to the point. Life is short, so rather that make you build the app from scratch, I've given you an assembled app so you can investigate the particularly interesting bits.

There are two code repositories for the app: one that uses Electron as the desktop app framework, and another that uses NW.js. You'll find them under the names Facebomb-NW.js and Facebomb-Electron in the book's GitHub repository at http://mng.bz/dST8 and http://mng.bz/TX1k.

You can download whichever version of the app you're interested in inspecting, and run the installation instructions for it from the README.md file. Then, you can run the app and see it in action.

11.1.1 Inspecting the NW.js version of the app

A lot of the code is pretty standard boilerplate code for an NW.js app. We'll narrow focus to the index.html and app.js files, which contain code unique to the app, starting with the index.html file.

Listing 11.1 The index.html file for the Facebomb NW.js app

```html
<html>
  <head>
    <title>Facebomb</title>
    <link href="app.css" rel="stylesheet" />
    <link rel="stylesheet" href="css/font-awesome.min.css">
    <script src="app.js"></script>
  </head>
  <body>
    <input type="file" nwsaveas="myfacebomb.png" id="saveFile">
    <canvas width="800" height="600"></canvas>
    <video autoplay></video>
    <div id="takePhoto" onclick="takePhoto()">
      <i class="fa fa-camera" aria-hidden="true"></i>
    </div>
  </body>
</html>
```

Triggers the Save File dialog in NW.js

Captures an image from the video

Video feed is streamed into this element

Button that's clicked to trigger taking a photo

The HTML file contains the following:

- An input element that's used for the file save. Inside it is a custom NW.js attribute called nwsaveas that contains the default filename to save the file as.

- The `canvas` element is used to store the picture data of the photo snapshot you take from the video feed.
- The `video` element will display the video feed from the webcam, which is the source for the photo.
- The `div` element with the id `takePhoto` is the round button in the bottom right of the app window that you'll use to take the photo and save it as a file on the computer. Inside it is a Font Awesome icon for the camera. The advantages of using the camera icon in place of text are that icons use less screen space than words and can be easier to visually process as a result, and if the icon is universally recognizable, you don't need to consider implementing internationalization. Not everyone speaks English—in fact, English is the third-most-commonly spoken language after Mandarin Chinese and Spanish.

Most of this code is compatible with running inside a web browser. The notable element unique to NW.js is the `nwsaveas` attribute (which brings up the Save As dialog for the file) on the `input` element. To read more about this custom attribute, see the docs at http://mng.bz/nU1c.

That covers the index.html file. The app.js file is around 39 lines of code, so we'll look at it in chunks. We'll start with the dependencies and the `bindSavingPhoto` function.

Listing 11.2 The initial code in the app.js file for the Facebomb NW.js app

```
'use strict';

const fs = require('fs');
let photoData;
let saveFile;
let video;

function bindSavingPhoto () {                        ◁─── Function binds on
  saveFile.addEventListener('change', function () {        the input element
    const filePath = this.value;                     ◁─── in the HTML
    fs.writeFile(filePath, photoData, 'base64', (err) => {   ◁─── File path for photo
      if (err) {                                              is set by value in
        alert('There was a problem saving the photo:', err.message);   input element
      }
      photoData = null;         ◁─── Attempts to save
    });                              file to disk as
  });                              Base64-encoded
}                                  image
```

Function binds on the input element in the HTML

File path for photo is set by value in input element

Attempts to save file to disk as Base64-encoded image

photoData variable that held photo data reset to null

If error saving the file, displays alert dialog with error message

Here, you require some dependencies, define a few empty variables, and then define a function that's used for binding on when a photo is saved. Inside that function, you add an event listener on the `input` element for when its value changes. When it changes, it's because the Save As dialog has been triggered. When an action is taken to save a photo under a given file name or to cancel it, you attempt to save the photo data to the computer as a Base64-encoded image file. If the file write is successful,

nothing else happens. But if there's an error, you report it to the user in an alert dialog. Finally, you reset the photoData variable that was holding the photo snapshot.

Next, we'll look at the initialize function in the app.js file.

Listing 11.3   The initialize function in the app.js file for the Facebomb NW.js app

```
function initialize () {                              ◁─── initialize function called
  saveFile = window.document.querySelector('#saveFile');      when app window
  video = window.document.querySelector('video');             finishes loading

  let errorCallback = (error) => {                   ◁─── Creates error-
    console.log(                                          Callback function
      'There was an error connecting to the video stream:', error    to handle error
    );                                                    on creating video
  };                                                      stream

  window.navigator.webkitGetUserMedia(
    {video: true},                                   ◁─── Media Capture API
    (localMediaStream) => {                               request to access
      video.src = window.URL.createObjectURL(localMediaStream);   video stream from
      video.onloadedmetadata = bindSavingPhoto;   ◁──   user's computer
    }, errorCallback);         ◁─                         Binds on
}                                                         saving photo
```

Attaches video stream to video element → (at `video.src = ...` line)

If you can't access video stream, then calls the error callback → (at `}, errorCallback);`)

This bit of code does the key actions of requesting the video stream from the user's
media capture device (be it a webcam built into their computer or an external video
device) and inserting that video stream into the video element in the app window. It
also attaches the bindSavingPhoto element to the video's loadedmetadata event. This
event is triggered when the video stream starts to be fed into the video element (it
usually takes a second or two before the video stream kicks in).

Once you've got the initialize function defined, you define the takePhoto function that's triggered when the takePhoto div element is clicked in the app window.
The code for this is shown in the following listing.

Listing 11.4   The takePhoto function in the Facebomb NW.js app's app.js file

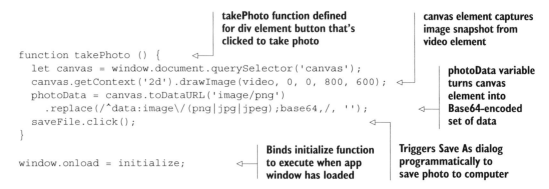

takePhoto function defined for div element button that's clicked to take photo

canvas element captures image snapshot from video element

```
function takePhoto () {            ◁─
  let canvas = window.document.querySelector('canvas');
  canvas.getContext('2d').drawImage(video, 0, 0, 800, 600);   ◁─
  photoData = canvas.toDataURL('image/png')
    .replace(/^data:image\/(png|jpg|jpeg);base64,/, '');   ◁─
  saveFile.click();                                     ◁─
}

window.onload = initialize;   ◁─
```

photoData variable turns canvas element into Base64-encoded set of data

Binds initialize function to execute when app window has loaded

Triggers Save As dialog programmatically to save photo to computer

Here, the canvas element is used to capture an image snapshot from the video element. You tell it to use a 2D context and to then draw an image from the video element that begins at 0 pixels left and 0 pixels top, and then goes 800 pixels wide and 600 pixels high. These dimensions mean that you capture the full picture of the video.

You then take the image that has been recorded in the canvas element and convert the data format to one for a PNG image. To make the data suitable for saving as a file to the computer, you have to remove a bit of the data that's used to make the image render as an inline image in a web browser. The string replace method uses a regular expression to find that bit of data and strip it out.

You programmatically trigger clicking the input element that displays the Save As dialog to the user. This means that when the #takePhoto div element is clicked in the app window, you'll create an image snapshot from the video element at that point in time and then trigger the Save As dialog so that the user can save the image to their computer.

With that function defined, the final bit of code left is to bind the initialize function on when the app window has loaded. You do it this way because you want to make sure the app window has finished loading the HTML—otherwise, it will attempt to bind on DOM elements that haven't yet been rendered in the app window, which would cause an error.

With all that code defined in the app.js file, there's a bit of configuration in the package.json file that ensures that the app window is set to 800 pixels wide and 600 pixels high and ensures that the app window cannot be resized or set into full-screen mode. The next listing shows the code for the package.json file.

Listing 11.5　The package.json file for the Facebomb NW.js app

```json
{
  "name": "facebomb",
  "version": "1.0.0",
  "main": "index.html",
  "window": {
    "toolbar": false,
    "width": 800,
    "height": 600,
    "resizable": false,
    "fullscreen": false
  },
  "dependencies": {
    "nw": "^0.15.2"
  },
  "scripts": {
    "start": "node_modules/.bin/nw ."
  }
}
```

You also have an app.css file with some styling.

Listing 11.6   The app.css file for the Facebomb NW.js app

```css
body {
  margin: 0;
  padding: 0;
  background: black;
  color: white;
  font-family: 'Helvetica', 'Arial', 'Sans';
  width: 800px;
  height: 600px;
}

#saveFile, canvas {
  display: none;
}

video {
  z-index: 1;
  position: absolute;
  width: 800px;
  height: 600px;
}

#takePhoto {
  z-index: 2;
  position: absolute;
  bottom: 5%;
  right: 5%;
  text-align: center;
  border: solid 2px white;
  box-shadow: 0px 0px 7px rgba(255,255,255,0.5);
  margin: 5px;
  border-radius: 3em;
  padding: 1em;
  background-color: rgba(0,0,0,0.2);
}

#takePhoto:hover {
  background: #FF5C5C;
  cursor: pointer;
}
```

Now, you can look at what the app would look like when it's run. Figure 11.1 shows an example of the app running on Windows 10.

Figure 11.1 Facebomb in action (that's me by the way—I could use a shave)

Why isn't the app asking for permission to use the camera?

The HTML5 Media Capture API has a security policy of asking users if they want a web page to be allowed to access their camera or microphone before the web app can use them. This is to prevent malicious use of the camera or microphone to take photos or record audio.

With Electron and NW.js, because the app is running on the user's computer, the app is trusted with access to the computer's devices, so there's no permission bar appearing in the app. This means you can create apps that have direct access to the camera and microphone, but as Peter Parker's (Spider-Man's) uncle said, "With great power comes great responsibility."

With the app, you can take a photo of yourself and the file is saved to the computer. Nice and simple—but the key thing here is that it demonstrates how easy it is to build an app that takes in the camera feed and can do all kinds of things with it.

That shows how you can do it with NW.js, but what about Electron?

11.1.2 Creating Facebomb with Electron

If you want to have the cake and eat it straightaway, you can grab the Facebomb-Electron app from the book's GitHub repository. I'll walk you through the differences of Electron's approach to implementing Facebomb. First, as expected, the entry point of the app differs from NW.js—you have a main.js file that handles the responsibility of loading the app window and applying constraints to it so it can't be resized or enter fullscreen mode. Other differences with Electron are in how it implements the Save As dialog, as well as the level of customization you can apply to the dialog.

You'll take a look first at the entry point of the app to see how the constraints are applied to the app window. The following listing shows the code for the main.js file.

Listing 11.7   The main.js file for the Facebomb Electron app

```
'use strict';                                             Requires Electron;
                                                          loads app and browser
const electron = require('electron');                     window dependencies
const app = electron.app;
const BrowserWindow = electron.BrowserWindow;      ◁──────┐ Creates empty
                                                            mainWindow variable to
let mainWindow = null;                              ◁──────┘ hold app window reference

app.on('window-all-closed', () => {                       If all windows are closed
  if (process.platform !== 'darwin') app.quit();   ◁───── and you're not running app
});                                                       on Mac OS, quits app

app.on('ready', () => {                                   Creates browser window with
  mainWindow = new BrowserWindow({                 ◁───── width, height, resizable, and
    useContentSize: true,                                 full-screen properties
    width: 800,
    height: 600,
    resizable: false,
    fullscreen: false                                     Gets main app window
  });                                                      to load index.html file
  mainWindow.loadURL(`file://${__dirname}/index.html`);  ◁── inside it
  mainWindow.on('closed', () => { mainWindow = null; });  ◁──┐
});                                                          │
                   Adds event binding to reset mainWindow ───┘
                          variable when window is closed
```

This is pretty much standard boilerplate for an Electron app, but the key bit of interest is the configuration object that's passed into the initialization of the `Browser-Window` instance.

The first property passed in the configuration object is called `useContentSize`. It ensures that the `width` and `height` properties of the app window are referring to the content of the app window and not to the entire app window. If you don't pass this property (or explicitly set it to `false`), you'll see scrollbars appear in the app window. This is because Electron treats the `width` and `height` properties as referring to not only the app window's content size, but also the title bar at the top of the app window, as well as any trim around the edges of the app window.

If you didn't pass this, you would otherwise have to tweak the `width` and `height` properties to make sure that the app window didn't have any scrollbars. This is the kind of pixel pushing that you don't want to have to deal with—plus, if your app is running across multiple OSs, you would have to tweak these numbers for each build you want to target. Not ideal. I recommend you always pass the `useContentSize` attribute if you're going to define `width` and `height` properties to your app windows. For more on this attribute and other options that can be passed to the window configuration, see http://electron.atom.io/docs/api/browser-window/.

You also pass the options for disabling the ability to resize the window or make it allow full-screen mode here. Whereas in NW.js these options are configured in the package.json file, Electron passes the configuration at the point of creating the app window. The advantage of this approach is that it's easier to give separate app windows different configurations rather than inherit the same configuration from the package.json file.

Now, take a quick look at the index.html file.

Listing 11.8   The index.html file for the Facebomb Electron app

```html
<html>
  <head>
    <title>Facebomb</title>
    <link href="app.css" rel="stylesheet" />
    <link rel="stylesheet" href="css/font-awesome.min.css">
    <script src="app.js"></script>
  </head>
  <body>
    <canvas width="800" height="600"></canvas>
    <video autoplay></video>
    <div id="takePhoto" onclick="takePhoto()">
      <i class="fa fa-camera" aria-hidden="true"></i>
    </div>
  </body>
</html>
```

The index.html file that's loaded for the app window is almost identical to the one used in the NW.js variant. The only difference is that there's no `input` element in the Electron version, and that's because it's not needed. If you remember, the `input` element was used for storing the filename for the photo, as well as containing the custom attribute `nwsaveas`, which NW.js uses to bind a Save File dialog.

Electron handles dialog windows differently than NW.js, and to see how differently, you need to take a look at the app.js file. The app.js file is around 40 lines of code, so we'll scan through it bit by bit, starting with the dependencies and the alternative to the `bindSavingPhoto` function.

Listing 11.9   The dependencies in the app.js file for the Facebomb Electron app

```
'use strict';

const electron = require('electron');          ◁── Loads Electron and
const dialog = electron.remote.dialog;               requires dialog module
const fs = require('fs');                            through remote API
let photoData;
let video;
                                        savePhoto function              Checks for file path
                                        receives file path from         in case user clicked
function savePhoto (filePath) {    ◁──  Save File dialog                Cancel on Save File
  if (filePath) {                                                  ◁──  dialog
    fs.writeFile(filePath, photoData, 'base64', (err) => {
      if (err) {
        alert(`There was a problem saving the photo: ${err.message}`);
      }
      photoData = null;
    });
  }
}
```

In the dependencies at the top of the app.js file, you require Electron and then use the remote API to load Electron's dialog module from a renderer process (the app.js file). You then define a function called `savePhoto`. The purpose of this function is to save the photo to disk when a file path is passed to it from Electron's Save File dialog. If it manages to successfully save the file to disk, you're good, but if it encounters an error, you alert the user. You also reset the `photoData` variable afterward.

Let's look at the `initialize` function in the app.js file.

Listing 11.10   The app.js file's `initialize` function for the Facebomb Electron app

```
function initialize () {
  video = window.document.querySelector('video');
  let errorCallback = (error) => {
    console.log(`There was an error connecting to the video stream:
      ${error.message}`);
  };

  window.navigator.webkitGetUserMedia({video: true}, (localMediaStream) => {
    video.src = window.URL.createObjectURL(localMediaStream);
  }, errorCallback);
}
```

This code is almost identical to the same-named function in the NW.js variant, but with a slight difference: you don't need to define a `saveFile` variable as there is no `input` element in the HTML, and you don't need to bind on the video's `loadedmetadata` event triggering, because you pass the data and file in another location in the app's code.

Finally, let's take a look at the `takePhoto` function and the `window.onload` event binding that makes up the rest of the app.js file.

Listing 11.11 The app.js file's `takePhoto` function for the Facebomb Electron app

```
function takePhoto () {
  let canvas = window.document.querySelector('canvas');
  canvas.getContext('2d').drawImage(video, 0, 0, 800, 600);
  photoData =
    canvas.toDataURL('image/png').replace(/^data:image\/(png|jpg|jpeg);base6
    4,/, '');
  dialog.showSaveDialog({                    ◁─────┐ Calls dialog module to
    title: "Save the photo",            ◁────┐    └ create Save File dialog
    defaultPath: 'myfacebomb.png',    ◁──┐   │
    buttonLabel: 'Save photo'  ◁──┐    │   │   Sets title of Save File
  }, savePhoto);            ◁──┐  │    │   │   dialog window
}                            │  │    │   │
                             │  │    │   └ Passes default
window.onload = initialize;  │  │    │     filename for the file
                             │  │    │
                             │  │    └ Sets label of success
                             │  │      action button to
                             │  │      "Save photo"
                             │  │
                             │  └ Passes savePhoto function
                             │    as callback to dialog, which
                             │    will pass final file path
```

In this version of the app, the `takePhoto` function does a bit more work. It directly triggers the rendering of the Save File dialog window. You set the title, default file path, and Success button's labels, and then pass the `savePhoto` function as the callback function that the dialog window will call once the user has either clicked Save Photo or Cancel on the dialog window. When the `savePhoto` function is called, it will receive the file path with the name of the file given by the user, or it will receive a null value if the user cancelled. Last but not least, you bind the `initialize` function on triggering when the window has loaded the HTML.

Here, you can see that to bring about a dialog window for saving a file, you call a function in Electron's dialog module. The `showSaveDialog` function is one of a number of functions you can call from the module. If you want to trigger other behaviors, like a dialog for opening a file or displaying a message dialog with an icon, the API methods and their arguments are available at http://electron.atom.io/docs/api/dialog/.

What does the Electron version of the app look like? It's almost identical to the NW.js version, as figure 11.2 shows.

The key takeaway here is that you've been able to build an app with embedded video and photo-saving features. Imagine the effort involved in trying to replicate the same app in native frameworks! It's fair to say that HTML5 Media Capture has taken away a lot of the pain, so the ability to build desktop apps on top of that kind of work is a massive timesaver.

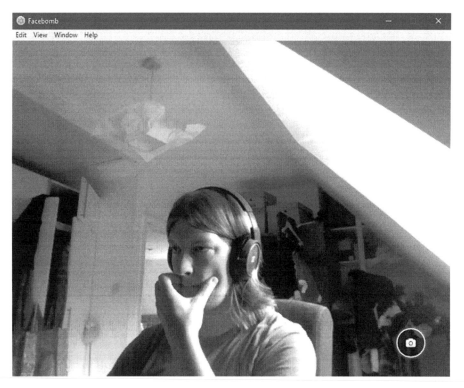

Figure 11.2   Facebomb Electron on Windows 10. Notice how the app looks exactly the same, except for the app icon in the app title.

11.2   Summary

In this chapter, you created a photo booth–like app called Facebomb and explored different implementations of it in NW.js and Electron. This discussion has introduced you to the idea that you can leverage the HTML5 Media Capture API to access video and use it in creative ways. Some of the key takeaways from the chapter include these:

- You don't need to worry about asking for permission to access the webcam or microphone when using HTML5 Media Capture APIs, because both Electron and NW.js apps run locally on the user's computer and are therefore trusted.
- You can use the `video` element to display the video feed in your app, and the HTML5 `canvas` element to record an image from it to be saved to your computer.

That was fun. In chapter 12, we'll turn our attention to ways of storing app data.

Storing app data

Applications need to store data; when you're playing a game and loading from a saved level, or configuring settings for how you use a particular app, or even storing structured data in a line-of-business app, data must be stored somewhere and must be accessed by the app with ease.

Options for how to store data in your app range from using the HTML5 `localStorage` API to using embedded databases in your desktop app. In this chapter, we'll explore some options and see how you can use them with your desktop apps.

12.1 What data storage option should I use?

In the old days, this was a simple question—there were fewer options. Traditionally, web apps relied solely on storing data in databases that lived on back-end servers. With the advent of client-side storage APIs for HTML5, the ability to store data on the client has resulted in the emergence of new libraries for that purpose, and for synchronizing that data with an external database.

Table 12.1 lists options for storing your data in web apps, and these can therefore be used in both Electron and NW.js apps.

Table 12.1   Options for storing data

Name	Database type	Type	URL
IndexedDB	Key/Value	Browser API	https://is.gd/wwDSgj
localStorage	Key/Value	Browser API	https://is.gd/3XbaFQ
Lovefield	Relational	Client-side library	https://github.com/google/lovefield
PouchDB	Document	Client-side library	https://pouchdb.com/
SQLite	Relational	Embedded	http://sqlite.com/
NeDB	Document	Embedded	https://is.gd/f44eap
LevelDB	Key/Value	Embedded	http://leveldb.org/
Minimongo	Document	Client-side library	https://is.gd/yTRXhe

Lots of options are available, sure, but which one should you use? That depends on what data you're storing, how much of it you're storing, and how you'll need to query that data.

If you have a good idea what kind of data you're going to be storing, and the schema for that data is known up front and is unlikely to change while the app is in use, relational databases are worth considering due to the benefits of their powerful querying capabilities.

If you need to store no more than 5 MB of data for your app (for example, user settings), you can get away with using the browser-based API options, which impose limits of 5 MB on how much data can be stored on them.

Another thing to consider is how you'll need to query the data. If the data is denormalized and stored in tables with references to data in other tables, then a document-based approach might not be the most efficient when it comes to querying the data. The design of the data schemas and whether the data is denormalized or not will go some way toward helping you choose whether to opt for a SQL-based or NoSQL-based database for data storage.

Enough debating about which option to pick. Let's give some of them a spin.

12.2   Storing a sticky note with the localStorage API

You'll create a simple single sticky note app called Let Me Remember. It's a dead-simple app that will demonstrate what localStorage is handy for (storing text-based data in a key/value data store). There are two separate versions of the app for the different frameworks, one for NW.js (called let-me-remember-nwjs) and one for Electron (called let-me-remember-electron). Both apps can be found in the book's GitHub repository at http://mng.bz/fYrm and http://mng.bz/COlh.

You can either take a look at one of those apps and run the code according to the README instructions or assemble it from scratch. We'll look at the Electron version of the app first, for a change.

12.2.1 Creating the Let Me Remember app with Electron

The app is mostly a vanilla boilerplate, but with a few distinct touches. Let's start with the package.json file and work from there. First, you create a folder for the app. You can use the following commands in a terminal:

```
mkdir let-me-remember
cd let-me-remember
```

Now, you can create a package.json file inside the folder and insert the code shown in the next listing.

Listing 12.1 Making the package.json file for the Let Me Remember Electron app

```
{
  "name": "let-me-remember-electron",
  "version": "1.0.0",
  "description": "A sticky note app for Electron",
  "main": "main.js",
  "scripts": {
    "start": "node_modules/.bin/electron .",
    "test": "echo \"Error: no test specified\" && exit 1"
  },
  "keywords": [
    "electron"
  ],
  "author": "Paul Jensen <paulbjensen@gmail.com>",
  "license": "MIT",
  "dependencies": {
    "electron ": "^1.3.7"
  }
}
```

The main property in the package.json file indicates that the main.js file is the app's point of entry. The main.js file is mostly vanilla boilerplate, but there's a bit of code that you need to make the app window frameless, as well as to apply width/height constraints. This is so the app can have the look and feel of a sticky note to the user.

Don't forget to run `npm install` after saving the package.json to install the Electron dependency.

Let's create the main.js file next and add the code to it shown next.

Listing 12.2 Making the main.js file for the Let Me Remember Electron app

```
'use strict';

const electron = require('electron');
const app = electron.app;
const BrowserWindow = electron.BrowserWindow;
```

```
let mainWindow = null;

app.on('window-all-closed', () => {
  if (process.platform !== 'darwin') app.quit();
});

app.on('ready', () => {
  mainWindow = new BrowserWindow({
    width: 480,
    height: 320,
    frame: false
  });
  mainWindow.loadURL(`file://${__dirname}/index.html`);
  mainWindow.on('closed', () => { mainWindow = null; });
});
```

> Sets frame attribute to
> false to make app
> window frameless

The main.js file configures the app window to be of a fairly small size so that it resembles the dimensions of a sticky note and has a frameless app window. Inside the app window is the index.html file that will be the only visible element of the app. Let's now flesh out the index.html file with the content from the next listing.

Listing 12.3   Making the index.html file for the Let Me Remember Electron app

```
<html>
  <head>
    <title>Let Me Remember</title>
    <link rel="stylesheet" type="text/css" href="app.css">
    <script src="app.js"></script>
  </head>
  <body>
    <div id="close" onclick="quit();">x</div>
    <textarea onKeyUp="saveNotes();"></textarea>
  </body>
</html>
```

> Triggers call to quit
> when clicking X

> textarea element saves
> text on every keystroke

The index.html file is fairly simple, because the app itself is quite simple. There's no app frame, so you implement a custom close button that, when clicked, will quit the app. You then also define a `textarea` element, which is responsible for displaying the text of the sticky note as well as allowing the user to edit it.

At the top of the index.html file, you load two front-end files: an app.css stylesheet and an app.js JavaScript file. We'll look at the stylesheet first. In the app's folder, create an app.css file, and put the CSS shown next inside.

Listing 12.4   Creating the app.css file for the Let Me Remember Electron app

```
body {
  background: #ffe15f;
  color: #694921;
  padding: 1em;
}
```

```
textarea {
  font-family: 'Hannotate SC', 'Hanzipen SC','Comic Sans', 'Comic Sans MS';
  outline: none;
  font-size: 18pt;
  border: none;
  width: 100%;
  height: 100%;
  background: none;
}

#close {
  cursor: pointer;
  position: absolute;
  top: 8px;
  right: 10px;
  text-align: center;
  font-family: 'Helvetica Neue', 'Arial';
  font-weight: 400;
}
```

The CSS code here uses fairly common CSS rules and could be repurposed in a web app if you wanted. The body is styled to look like the yellow paper commonly associated with a sticky note, and the textarea is styled to look like handwriting—it even uses Comic Sans as a last resort (the last time I saw Comic Sans in use was at AOL). Finally, the close button is given a different styling to make the X character look like the one used for a close button.

With the styling applied, all that's left to do now is create the app.js file that contains the quit and saveNotes functions. In the same app folder, create the app.js file and insert the code shown here.

Listing 12.5 The app.js file for the Let Me Remember Electron app

```
'use strict';                                    ← Loads app module via remote API to enable quitting app

const electron = require('electron');
const app = electron.remote.app;                 ← Calls HTML5 localStorage API to check for notes data

function initialize () {
  let notes = window.localStorage.notes;         ← If none, sets it to default value
  if (!notes) notes = 'Let me remember...';
  window.document.querySelector('textarea').value = notes;   ← Loads notes data for display in textarea element
}

function saveNotes () {                           ← Gets text content in textarea element
  let notes = window.document.querySelector('textarea').value;
  window.localStorage.setItem('notes',notes);    ← Saves text content to HTML5 localStorage API
}

function quit () { app.quit(); }                 ← quit function wraps call to quit function on the app module

window.onload = initialize;
```

The app.js file helps implement the loading of data from the computer via the HTML5 `localStorage` API and then allows the user to record notes on the sticky and close the app down. When they type some notes, the notes are saved. When they reopen the app, the notes they saved will be displayed in the sticky, as shown in figure 12.1.

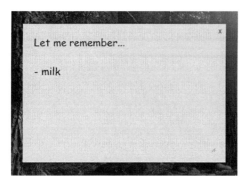

Figure 12.1   The Let Me Remember Electron app running on Windows 10. If you type some notes, close the app, and reopen it, it will load with the notes that you typed.

With the help of the HTML5 `localStorage` API, you've been able to add *data persistence* to your app and make it work in such a way that saving the notes happens invisibly in the background. It's the kind of user experience you want the app to provide—seamless.

Now, you can take a look at how the NW.js implementation differs in its approach.

12.2.2 *Implementing the Let Me Remember app with NW.js*

The NW.js implementation of the app varies slightly. It has the same CSS as the Electron variant of the app and almost identical versions of the app.js and index.html files. You'll work from the package.json and look at the files from there.

Create a folder for the app, and then create a package.json file inside it and insert the following code:

```
{
  "name" : "let-me-remember",
  "version": "1.0.0",
  "main": "index.html",
  "window": {
    "width": 480,
    "height": 320,
    "frame": false
  }
}
```

The package.json file is pretty much vanilla, with the exception of the `window` properties. You've set the initial `width` and `height` to a relatively small size (similar to a large sticky note stuck on the screen) and turned off the window frame so that it will look like a sticky note stuck on the screen.

Next, you'll add the index.html file in the folder, and put the following code in there:

```html
<html>
  <head>
    <title>Let Me Remember?</title>
    <link rel="stylesheet" type="text/css" href="app.css">
    <script src="app.js"></script>
  </head>
  <body>
    <div id="close" onclick="process.exit(0)">x</div>
    <textarea onKeyUp="saveNotes();"></textarea>
  </body>
</html>
```

The HTML file is a simple file as well. You use a `textarea` element to capture the notes that you want to jot down inside the sticky note. You could have used a p element with a `contenteditable` attribute, but you need to be able to capture the event when new content enters the p element, and currently there isn't a way to do that. You also have a `div` element with the ID attribute of `"close"`, which when clicked will trigger the process of exiting the app (because you've hidden the window frame around the app, and therefore you wouldn't have a way to close the app graphically, except for navigating to the menu bar and closing the app from there). Note that this doesn't call a `quit()` function, because you can directly call Node.js's process global variable from the JavaScript context in the HTML.

The app.css file is identical to the one used in the Electron app, shown in listing 12.4, so you can avoid repeating yourself on that. As for the app.js file, the code is similar but has a little less code, as shown next.

Listing 12.6   The app.js file for the Let Me Remember NW.js app

```javascript
'use strict';

function initialize () {
  let notes = window.localStorage.notes;
  if (!notes) notes = 'Let me remember...';
  window.document.querySelector('textarea').value = notes;
}
function saveNotes () {
  let notes = window.document.querySelector('textarea').value;
  window.localStorage.setItem('notes',notes);
}

window.onload = initialize;
```

It's quite a nice, compact bit of code, so let's go through it. When the app and the DOM have loaded, you call an `initialize` function to retrieve any notes that are stored under the key name of `notes`. If there are no notes, then you provide some default copy, "Let me remember. . ." and insert that into the `textarea` element in the page.

If you take a quick glance back to the index.html file, you'll notice that the text-area element had an `onKeyUp` attribute that called a function named `saveNotes`. Well, the `saveNotes` function does what the name suggests—it gets the text that's currently in the `textarea` element of the app and calls the `localStorage` API's `setItem` function to set the value of `notes` to that text.

If you type in some items you want to get, such as a grocery list, and then close the app, you should find that when you reopen the app, the notes have been saved and will be displayed as before, as in figure 12.2.

Figure 12.2   The Let Me Remember NW.js app. I've added some grocery list items for shopping later.

The `localStorage` API is ideal for storing unstructured text with a simple key/value storage mechanism (`getItem`, `setItem`). The Let Me Remember app example you went through is an ideal use case for it, but a lot of other apps will need to store structured data that's not necessarily in string format—it might be an array of strings, or integers, or other kinds of data types.

One potential approach to storing that kind of data is serializing and deserializing the data with `JSON.stringify()` and `JSON.parse()`. If the use case of your app is well defined, then this approach can work. An example of this is the popular TodoMVC project. To demonstrate this, you'll port one of the TodoMVC app examples to become a desktop app, with a few changes.

12.3   *Porting a to-do list web app*

Storing a to-do list with the `localStorage` API is possible—in fact, this is how the TodoMVC project handles data persistence.

The TodoMVC project is a collection of examples of the same to-do list app, implemented using different JavaScript frameworks. Its purpose is to show developers how each framework approaches implementing a to-do list app so that users can find the right framework for their needs.

There are lots of different implementations of the TodoMVC app, including Socketstream (a framework for real-time web apps that I've been involved with in the past).

You'll take a popular framework called React and use its implementation as the example that you'll port to a desktop app.

Porting this app will demonstrate a major key benefit of both Electron and NW.js: how easy it is to reuse code from a web app inside a desktop app.

12.3.1 *Porting a TodoMVC web app with NW.js*

First, you need to make a copy of the TodoMVC GitHub repository. Find a folder where you want to install a local copy of the repository and clone it to there with Git from the Terminal:

```
git clone git@github.com:tastejs/todomvc.git
```

Inside the cloned GitHub repository, you'll find an examples folder containing all the different implementations of the TodoMVC app. You're interested in the folder named react. Open the folder in your text editor/IDE of choice and add these lines to the package.json file:

```
"name":"todo-mvc-app",
"version":"1.0.0",
"main":"index.html",
"window": {
  "toolbar":false
}
```

Save the package.json file, and run nw inside the folder in the Terminal. You should see the app running on your desktop. Add some to-do list items to it and then close the app and reopen it. What you'll see is something like figure 12.3.

Figure 12.3 The TodoMVC app running as a desktop app via NW.js, with data being stored in the app via the HTML5 `localStorage` API

What's so cool about this is that with six lines of code added to one file, you've turned a web app into a desktop app. If only all apps could be ported that easily! If you're interested in seeing what's going on behind the scenes, take a look at the js/utils.js file, particularly at the `store` function that begins on line 28. The function is a getter/setter that wraps access to the HTML5 `localStorage` API and makes use of the `JSON.stringify()` and `JSON.parse()` methods to handle storing and retrieving data.

Why not store structured data using Web SQL?

It's a good question. Naturally, SQL would make a good fit for storing structured data such as the data inside the TodoMVC project. The reason that it isn't used, and why I don't mention it in the book, is because Web SQL as a web standard is being deprecated and hence will enter a graveyard of web standards that have been abandoned over time.

12.3.2 Porting a TodoMVC app with Electron

I'd like to say that the Electron app version is as simple, but it requires a few more steps. First, you need to modify the package.json file for the TodoMVC React example so that it looks like the code in the following listing.

Listing 12.7   The package.json file for the TodoMVC React Electron app

```
{
  "private": true,
  "dependencies": {
    "classnames": "^2.1.5",
    "director": "^1.2.0",
    "electron-prebuilt": "^1.2.5",      ◁── Adds Electron as
    "react": "^0.13.3",                     dependency to list of
    "todomvc-app-css": "^2.0.0",            dependencies for repo
    "todomvc-common": "^1.0.1"
  },                                      Adds main field for app's
  "main":"main.js",                   ◁── entry point, pointing to
}                                         main.js file you'll make
```

The modifications to the package.json file are so that you can get Electron to run the app. Next, we'll look at implementing the main.js file that you need to make the Electron app load. Create a file called main.js, and put the following code into it:

```
'use strict';

const electron = require('electron');
const app = electron.app;
const BrowserWindow = electron.BrowserWindow;

let mainWindow = null;
```

```
app.on('window-all-closed', () => {
  if (process.platform !== 'darwin') app.quit();
});

app.on('ready', () => {
  mainWindow = new BrowserWindow();
  mainWindow.loadURL(`file://${__dirname}/index.html`);
  mainWindow.on('closed', () => { mainWindow = null; });
});
```

The main.js file is pretty standard and is used to load the index.html file in the React example app. If you try to load the app, you'll find that the example doesn't work. Opening the developer tools on the app and looking at the Console Tab reveals a JavaScript error: 'classNames' is not defined. This error is occurring in the todoItem.jsx file located inside the js folder of the React example folder. The classNames variable is coming from a Node.js module that's loaded in the index.html file as a script tag.

One way to fix this error is to require the classnames module inside the todoItem.jsx file so you can guarantee the module is loaded by the time the React code is evaluated. In the todoItem.jsx file, add the following line of code on line 8, before the instantly invoked function expression:

```
const classNames = require('classnames');
```

Now, you can run the app from the command line by running this in the same directory as the TodoMVC app:

```
electron
```

This will get the TodoMVC app to run. What this demonstrates is that when you port a web app to Electron, there are a few more steps involved; but also, loading libraries in the DOM can't be guaranteed to happen in the order you expect, so you should be aware of that.

12.4   *Summary*

In this chapter, we've looked at how you can go about storing data for your desktop apps. You looked at what options exist for storing your app's data, and explored using the HTML5 localStorage API to implement a notes app. You then explored how versatile NW.js and Electron are by using them to convert a web app into a desktop app that persists its data locally.

You can store simple datasets in your desktop app using HTML5's localStorage API and, if needed, serialize and deserialize structured data with that too; but you're better off using an embedded database for that kind of data.

Now that we've covered ways to store and retrieve data for your apps, we can explore another element of handling data in your apps—specifically, how you get and set data from the OS clipboard.

Copying and
pasting contents
from the clipboard

This chapter covers

- Accessing the clipboard in NW.js and Electron
- Copying text content to the clipboard
- Clearing the clipboard
- Copying Electron's other data types to the clipboard

Copying data from one source and using it in another is a function that's pretty standard with today's apps. Some utility apps add value to this functionality by automatically copying screenshots to the clipboard, or keeping track of multiple data items that are copied to the clipboard.

In this chapter, we'll look at how NW.js and Electron enable you to use the OS's clipboard to copy and paste content, as well as how to clear the clipboard (a good practice, especially when copying/pasting sensitive data).

By the end of the chapter, you'll have a good understanding of how to access and alter the user's clipboard.

13.1 Accessing the clipboard

Copying and pasting from the OS clipboard improves the UX by taking a manual step out of the user journey. Take, for example, the password manager app 1Password by AgileBits. When you enter your password in a website login, the app automatically copies the password to your clipboard for pasting into the password field of the login form the next time you log in.

The clipboard APIs in Electron and NW.js allow you to store and retrieve text-based data to and from the clipboard. To illustrate how this works, you'll build a very simple app that lists a number of common phrases, film quotes, and things you might want to type into a chat window, and saves some nuggets that you want to keep for later. You'll call it Pearls.

If you want to have a look at premade versions of these apps, the NW.js and Electron versions of the app are available in the pearls-nwjs app in the book's GitHub repository at http://mng.bz/4V2D. You can download the code and run it per the instructions, or if you prefer to see how the app is made from scratch, read on.

13.1.1 Creating the Pearls app with NW.js

You'll start by creating a folder called pearls-nwjs to store the app's files. Then, add the package.json file. In your text editor, create the package.json file and add the following content to it:

```
{
  "name":"pearls",
  "version":"1.0.0",
  "main":"index.html",
  "window": {
    "width": 650,
    "height": 550,
    "toolbar": false
  },
  "scripts": {
    "start": "node_modules/.bin/nw ."
  },
  "dependencies": {
    "nw": "^0.15.3"
  }
}
```

The package.json file is much like the package.json for other NW.js apps, with the only unique bits being the window `width` and `height` properties. Next, implement the index.html file, and put the following code into it:

```
<html>
  <head>
    <title>Pearls</title>
    <link href="app.css" rel="stylesheet" />
    <script src=" app.js"></script>
  </head>
```

```
<body>
  <template id="phrase">
    <div class="phrase"
    onclick="copyPhraseToClipboard(this.innerText);"></div>
  </template>
  <div id="phrases"></div>
</body>
</html>
```

The index.html file does a few things: It loads an app stylesheet as well as an app.js file for loading the phrases and copying them into the clipboard. It then also contains a `template` tag for the phrase, used for each phrase you want to display in the app window. The following listing shows the CSS for the Pearls app.

Listing 13.1   The app.css file for the Pearls NW.js app

```
body {
  padding: 0;
  margin: 0;
  background: #001203;
}

#phrases {
  padding: 0.5em;
}

.phrase {
  float: left;
  padding: 1em;
  margin: 1em;
  border-radius: 12px;
  border: solid 1px #ccc;
  font-family: 'Helvetica Neue', 'Arial' 'Sans-Serif';
  font-style: italic;
  width: 9em;
  min-height: 7em;
  text-align: center;
  color: #fff;
}

.phrase:hover {
  cursor: pointer;
  background: #1188de;
}
```

The CSS for the app is designed so that the app has a dark background, and the phrases are highlighted against that dark background with white text surrounded by a white border. When a phrase is hovered over, the background color of that phrase turns blue.

Next, load the app.js file, shown here.

Listing 13.2   The app.js file for the Pearls NW.js app

```
'use strict';

const gui = require('nw.gui');
const clipboard = gui.Clipboard.get();
const phrases = require('./phrases');
let phrasesArea;
let template;

function addPhrase (phrase) {
  template.content.querySelector('div').innerText = phrase;
  let clone = window.document.importNode(template.content, true);
  phrasesArea.appendChild(clone);
}

function loadPhrasesInto () {
  phrasesArea = window.document.getElementById('phrases');
  template = window.document.querySelector('#phrase');
  phrases.forEach(addPhrase);
}

function copyPhraseToClipboard (phrase) {
  clipboard.set(phrase, 'text');
}

window.onload = loadPhrasesInto;
```

Loads NW.js's Clipboard API through NW.gui module

Loads example phrases to use in app

Adds a phrase to app window

Function loads phrases from phrases.js file into app window

When phrase is clicked, function is triggered to copy phrase into clipboard

When app is done loading HTML, triggers loading phrases

The key bit of the app is the function copyPhraseToClipboard, which uses the clipboard API to set a value to the clipboard—in this case, the phrase that was clicked. The phrases.js file contains a list of quotes from various films like *Kindergarten Cop* and others (I'll let you figure out the rest). Here's the list of phrases:

```
'use strict';

module.exports = [
  'I have to return some videotapes',
  'Do not attempt to grow a brain',
  'So tell me, do you feel lucky? Well do ya, Punk!',
  'We\'re gonna need a bigger boat',
  'We can handle a little chop',
  'Get to the choppa!',
  'Hold onto your butts',
  'Today we\'re going to play a wonderful game called "Who is your daddy, and
    what does he do?"',
  'Yesterday we were an army without a country. Tomorrow we must decide...
    which country we want to buy!'
];
```

The phrases.js file exports a list of strings that are movie quotes from various films. That list is then loaded by the app.js file into the app window.

Now, you can run the app with npm start, and you should see an app that looks like figure 13.1.

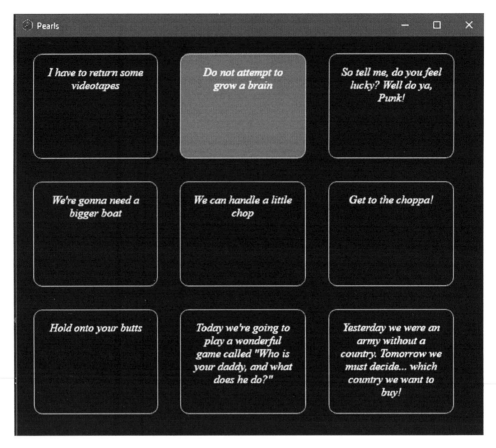

Figure 13.1   The Pearls app running with NW.js on Microsoft Windows 10

What content can I store and retrieve from the clipboard?

NW.js currently only allows text-based content to be stored and retrieved from the OS clipboard—unfortunately, images can't be accessed or stored. It is hoped that other content types will be able to be stored and accessed from the clipboard in the future, but for now text will have to do.

If you want to get/set other types of content to the clipboard, you may be better off going with Electron because that has support for other data types.

If you wanted to access the contents of the clipboard (say you had a quotation from a web page that you copied to the clipboard but hadn't pasted anywhere), you could do that by using the following line of code in your app:

```
let copiedText = clipboard.get('text');
```

This can be useful in cases where you want to automatically record copied content (such as for a note-taking app where content is being copied out of pages and documents). Sometimes you want the clipboard cleared (such as when it's used to store sensitive information). To do that, call this line on the API:

```
clipboard.clear();
```

The clipboard API offers the ability to store and retrieve text-based content from the OS clipboard, but if you need to work with other data (such as files), then you might still be in luck.

What does the clipboard API in Electron look like in comparison?

13.1.2 *Creating the Pearls app with Electron*

The Pearls app Electron example's source code can be found in the pearls-electron app folder in the book's GitHub repository.

The app's code is similar to that of the Pearls app NW.js example, with the exceptions of the package.json file, the app.js file, and the main.js file required by Electron to load an app. The next listing shows the package.json file for this app.

> **Listing 13.3   The package.json file for the Pearls Electron app**

```
{
  "name": "pearls-electron",
  "version": "1.0.0",
  "description": "A clipboard API example for Electron and the book 'Cross
    Platform Desktop apps'",
  "main": "main.js",
  "scripts": {
    "start": "node_modules/.bin/electron .",
    "test": "echo \"Error: no test specified\" && exit 1"
  },
  "keywords": [
    "electron",
    "clipboard"
  ],
  "author": "Paul Jensen <paulbjensen@gmail.com>",
  "license": "MIT",
  "dependencies": {
    "electron ": "^1.3.7"
  }
}
```

The package.json file is generated by running npm init from the command line and is modified slightly to include the Electron npm dependency, as well as the start command so that you can run npm start to make the app boot. It also loads the main.js file as the Electron app's first entry point. The code for the main.js file is shown next.

Listing 13.4   The main.js file for the Pearls Electron app

```
'use strict';

const electron = require('electron');
const app = electron. app;
const BrowserWindow = electron.BrowserWindow;

let mainWindow = null;

app.on('window-all-closed', () => {
  if (process.platform !== 'darwin') app.quit();
});

app.on('ready', () => {
  mainWindow = new BrowserWindow({
    width: 670,
    height: 550,
    useContentSize: true
  });
  mainWindow.loadURL(`file://${__dirname}/index.html`);
  mainWindow.on('closed', () => { mainWindow = null; });
});
```

The main.js file loads a standard app window with a specific width and height so you
can display the phrases in a 3 x 3 grid initially, as well as ensure that the app window
size is based on the size of the content window.

The index.html, app.css, and phrases.js files are identical to the NW.js equivalent
of the app, so there's no point repeating those here. What is different, though, is how
the clipboard API methods are called in Electron, which you can see in the app.js file.

Listing 13.5   The app.js file for the Pearls Electron app

```
'use strict';

const electron = require('electron');
const clipboard = electron.clipboard;        ◁┐ Loads Electron's
const phrases = require('./phrases');             clipboard API
let phrasesArea;
let template;

function addPhrase (phrase) {
  template.content.querySelector('div').innerText = phrase;
  let clone = window.document.importNode(template.content, true);
  phrasesArea. app endChild(clone);
}

function loadPhrasesInto () {
  phrasesArea = window.document.getElementById('phrases');
  template = window.document.querySelector('#phrase');
  phrases.forEach(addPhrase);
}

function copyPhraseToClipboard (phrase) {        Make3 call to clipboard
  clipboard.writeText(phrase);        ◁┐ API to write some text to
}                                         clipboard

window.onload = loadPhrasesInto;
```

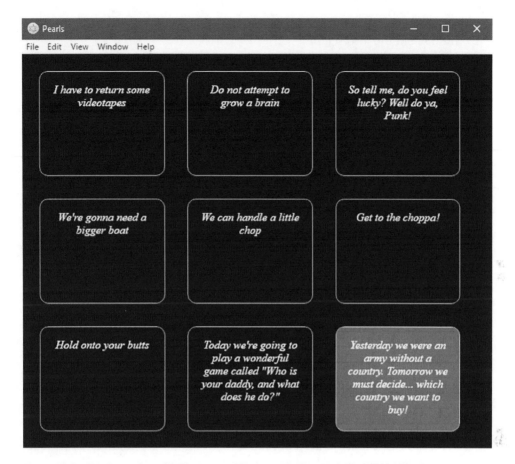

Figure 13.2 Pearls running with Electron on Windows 10. The app looks almost identical to the one shown in figure 13.1, with the exception of the toolbar and the app icon.

If you run the app via `npm start`, you'll see the app looking like figure 13.2.

The way in which you access the clipboard from Electron follows a semantic naming convention of read and write. In the app.js file for the Pearls app, the call to put some text content in the clipboard is `clipboard.writeText`. To read the content in the clipboard, you can make the following code call:

```
const content = clipboard.readText();
```

To clear the clipboard's content, you can make an identical function call to the clipboard API:

```
clipboard.clear()
```

The API method call is identical to the one used in NW.js—another signal of how much the two frameworks share in common. That said, Electron has evolved more

API methods that allow it to do more than copy and paste text from the clipboard, as you'll see in the next section.

13.1.3   *Setting other types of content to the clipboard with Electron*

Unlike NW.js, Electron allows you to put RTF, HTML, and even images on the clipboard. The API methods follow the same patterns as the `readText` and `writeText` functions that the clipboard API exposes. We'll briefly walk through some of them, but to read more, see the API documentation at http://electron.atom.io/docs/api/clipboard/.

The clipboard API has methods for the following content types:

- Text
- HTML
- Images
- RTF

Calling the API methods from the clipboard API looks like this:

```
const electron = require('electron');
const clipboard = electron.clipboard;

let image = clipboard.readImage();
let richText = clipboard.readRTF();
let html = clipboard.readHTML();

clipboard.writeImage(image);
clipboard.writeRTF(richText);
clipboard.writeHTML(html);
```

Here, you can see the pattern of read/write for getting content from the clipboard as well as setting content to it.

13.2   *Summary*

In this chapter, we worked through an app that copied movie quotes into the user's clipboard, and explored the API methods available to the developer for copying text-based and other types of data into the clipboard.

The key takeaway from this chapter is that you can only copy and paste text-based content with the clipboard API in NW.js, but Electron can handle multimedia content like images and RTF.

In chapter 14, we'll take a look at how the various desktop app frameworks go about implementing keyboard shortcuts. We'll make it fun by putting them into a well-known 2D game called Snake.

Binding on
keyboard shortcuts

14

This chapter covers

- Learning how NW.js and Electron work with keyboard shortcuts
- Adding keyboard shortcuts to a 2D game
- Adding global hotkey shortcuts

Power users of applications (and users of Vim) will tell you that learning keyboard shortcuts is invaluable for using apps in a fast and productive manner. For other apps, like arcade games, they can also be an essential interface method.

Programmatically binding keyboard shortcuts to your desktop app in Electron and NW.js offers your users faster ways to perform common tasks, takes some of UI scanning out of the user experience, and makes your apps easier and more pleasant to use. In this chapter, we'll explore how to add keyboard shortcuts to a video game known as Snake.

Years ago, I built the Snake game as a Christmas/New Year project at a Ruby on Rails consultancy called New Bamboo (now part of Thoughtbot) and wrote up a tutorial about it on their site. Step forward to now, and what better example than to re-create the same game as a desktop app.

Although you could port the original source code of the game from the repository I created six years ago, it would be better to create it fresh, learning from how it was developed. That way you can better understand the mechanics of the game as well as how you can use Electron and NW.js's keyboard shortcuts APIs to bind direction keys to the movement of the snake. If you want to see the app in action, you can grab the app's source code for snake-nwjs and snake-electron from the book's GitHub repository at http://mng.bz/kxdd and http://mng.bz/Wis3.

14.1   *Creating the Snake game with NW.js*

First off, create a new folder called snake-nwjs, and generate some default boilerplate code for it:

```
mkdir snake-nwjs
cd snake-nwjs
touch app.js
touch app.css
touch index.html
touch package.json
```

You next need to put some initial configuration into the package.json file. Add the following code to it:

```
{
  "name": "snake-nwjs",
  "version": "1.0.0",
  "description": "A Snake game in NW.js for 'Cross Platform Desktop
    Applications'",
  "main": "index.html",
  "scripts": {
    "start": "node_modules/.bin/nw .",
    "test": "echo \"Error: no test specified\" && exit 1"
  },
  "keywords": [
    "snake",
    "nwjs"
  ],
  "author": "Paul Jensen <paulbjensen@gmail.com>",
  "license": "MIT",
  "window": {
    "width": 840,
    "height": 470,
    "toolbar": false
  },
  "dependencies": {
    "nw": "^0.15.3"
  }
}
```

IS THERE ANOTHER WAY TO CREATE THE PACKAGE.JSON FILE? Yes. If you get bored with creating the package.json file from scratch, there's a convenience command from npm called init. It will ask you a bunch of questions from the CLI and create the package.json file for you. To use it, open a Terminal or Command Prompt and type npm init in the location where you would like the package.json file to exist. To find out more about npm init, check out https://docs.npmjs.com/cli/init.

Now, turn your attention to the index.html file and put the following code in it:

```html
<html>
  <head>
    <title>Snake</title>
    <link href="app.css" rel="stylesheet" />
    <script src="app.js"></script>
  </head>
  <body>
  </body>
</html>
```

Now, you can start building the game. The first decision is what content you want to display for the Snake game. A few items should be displayed visually:

- The score
- The game area, the snake inside it, and the item that the snake eats
- Buttons for starting, pausing, and restarting the game.

We'll focus on the UI first and then flesh out various bits of the game. Let's define the main scoreboard and the game area in the UI.

First, define the game area and the scoreboard. For the game area, you'll use a canvas element, a simple div element for the scoreboard, and a bar element containing the buttons to pause, resume, and restart the game. Inside the body element of the index.html file, add the following snippet:

```html
<div id="scoreboard">
  <span id="label">Score:</span>
  <span id="score"></span>
  <div id="bar">
    <div id="play_menu">
      <button onclick="pause();">Pause</button>
    </div>
    <div id="pause_menu">
      <button onclick="play();">Resume</button>
      <button onclick="restart();">Restart</button>
    </div>
    <div id="restart_menu">
      <button onclick="restart();">Restart</button>
    </div>
  </div>
</div>
<canvas></canvas>
```

The canvas tag will be used to render the area in which the snake will move, as well as where the food will appear. You'll add some styling to it to make it look presentable, too. In the app.css file, add the following styling:

```css
body {
  margin: 1em;
  padding: 0;
  background: #111;
  color: white;
  font-family: helvetica;
}

canvas {
  border: solid 1px red;
  width: 800px;
  height: 400px;
}

#scoreboard {
  padding-bottom: 1em
}

#label, #score, #bar {
  float: left;
  padding: 8px;
}

#pause_menu, #restart_menu {
  display: none;
}
```

Now you have the area for the snake to move around in, as well as the scoreboard, so now you need a snake moving around and eating food. You'll use the HTML5 canvas API to handle rendering the snake. In the app.js file, add the following code:

```js
'use strict';

let canvas, ctx, gridSize, currentPosition, snakeBody, snakeLength,
    direction, score, suggestedPoint, allowPressKeys, interval, choice;

function updateScore () {
  score = (snakeLength - 3) * 10;
  document.getElementById('score').innerText = score;
}
```

The updateScore function is a simple UI helper function that updates the div element, displaying the current score. Add the following code:

```js
function hasPoint (element) {
  return (element[0] === suggestedPoint[0] && element[1] === suggestedPoint[1]);
}
```

The hasPoint function is a helper function to check whether a given element's x and y coordinates match a suggested point's x and y coordinates, which are stored as an array. The suggested point is where to place the food item that the snake will eat. Now, add the following:

```
function makeFoodItem () {
  suggestedPoint =
      [Math.floor(Math.random()*(canvas.width/gridSize))*gridSize,
       Math.floor(Math.random()*(canvas.height/gridSize))*gridSize];
  if (snakeBody.some(hasPoint)) {
    makeFoodItem();
  } else {
    ctx.fillStyle = 'rgb(10,100,0)';
    ctx.fillRect(suggestedPoint[0], suggestedPoint[1], gridSize, gridSize);
  }
}
```

makeFoodItem does what it says—makes the food items for the snake to eat. It finds a random point on the canvas and checks if it is currently occupied by the snake. If it is, it calls itself in order to find another spot. If not, it creates the food item at that spot. Add the following code:

```
function hasEatenItself (element) {
  return (element[0] === currentPosition.x && element[1] === currentPosition.y);
}
```

Another semantically named function, hasEatenItself, checks whether the snake has managed to wander into its own path. Now add this code:

```
function leftPosition(){
 return currentPosition.x - gridSize;
}

function rightPosition(){
  return currentPosition.x + gridSize;
}

function upPosition(){
  return currentPosition.y - gridSize;
}

function downPosition(){
  return currentPosition.y + gridSize;
}
```

These helper functions report back the edge of the snake's head, depending on the direction in which the snake is heading. It's used to track the next coordinate that the snake would occupy on the axis so you can check if it's about to hit the edge of the movement area, or eat a food item, or itself. Insert the following:

```
function whichWayToGo (axisType) {
  if (axisType === 'x') {
    choice = (currentPosition.x > canvas.width / 2) ? moveLeft() : moveRight();
```

```
    } else {
      choice = (currentPosition.y > canvas.height / 2) ? moveUp() : moveDown();
    }
}
```

A slight variation on the original Snake game, now, when the snake hits the edge of the movement area, it will go sideways rather than continue from the opposing end of the movement area. The idea is that the snake will move in the general direction of where most of the space is, so if the snake is toward the bottom limit of the movement area and hits the right side, then the snake will move upward—that's where the space is. Add the following:

```
function moveUp(){
  if (upPosition() >= 0) {
    executeMove('up', 'y', upPosition());
  } else {
    whichWayToGo('x');
  }
}

function moveDown(){
  if (downPosition() < canvas.height) {
    executeMove('down', 'y', downPosition());
  } else {
    whichWayToGo('x');
  }
}

function moveLeft(){
  if (leftPosition() >= 0) {
    executeMove('left', 'x', leftPosition());
  } else {
    whichWayToGo('y');
  }
}

function moveRight(){
  if (rightPosition() < canvas.width) {
    executeMove('right', 'x', rightPosition());
  } else {
    whichWayToGo('y');
  }
}
```

These functions will execute moving in a given direction, so long as there's space to do so. It will then move the snake in that direction. Now, add more code:

```
function executeMove(dirValue, axisType, axisValue) {
  direction = dirValue;
  currentPosition[axisType] = axisValue;
  drawSnake();
}
```

The executeMove function handles setting the direction of the snake, its current position, and then drawing the body of the snake onto the movement area. Next, add this code:

```
function moveSnake(){
  switch (direction) {
    case 'up':
      moveUp();
      break;

    case 'down':
      moveDown();
      break;

    case 'left':
      moveLeft();
      break;

    case 'right':
      moveRight();
      break;
  }
}
```

moveSnake handles moving the snake, based on the direction given. Next, you want to add the buttons for restarting, pausing, and resuming the game. Insert the following:

```
function restart () {
  document.getElementById('play_menu').style.display='block';
  document.getElementById('pause_menu').style.display='none';
  document.getElementById('restart_menu').style.display='none';
  pause();
  start();
}

function pause(){
  document.getElementById('play_menu').style.display='none';
  document.getElementById('pause_menu').style.display='block';
  clearInterval(interval);
  allowPressKeys = false;
}

function play(){
  document.getElementById('play_menu').style.display='block';
  document.getElementById('pause_menu').style.display='none';
  interval = setInterval(moveSnake,100);
  allowPressKeys = true;
}
```

Now, the player can restart, pause, and play the game. Now add this:

```
function gameOver(){
  pause();
  window.alert('Game Over. Your score was ' + score);
  ctx.clearRect(0,0, canvas.width, canvas.height);
```

```
  document.getElementById('play_menu').style.display='none';
  document.getElementById('restart_menu').style.display='block';

}
```

When the game is finished, the player is shown what their score is, and the movement area resets. Now you'll add the animation function:

```
function drawSnake() {
  if (snakeBody.some(hasEatenItself)) {
    gameOver();
    return false;
  }
  snakeBody.push([currentPosition.x, currentPosition.y]);
  ctx.fillStyle = 'rgb(200,0,0)';
  ctx.fillRect(currentPosition.x, currentPosition.y, gridSize, gridSize);
  if (snakeBody.length > snakeLength) {
    let itemToRemove = snakeBody.shift();
    ctx.clearRect(itemToRemove[0], itemToRemove[1], gridSize, gridSize);
  }
  if (currentPosition.x === suggestedPoint[0] && currentPosition.y ===
    suggestedPoint[1]) {
    makeFoodItem();
    snakeLength += 1;
    updateScore();
  }
}
```

The drawSnake function is the most complex of all of the functions in terms of the number of things it needs to do, which include the following:

- Check whether the snake has eaten itself, and if it has, end the game
- Track where the snake is in terms of coordinates
- Draw the snake's body on the canvas
- Clear areas where the snake was, and draw areas where the snake now is, giving the illusion of the snake moving around in the area.
- Track whether the snake has eaten the food item, and if so, make another food item, make the snake that much bigger, and update the score

Add this to start a new game:

```
function start () {
  ctx.clearRect(0,0, canvas.width, canvas.height);
  currentPosition = {'x':50, 'y':50};
  snakeBody = [];
  snakeLength = 3;
  updateScore();
  makeFoodItem();
  drawSnake();
  direction = 'right';
  play();
}
```

The start function takes care of kicking off the game, setting up the initial state of the game, and then calling play in order to get the game going. Add the following to get the game to load and begin from the start:

```
function initialize () {
  canvas = document.querySelector('canvas');
  ctx = canvas.getContext('2d');
  gridSize = 10;
  start();
}

window.onload = initialize;
```

The initialize function runs when the app loads. It takes care of initializing the HTML5 canvas object for interaction and calls the start function to begin the game.

This is quite a sizeable amount of code, but now you have most of the game implemented. If you were to open the game and run it with NW.js, you should see something like figure 14.1.

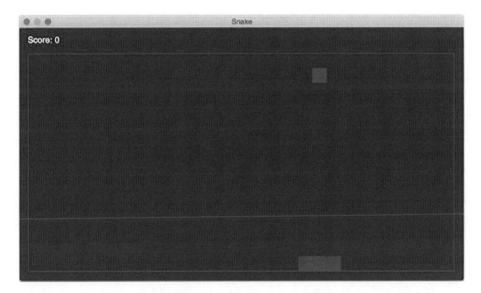

Figure 14.1   The Snake game running, but no keyboard controls implemented yet

The game is functional, but you can't control the snake yet—it's going to go round and round in circles. You need to implement keyboard controls.

14.1.1   Implementing window focus keyboard shortcuts with NW.js

If you need to control the app when the window is in focus, you can add keyboard shortcuts to JavaScript in the app without using NW.js's keyboard shortcuts API. You can use browser-specific JavaScript to handle that.

Add this code to the app.js file above the `start` function:

```
window.document.onkeydown = function(event) {
  if (!allowPressKeys){
    return null;
  }
  let keyCode;
  if(!event)
  {
    keyCode = window.event.keyCode;
  }
  else
  {
    keyCode = event.keyCode;
  }

  switch(keyCode)
  {
    case 37:
      if (direction !== 'right') {
        moveLeft();
      }
      break;

    case 38:
      if (direction !== 'down'){
        moveUp();
      }
      break;

    case 39:
      if (direction !== 'left'){
        moveRight();
      }
      break;

    case 40:
      if (direction !== 'up'){
        moveDown();
      }
      break;

    default:
      break;
  }
};
```

Here, you add an event listener for any keypress. You then look at which key is pressed, and if it's a keycode for a direction key, then you move the snake in that direction. If you were to save this file and reload the app with nw on the Terminal, you could play the game by using the up, down, left, and right keys.

This is okay in the context of playing a video game, but what if you want to trigger a command from the keyboard without the app window necessarily being in focus?

This is where NW.js's keyboard shortcuts API comes into action. You can link global keyboard shortcuts to the game so users can pause the game, even when the window isn't in focus.

14.1.2 *Creating global keyboard shortcuts with NW.js*

NW.js's keyboard shortcuts API is used to create global shortcuts for apps that execute even when the app window isn't in focus; for example, the media keys on your desktop music player app, which you can use to pause music even when the music player isn't in focus.

Let's say, for the sake of putting the API to use, that you want to be able to pause the Snake game, even when the app window isn't in focus. You propose that pressing Ctrl-P will pause the game, or resume it if it was paused.

You'll start by adding a variable for tracking whether the game is currently in play, or is paused:

```
let currentState;
```

Next, add a function to handle toggling between the play and pause states of the game so you can press a key combination that will either pause or resume the game, depending on the current state:

```
function togglePauseState () {
  if (currentState) {
    if (currentState === 'play') {
      pause();
      currentState = 'pause';
    } else {
      play();
      currentState = 'play';
    }
  } else {
    pause();
    currentState = 'play';
  }
}
```

Upon the first attempt to run the code, the currentState variable hasn't been set, so you set it to play (as the game app automatically plays when it's started) and then pause the game. If the variable is then set to pause, you call the play command and set the current state to that, and vice versa.

The functionality of the togglePauseState function means you can bind the Ctrl-P keys to this command, keeping the binding nice and simple. To attach this function to the Ctrl-P keypresses, you insert this little bit of code:

```
const pauseKeyOptions = {
  key:'Ctrl+P',
  active: togglePauseState,
  failed: () => {
```

```
    console.log('An error occurred');
  }
};
```

The `pauseKeyOptions` variable specifies the key combination, what action to run when the key combo is triggered, and a function to execute if it fails for any reason. You then pass this variable to a new instance of NW.js's `Shortcut` class:

```
const pauseShortcut = new nw.Shortcut(pauseKeyOptions);
```

To confirm that this key combo works with the OS, add this line of code:

```
nw.App.registerGlobalHotKey(pauseShortcut);
```

This ensures that the OS will recognize the key combination and trigger the pause/resume action on combo keypress. You could leave it there and say that's all that needs to be done, but one thing to bear in mind is that you need to release this global hotkey combination when the game is closed. For this, add one final snippet of code:

```
process.on('exit', () => {
  nw.App.unregisterGlobalHotKey(pauseShortcut);
});
```

This snippet ensures that when the app is about to be closed, the hotkey combination is released. If you now save the file and reload the app from the Terminal, you should now find that pressing Ctrl-P pauses the game, even when the window is not in focus.

> ### Ctrl-P keys work as Command-P on Macs, why?
> This is a bit odd, but NW.js treats the Ctrl key specified in the keyboard shortcuts API as the Command key on Mac OS; even though you specified the Ctrl-P key combo in the example, it triggers with Command-P on the Mac.
>
> Macs use the Command key rather than the Control key for shortcuts (for example, Command-C for copy on Macs is equivalent to Ctrl-C for copy on Windows).

The use case given is perhaps a bit unusual, but it demonstrates how you can use NW.js to work with your keyboard even when an app window isn't in focus. Apps that would use this include music-playing apps, and even screen-recording software, which do not depend on the mouse to click a button to start and stop recording.

We'll now take a look at how Electron handles implementing keyboard shortcuts.

14.2 Creating global shortcuts for the Snake game with Electron

To compare how Electron implements keyboard shortcuts, you'll re-create the game with Electron. If you want to skip ahead to a working version of the game, you can check out the source code on the book's GitHub repository for the snake-electron app.

The two versions of the app share a lot of similar code, but how they go about implementing support for keyboard shortcuts differs quite a bit. Not only are the API methods different, but the way in which they're accessed also needs to be taken into consideration.

To illustrate this, I'll skip showing the identical files and focus exclusively on the parts of the app that involve implementing the global keyboard shortcuts.

The index.html and app.css files look exactly the same. The bits that have changes in them are the app.js and main.js files. You'll start with the main.js file, which is important because it's the place from which you'll call Electron's `globalShortcut` API. The following listing shows the main.js file.

Listing 14.1   The main.js file in the Snake Electron app

```
'use strict';

const {app, globalShortcut, BrowserWindow} = require('electron');    ⟵ Requires the
                                                                        globalShortcut
let mainWindow = null;                                                  dependency
                                                                        from Electron
app.on('window-all-closed', () => {
  if (process.platform !== 'darwin') app.quit();
});

app.on('ready', () => {
  mainWindow = new BrowserWindow({                          When keyboard
    width: 840,                                        shortcut is triggered,
    height: 470,                                            emits event to
    useContentSize: true                                        app window
  });
  mainWindow.loadURL(`file://${__dirname}/index.html`);
  mainWindow.on('closed', () => { mainWindow = null; });
  const pauseKey = globalShortcut.register('CommandOrControl+P', () => {
    mainWindow.webContents.send('togglePauseState');           ⟵
  });
  if (!pauseKey) alert('You will not be able to pause the game from the
    keyboard');                                    ⟵ If you couldn't register
});                                                   keyboard shortcut,
                                                      alerts user
app.on('will-quit', () => {
  globalShortcut.unregister('CommandOrControl+P');    ⟵ When app quits,
});                                                      unregisters keyboard
                                                         shortcut from computer
```

Registers the keyboard shortcut ⟶

The `globalShortcut` API is available from the main process in Electron, so you require it from the main.js file and then use it to register a keyboard shortcut. Once the module is required, you're then able to add and remove keyboard shortcuts by calling the register and unregister API methods. What's different with Electron's approach to creating keyboard shortcuts is that the string passed for the keyboard shortcut binding says `"CommandOrControl"` rather than `"Ctrl"` in NW.js. This reflects the way in which Mac OS favors the use of Command as the main keyboard shortcut key, and Windows and Linux favor the Ctrl key. Electron is smart enough to detect which OS the app is running on and use the appropriate keyboard shortcut.

Because the keyboard shortcut is registered in the main process, you need a way to pass the message on to the renderer process where the app window is so the game can be paused there. To do this, you need to use the webContents module to send a message to the app window so the message can be received by the renderer process and acted on. To demonstrate how this works, here's the bit of code that handles this in the app.js file.

Listing 14.2   The app.js file for the Snake Electron app

```
const ipcRenderer = require('electron').ipcRenderer;          ◁─┐ Loads ipcRenderer
                                                                 │ module from Electron
function togglePauseState () {            ◁─┐                     │ via ES2015 shorthand
  if (currentState) {                       │
    if (currentState === 'play') {          │ Function to trigger
      pause();                              │ when keyboard
      currentState = 'pause';               │ shortcut is pressed
    } else {
      play();
      currentState = 'play';
    }
  } else {
    pause();
    currentState = 'play';                            ┌─ When message with
  }                                                   │  event name
}                                                     │  "togglePauseState"
                                                      │  is received, triggers
ipcRenderer.on('togglePauseState', togglePauseState);  ◁─┘ that function
```

The ipcRenderer module receives events emitted via the webContents module in the main process. When the Ctrl (or Command) and P keyboard combination is pressed, the `webContents.send` call sends an event with the name `togglePauseState`. This event is then received by the ipcRenderer module in the app window, which is then able to trigger the function of the same name.

Comparing the different approaches of NW.js and Electron in implementing this feature in the game, you can see that Electron involves a bit more code in order to facilitate using the `globalShortcut` API via IPC. This is where NW.js's shared JavaScript context between the back end and front end makes implementing this feature simpler.

If you want to read more about the `globalShortcut` API in Electron, the documentation for it is available at http://electron.atom.io/docs/api/global-shortcut/.

14.3   *Summary*

In this chapter, we've looked at how keyboard shortcuts can be added to a 2D game with both NW.js and Electron and studied how each of them approaches implementing shortcuts. We also looked at how global hotkeys can be added that can be accessed at any time on the computer, even when the desktop app isn't in focus. Some of the key takeaways from the chapter include the following:

- You can use the `document.onkeydown` event to listen for keystrokes in an app, as you would in a web page.
- When it comes to implementing global hotkeys in NW.js, the Ctrl key refers to the Command key on Mac OS.
- Make sure to unregister global hot keys if you use the keyboard shortcuts API in your app; otherwise, other apps' keyboard shortcuts will be overridden.

In chapter 15, we'll look at another way to interact more closely with the OS—through emitting desktop notifications.

15
Making desktop notifications

This chapter covers

- Seeing how Electron supports desktop notifications through a third-party npm module
- Using the HTML5 notification API to make desktop notifications in NW.js
- Working with Twitter to create a live tweet notification app

When working day-to-day with computers, users tend to have a number of apps open and running while focusing on one app at a time. Applications such as chat apps, file downloaders, and music players may have activity, but if the user doesn't have them in direct view or focus, they might miss that activity.

One feature provided by OSs is allowing notifications to be displayed as small dialogs that overlay all open and focused windows, usually in the top-right corner of the desktop window, helping users stay informed of important activity. Both NW.js and Electron provide notification APIs to ensure that your apps can communicate events using the OS's notifications system.

15.1 About the app you'll make

In the world of social media, events need to be monitored and tracked in real time. As busy users of our computers, we can't afford to be glued to our screens waiting for an event to happen. Say, for example, your app monitors mentions of a topical item, and you want your app to display the contents of any tweet that mentions that topic. You'd like to alert the user that someone mentioned *X*, whether it's a laundry detergent brand (after seeing an amusing TV ad that made them laugh), or a tweet about a rather slow football game, and the user wants to know when a goal is scored.

For this use case, I've created an app called Watchy. You type in a term that you want to monitor mentions of on Twitter, and the app connects to Twitter's Streaming API, displaying as desktop notifications any tweets mentioning the term.

If you'd like the Electron version of the app, you can download the source code for it from the watchy-electron app in the book's GitHub repository at http://mng.bz/URx8.

We'll first look at how you can make this app in Electron, and then look at NW.js's implementation.

15.2 Creating the Watchy app in Electron

Watchy is a small app that combines the use of Twitter and a third-party library for desktop notifications. You'll start by creating the app folder. Create a folder named watchy-electron, and then create the package.json file shown next.

Listing 15.1 The package.json file for the Watchy Electron app

```json
{
  "name": "watchy-electron",
  "version": "1.0.0",
  "description": "A Twitter client for monitoring topics, built with Electron
     for the book 'Cross Platform Desktop Applications'",
  "main": "main.js",
  "scripts": {
    "start": "node_modules/.bin/electron .",
    "test": "echo \"Error: no test specified\" && exit 1"
  },
  "keywords": [
    "electron",
    "twitter"
  ],
  "author": "Paul Jensen <paulbjensen@gmail.com>",
  "license": "MIT",
  "dependencies": {
    "electron-notifications": "0.0.3",
    "electron ": "^1.3.7",
    "twitter": "^1.3.0"
  }
}
```

The package.json file has a few more app dependencies than other apps—you have a dependency on the Twitter API client, as well as on the electron-notifications module, documented at https://github.com/blainesch/electron-notifications.

You also download the Electron dependency, which you use in the `scripts` field to boot the app via `npm start`. This means you can simply start the app from the command line with a standard approach that's also used for the NW.js apps, as well as Node.js apps in general.

You'll take a look at the main.js file next, because that's what Electron boots first in the app. The main.js file contains the code for the configuration of the Twitter client and the code that uses Twitter's Streaming API to search for a query and provide tweets mentioning that query. These tweets are then hooked up with the desktop notifications.

Create a main.js file inside the watchy-electron folder and put the code shown in the next listing inside it.

Listing 15.2 The main.js file for the Watchy Electron app

```
'use strict';

const {app, ipcMain, BrowserWindow} = require('electron');        Loads electron-
const notifier = require('electron-notifications');               notifications module
const config = require('./config');                              for app
const Twitter = require('twitter');            Creates Twitter client
const client = new Twitter(config);           that uses your Twitter
                                              API credentials
let mainWindow = null;

app.on('window-all-closed', () => {
  if (process.platform !== 'darwin') app.quit();
});                                                          Listens for events to
                                                            monitor a term, such
ipcMain.on('monitorTerm', (event, term) => {                as "breakfast"
  client.stream('statuses/filter', {track: term}, (stream) => {
    stream.on('data', (tweet) => {                  Passes the term
      let notification = notifier.notify('New tweet', {   to Twitter's
        icon: tweet.user.profile_image_url,        streaming API
        message: tweet.text                        to get tweets
      });                                           mentioning
    });                                             that term
    stream.on('error', (error) => {
      console.log(error.message);             When you receive
    });                                       tweet with term,
  });                                         creates notification
});                                           with tweet's contents

app.on('ready', () => {
  mainWindow = new BrowserWindow({
    width: 370,
    height: 90,
    useContentSize: true
  });
  mainWindow.loadURL(`file://${__dirname}/index.html`);
  mainWindow.on('closed', () => { mainWindow = null; });
});
```

The main.js file is responsible for hooking up the Twitter client to the notifications module so that you can monitor for tweets that contain a term and display them as notifications. To do this, you need to create an instance of the Twitter client with your API credentials, which are stored in the config.js file. The config.js file is created from a copy of the config.example.js file, as shown in the following code:

```
module.exports = {
  consumer_key: null,
  consumer_secret: null,
  access_token_key: null,
  access_token_secret: null
};
```

The config.example.js file is an object with keys that have `null` values. The idea is to make a copy of the file, save it as config.js, and then populate the API credentials for your app from Twitter.

To get API credentials from Twitter, you'll need to create a Twitter app, which you can do at https://apps.twitter.com. Then, copy the following API credentials into the config.js file:

- Application consumer key
- Application consumer secret
- Access token key
- Access token secret

Now, you can implement the front-end part of the app. The app loads an index.html file for the front end, and the next listing shows what the code looks like.

> **Listing 15.3   The index.html file for the Watchy Electron app**

```
<html>
  <head>
    <title>Watchy</title>
    <link rel="stylesheet" href="app.css"/>
    <script src="app.js"></script>
  </head>
  <body>
    <form onsubmit="search();">
      <input type="text" placeholder="Monitor tweets about..." />
      <button type="submit">Monitor</button>
    </form>
  </body>
</html>
```

The index.html's UI is a simple use of the HTML `form` element, an `input` field for where the user will type in the term of interest, and a `button` element they can click to submit the term. An app.css stylesheet is loaded to apply styling to the UI, and an app.js file handles passing the term to the back end. Let's take a look at the app.css file first.

Listing 15.4   The app.css file for the Watchy Electron app

```
body {
  margin: 0px;
  padding: 0px;
  font-family: 'Helvetica Neue', 'Arial';
  background: #55acee;
}

input, button {
  padding: 1em;
  font-size: 12pt;
  border-radius: 10px;
  border: none;
  outline: none;
}

button {
  background: linear-gradient(0deg, #bbb, #fff);
  cursor: pointer;
}

form {
  margin: 1em;
}
```

The styling produces a small app, as shown in figure 15.1.

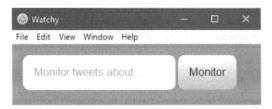

**Figure 15.1   Watchy running
on Electron and Windows 10**

With the UI styled, the main question now is how you get the term entered in the form sent to the back end, where the Twitter client can receive it and stream related tweets as desktop notifications.

In the index.html file, you see that submitting the form triggers a JavaScript function named `search`, which is located in the app.js file, the code for which is shown next.

Listing 15.5   The app.js file for the Watchy Electron app

```
'use strict';

const {ipcRenderer} = require('electron');    ⟵  Loads Electron's ipcRenderer
                                                  module so you can send data
function search () {                               to back end
  const formInput = window.document.querySelector('form input');
```

```
const term = formInput.value;
ipcRenderer.send('monitorTerm', term);
return false;
}
```

Gets ahold of term that was typed into form

Sends that term to back end via ipcRenderer module

The search function used by the form gets ahold of the term that was typed into the form and sends it to the back end, where the Twitter client is, via Electron's ipcRenderer module.

Now, if you try to run the app using npm start from the command line, the app should boot up. If you then type in a term that you want to search for and press Enter, you should see notifications appearing in the top-right corner, as shown in figure 15.2.

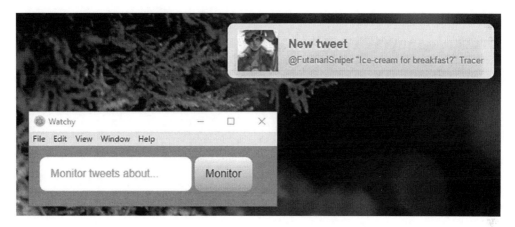

Figure 15.2   Watchy displaying a tweet that mentioned "breakfast"

What you can expect to see is a stream of tweets being displayed as notifications in the top-right corner of the desktop, depending on what term you typed into the app (you may find a nonstop selection of tweets appearing if your term is popular).

This demonstrates how to build a term-monitoring tool with Twitter and desktop notifications support with Electron. In the next section, we'll take a look at how to implement the same app with NW.js.

15.3   Creating the Watchy app in NW.js

NW.js's approach to implementing desktop notifications differs from Electron's, and the implementation has been in flux since the upgrade from 0.12 to 0.14, as well as from Google Chrome adding support for desktop notifications.

Between versions 0.12 and 0.14, NW.js switched from using native notifications to using Google Chrome's desktop notifications API. This means you can use the

Notifications API as documented at https://developer.mozilla.org/en-US/docs/Web/API/Notification. To use it in NW.js, though, there's a tiny little difference I'll show you—and it's important because quite a few people have had problems using notifications in NW.js. But first I'll walk you through creating the app. If you want to cut to the chase, the source code for the app can be found in the watchy-nwjs app in the book's GitHub repository at http://mng.bz/UD6r.

The best place to start is with the package.json file, shown next.

Listing 15.6   The package.json file for the Watchy NW.js app

```json
{
  "name": "watchy-nwjs",
  "version": "1.0.0",
  "description": "A Twitter client for monitoring topics, built with NW.js
    for the book 'Cross Platform Desktop Applications'",
  "main": "index.html",
  "scripts": {
    "start": "node_modules/.bin/nw .",
    "test": "echo \"Error: no test specified\" && exit 1"
  },
  "keywords": [
    "twitter",
    "nwjs"
  ],
  "window": {
    "toolbar": true,
    "width": 370,
    "height": 80
  },
  "author": "Paul Jensen <paulbjensen@gmail.com>",
  "license": "MIT",
  "dependencies": {
    "nw": "^0.15.3",
    "twitter": "^1.3.0"
  }
}
```

The package.json file has a couple of npm dependencies, as well as a convenience method for booting up the app via npm start on the command line. Next, install the dependencies via npm install, and then add the index.html file, which is identical to the file shown in listing 15.3 for the Electron version of the app. The index.html file loads the app.css file (which, again, is the same as the code shown in code listing 15.4 for the Electron app), and then add the app.js file, the code for which is shown here.

Listing 15.7   The app.js file for the Watchy NW.js app

```
'use strict';

const Twitter = require('twitter');
const config  = require('./config');
let term;
const client = new Twitter(config);
let notify = Notification;

function notifyOfTweet (tweet) {
  new notify(`New tweet about ${term}`,
    {
      body: tweet.text,
      icon: tweet.user.profile_image_url
    }
  );
}

function search () {
  const formInput = window.document.querySelector('form input');
  term = formInput.value;
  client.stream('statuses/filter', {track: term}, (stream) => {
    stream.on('data', notifyOfTweet);
    stream.on('error', (error) => {
      alert(error.message);
    });
  });
  return false;
}
```

Loads Twitter client with config for API credentials

Makes JS variable referring to Notification global variable

Refers to that variable when creating new notification

Passes tweet's text and user's profile image as body and icon for notification

After subscribing to streaming API, passes any tweets to notify Tweet function

You've almost finished writing all the code for the app. The last thing to do is create a copy of the config.example.js file, save it with the file name config.js, and add your Twitter API credentials to it:

```
module.exports = {
  consumer_key: null,
  consumer_secret: null,
  access_token_key: null,
  access_token_secret: null
};
```

Once you've copied your Twitter app's API credentials into that file, you can run the app with npm start. When the app starts, type in a term, and you should see notifications start to appear on the right-hand side of the screen, as in figure 15.3.

Because NW.js has a shared context between the front-end and back-end parts of the app, there isn't any need to pass data via inter-process communication. The Twitter client can be loaded in the same place the search function is defined, which gets the term from the UI. In some ways, it makes the app simpler because you don't need to worry about passing data between separate processes, but at the same time, in large

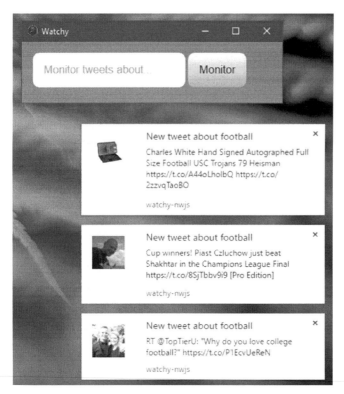

Figure 15.3   Watchy NW.js on Windows 10. Note how the desktop notifications are displayed on the right-hand side and look exactly the same as Google Chrome's desktop notifications.

desktop apps, the code can become disorganized quickly if it isn't refactored and cleaned up over time.

15.4   Summary

In this chapter, you implemented a live tweet-monitoring app in both Electron and NW.js. You looked at how each framework has different approaches to implementing desktop notifications and creating them. Some of the key takeaway points from the chapter are as follows:

- To use desktop notifications in Electron, you want to make use of the electron-notifications module via npm.
- With NW.js 0.14, there was a switch to using Google Chrome's notifications API. Previous versions of NW.js had been using another implementation.
- Be careful when using desktop notifications—they're a useful feature, but you don't want to spam your user's screens with notifications (as I found out trying to monitor tweets about NFL with the Watchy app).

In chapter 16, we'll move away from developing apps and look at how you can test them so you can add features and change code with confidence and build apps the right way.

Part 4

Getting ready to release

Once a desktop application is feature complete, there remain the last few steps of making sure the code is fully tested, issues are identified and fixed, and the app is built for various operating systems. This part shows how to write tests for your desktop apps, how to debug them and spot performance issues, and how to generate binary executables for your applications.

In chapter 16, we'll look at ways you can go about testing desktop apps, using tools like Mocha, Cucumber, and Devtron. We'll then continue to prepare your app for release by using debugging tools to help spot performance bottlenecks and root them out. In the final chapter of the book, I'll show the various ways in which you can prepare your app for installing on Windows, Mac, and Linux.

Testing desktop apps

When I started programming back in 2006, I had no idea how to test software, or why I should. Then, one day I was getting ready to deliver a product demo to a client, making some code changes 20 minutes before the demo. When I demoed the app to the client, it crashed. Perhaps if I had written some tests for the app, I would have foreseen that the app would crash, and I wouldn't have suffered that embarrassment. This is one of many reasons you don't want to write code without tests (or, for that matter, make last-minute changes before a product demo).

Thankfully, my colleague Matt Ford (who runs the digital consultancy Bit Zesty) sat down with me and introduced me to unit testing with RSpec in Ruby. From there, I was able to improve the quality of my work by writing tests for my code in a test-driven-development fashion.

I wasn't alone in being oblivious to the world of testing apps, and in my career I found places where testing was either unknown or sadly disregarded by people who "don't have time for tests" (as one product manager once told me). I can tell you from experience that apps written without tests don't stand the test of time. Besides, would you be comfortable flying on an airplane if the software powering it wasn't tested? What about apps that store data that's important to you—what if they keep crashing, or worse, lose your data? Testing is a safety net that you want when creating an app and a sane way to help others work on the app without causing unintentional breakages.

We'll look at different ways in which you can approach testing desktop apps. We'll start with a basic task—unit testing parts of your code with Mocha, a testing tool for Node.js. Then, we'll work up to testing functional components and test how the app works from a user's perspective with Cucumber. We'll also look at Spectron, a dedicated tool for testing Electron apps. You'll get an idea of what kind of software landscape to expect when you're testing apps.

The goal is that you gain a good understanding of how you can go about testing desktop apps. There's no point in building apps if they're going to be flaky and fall over on the user—users will give up on the app and try an alternative that works.

Ready to dive in? Great.

16.1   Different approaches to testing apps

There are different ways to approach testing apps—for example, test-driven development and behavior-driven development. What are they, and should you use them? The next couple of sections will answer those questions. You'll gain enough understanding of software testing to find an approach that works for you. If you already know about these techniques, feel free to skip ahead to section 16.2.

16.1.1   Test-driven-development (TDD)

Test-driven development involves developing a feature by first writing the code to test it. The tests will fail (because no code for the feature has been written yet). Then the developer writes code for the feature, which causes the tests to pass. Once the tests are passing, the developer can refine the code (if it needs improving) and then work on implementing the next feature. This process, called *red-green refactoring*, is illustrated in figure 16.1.

The idea behind the red-green cycle is to enhance developer productivity by providing a structured approach to developing software. It requires thinking and discipline to write tests before any product code is written. Once you have tests written for the app, then you're in a position to write the app code. Which part of the app code you choose to write first depends on what the tests require. This helps you make decisions about what to implement first, and reducing the number of decisions you have to make helps you stay focused and productive.

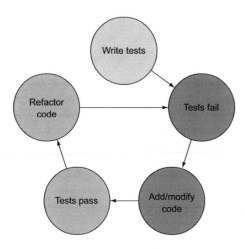

Figure 16.1 The red-green refactor cycle. First, you write the tests; then, they fail; then, you write/modify the app code; then, the tests pass and the feature is implemented; and finally, you can refactor, safe in the knowledge that the tests will fail if you break the feature.

As the code is written, the tests begin to pass, and as long as the tests sufficiently cover what things need to be implemented, the developer can have the confidence to refine their existing code and improve it via refactoring. If the tests still pass, then the solution is good—but if the tests fail, the developer can determine why they're failing and make the necessary adjustments. It's a safety net to help the developer.

TDD isn't to everyone's taste, admittedly. In 2014, David Heinemeier Hansson (the creator of Ruby on Rails) wrote a blog post called "TDD is dead. Long live testing." He described his experiences using TDD over the years and how he'd come to the conclusion that it was impacting his ability to design good software. It's worth a read at http://mng.bz/sXUJ. The discussions that followed online with Kent Beck and Martin Fowler are covered at http://mng.bz/Iy3O.

The interesting thing about the debate around TDD is that it shows that well-respected, accomplished members of the software community can hold different opinions about software—that there isn't necessarily a single right answer about these things.

So should you use TDD for building your apps? My suggestion is to give it a try and see if it works for you. If it doesn't, don't worry—there are other options, such as the one we'll look at next. The important thing is to find what works for you and for those around you.

16.1.2 *Behavior-driven development (BDD)*

Behavior-driven development, a variation on the concept of TDD, was influenced by the ideas behind *acceptance testing* (whereby you check with end users that the software does what they expect). Whereas TDD is focused on the workflow of the developer, BDD takes an interest in not just the developer's workflow, but also that of other stakeholders (such as the end user). Its goal is to aid collaboration between these stakeholders through the use of a common language to describe the requirements of the software. Figure 16.2 is a process chart showing how a product's feature requirements are gathered and implemented.

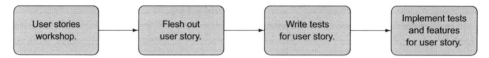

Figure 16.2   Process of gathering feature requirements and implementing them with BDD. Used in conjunction with an agile process, BDD complements the process shown by helping flesh out user stories, writing tests for them in a common language, and implementing those tests with tools like Cucumber.

From figure 16.2, we'll look at how BDD helps flesh out user stories. In a fashion similar to acceptance testing, BDD encourages the collection of user stories to help gather requirements for the app. These user stories, written in plain English, help describe how the feature in question should work. Take, for example, this feature:

```
Feature: Search
    In order to locate a file quickly
    As a user
    I want to filter files by their name

    Given I have opened the application
    And I am browsing the contents of my "documents" folder
    When I type "expenses" into the search bar
    Then I should see a file called "expenses"
    And I should not see "invoices"
```

This example of a user story is based on the Lorikeet app you made earlier in the book. It describes in simple terms how the app feature works from the perspective of the user and helps provide some acceptance criteria for the feature. With this user story, you're able to write code that can test the app—the documentation of how the feature works drives how the app is tested. This confirms that the product works according to the specification of the person who is actually going to use the product, something that's often known to be problematic in software development.

BDD allows developers to approach implementing the tests for their apps in a way that ensures that the feature does what the client expected. That said, testing an app isn't just a case of "write tests and make sure they pass." There are different levels at which software can be tested. In the next section, we'll go into more depth about how to approach these levels of testing.

16.1.3 *Different levels of testing*

For software developers writing tests for an app, there are three levels of testing that can occur:

- Unit testing
- Functional testing
- Integration testing

Unit testing is at the level of the individual functions in the code that are public API methods. *Functional* testing is at the level where the combination of those functions is checked (mainly as components). *Integration* testing is at the level where the components combine to support a user feature. Figure 16.3 shows an illustration of the different levels.

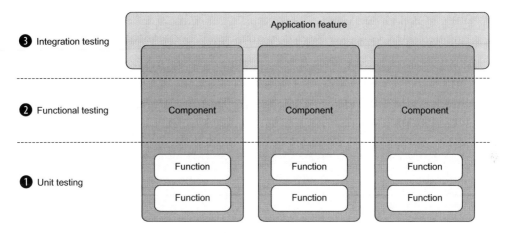

Figure 16.3 How the different levels of software testing stack up. Unit testing covers software at the smallest element of functionality. Functional testing builds on this by testing the interaction between those elements, at the level of components. The pattern repeats at the integration testing level, where interaction between app components is tested.

You can see from figure 16.3 that at the bottom of the stack is unit testing, which checks that each function works as expected. At the next level, functional testing checks that the functions within a component work well together. To ensure that the components themselves work together as expected, integration testing at the level of app features is performed.

In the next section, we'll explore these different levels of testing in greater detail, starting with unit testing.

16.2 Unit testing

Unit testing is the process of testing whether individual functions work. It's a bit like checking that each piece that makes up a car is in good working order. When it comes to unit-testing desktop apps— Node.js testing in general—the most widely used test framework is Mocha. In the next section, you'll find out what Mocha is and how you can use it for unit-testing your apps.

16.2.1 Writing tests with Mocha

Mocha is a testing framework for Node.js. It can run on both the server and the client (it's ideal for testing Node.js desktop apps) and offers a lot of features.

Say you wanted to unit test one of the functions provided in the Lorikeet file explorer app you built earlier. In the GitHub repository for the book, there's a copy of both the NW.js and Electron versions of the Lorikeet file explorer app: lorikeet-test-nwjs and lorikeet-test-electron.

These apps have the test code already, so you can run them and see what to expect. Follow the instructions in the README.md files to run the tests. If you want to write the tests yourself, you can revert to a point in the source code before the tests were added by checking out this `git` commit via the following command:

```
cd cross-platform-desktop-applications/chapter-16
git checkout -b before-tests-added
```

Feel free to use either app to run through the testing example with (the codebases are practically identical), and then we'll walk through implementing some unit tests with Mocha.

Navigate to the folder path of the Lorikeet app in your command-line Terminal program and run the following command to install `mocha` as a development dependency in the Lorikeet folder:

```
npm install mocha --save-dev
```

Now create a folder, called test, for storing your test code. There are two reasons for calling it *test*: it's pretty obvious what files are contained in that folder, and `mocha` looks for tests in the test folder by default when it's executed.

Next, you'll look at a particular file in the Lorikeet app and test one of its functions to ensure that it works as expected: the search.js file that handles filtering the files. You want to write a test that ensures that the following are true:

- A search returns results that match the term provided.
- That same search doesn't return results that don't match the term provided.

Create a file inside the test folder called search.test.js, and then insert the following snippet of code.

Listing 16.1   Writing a test using Mocha's API

```
'use strict';

const lunr = require('lunr');
const search = require('../search');

describe('search', () => {              describe function comes from Mocha and defines the context of the test
  describe('#find', () => {
    it('should return results when a file matches a term');    it function comes from Mocha as well and defines a test case
  });
});
```

I'll go through the DSL of Mocha now. At the top of the file, you have the usual declaration of libraries to load, and then the function `describe`, whose job is to receive a string with the name of the thing you're testing, and then a function that will execute either another nested `describe` or a set of tests to run using the keyword `it`. The `it` function is responsible for executing a test and is first passed the description of what it's testing. Because you haven't yet written the test implementation code, you leave it be, as it is now—a pending test.

If you now run the `node_modules/.bin/mocha` command on the Terminal, you should see the output shown in figure 16.4.

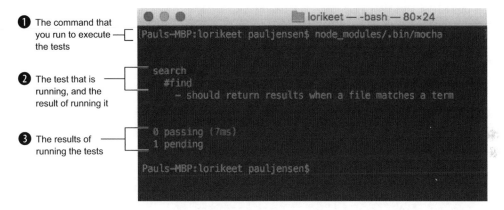

Figure 16.4   The Mocha tests running. Notice how there is a test marked in light blue text—this color indicates that the test is pending. (If you're looking at the printed book in grayscale, the light blue text says "should return results when a file matches a term" and "1 pending.")

You can see in figure 16.4 that there are no passing tests yet, and one pending test. The next thing to do is to start implementing that pending test.

16.2.2 *From pending test to passing test*

To test that finding a file based on a search term works, you need to follow the steps in figure 16.5.

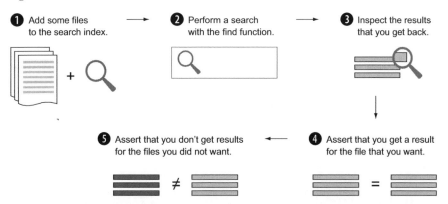

Figure 16.5   Process flow of the unit test. Test the search feature by getting it to index some example files, perform a search against that, check that the search results returned are to be expected, and ensure that you don't get back anything you shouldn't get back.

To implement the test code, start by requiring Node.js's `assert` library for performing assertions in the tests:

```
const assert = require('assert');
```

This library is used for doing the checks on the acceptance criteria being met for the test. If one of the criteria items is met, the library function returns true, and if not, it throws an error.

Next, look at providing some global scope for Lunr.js to bind to:

```
global.window = {};
global.window.lunr = lunr;
```

Because Lunr.js is a client-side library, it needs to attach to the `window` object, so you *stub out* (create a stand-in version of) the `window` object in Mocha to make sure that the library can be accessed and inspected. After that, add a function to the pending test to hold the test code, as shown next.

Listing 16.2   Setting up a Mocha test to be executed rather than be pending

```
it('should return results when a file matches a term', (done) => {

});                                       ⊲─┐ Where you'll insert
                                            │ your test code
```

Here, you extend the initial pending test to include a callback function named `done`. The `done` callback function is called once all the asynchronous code inside the test has finished. Inside the function, you add a few code comments to track the flow of the test code, fleshed out in the following listing.

Listing 16.3   Fleshing out the Mocha test with test code

```
  it('should return results when a file matches a term', (done) => {

    const seedFileReferences = [          ⊲──┐ Example data (seed file
      {                                       references), for search
        file: 'john.png',                     feature to index
        type: 'image/png',
        path: '/Users/pauljensen/Pictures/john.png'
      },
      {
        file: 'bob.png',
        type: 'image/png',
        path: '/Users/pauljensen/Pictures/bob.png'
      },
      {
        file: 'frank.png',
        type: 'image/png',
        path: '/Users/pauljensen/Pictures/frank.png'
      }
    ];
```

Performs a search for term 'frank' and checks results

```
    search.resetIndex();
    seedFileReferences.forEach(search.addToIndex);

    search.find('frank', (results) => {
      assert(results.length === 1);
      assert.equal(seedFileReferences[2].path, results[0].ref);
      done();
    });
  });
```

Resets search index to make sure it's clean before adding seed file references to search index

The final file for the search.test.js file should now look like the next listing.

Listing 16.4 The search.test.js file for the Lorikeet app

```javascript
'use strict';

const assert = require('assert');
const lunr = require('lunr');
const search = require('../search');

global.window = {};
global.window.lunr = lunr;

describe('search', () => {
  describe('#find', () => {

    it('should return results when a file matches a term', (done) => {

      const seedFileReferences = [
        {
          file: 'john.png',
          type: 'image/png',
          path: '/Users/pauljensen/Pictures/john.png'
        },
        {
          file: 'bob.png',
          type: 'image/png',
          path: '/Users/pauljensen/Pictures/bob.png'
        },
        {
          file: 'frank.png',
          type: 'image/png',
          path: '/Users/pauljensen/Pictures/frank.png'
        }
      ];

      search.resetIndex();
      seedFileReferences.forEach(search.addToIndex);

      search.find('frank', (results) => {
        assert(results.length === 1);
        assert.equal(seedFileReferences[2].path, results[0].ref);
        done();
      });

    });

  });
});
```

Here, you create some seed file references (which represent the kind of data that you want to pass to the module). You then pass these file references into the search module's `addToIndex` function, to populate the search index with them. Next, you call the `find` function (the bit that you want to test) with the term `'frank'` and check that you get back exactly one result, and that the result reference matches exactly with the file that has the name frank.png, by comparing the file paths. If that passes, you call the test's `done` function to let it know that you're finished.

If you now try to run this test, you can expect to see the result shown in figure 16.6.

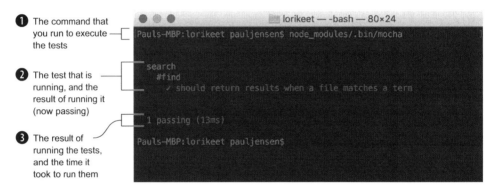

❶ The command that you run to execute the tests

❷ The test that is running, and the result of running it (now passing)

❸ The result of running the tests, and the time it took to run them

Figure 16.6   The unit test is now passing. The previously blue section is now green and has a tick against it. This means it's passing, and you can move on to testing other functions or refactoring the function to make its implementation better.

This is a simple example of implementing a unit test for the desktop app. What I hope you've been able to take away from this practical example is how you can go about unit testing a piece of functionality at the level of just a single JavaScript function using Mocha, because this will help you test your code at the simplest level. When it comes to writing tests, I suggest first making notes about what you want to test as code comments inside the test. Then, flesh them out once you know how to go about implementing that unit test.

Are there alternatives to Mocha?

Mocha is one of the more common testing libraries used in Node.js, but it's not the only one out there. A couple of other options are worth investigating.

Jasmine, a long-standing JavaScript testing framework from Pivotal Labs that works in JavaScript environments, has a DSL almost identical to Mocha's. You can read more about Jasmine at https://github.com/jasmine/jasmine.

Another option is Ava from Sindre Sorhus. Ava is a test runner for Node.js that executes tests faster by making them run in parallel as separate processes. The idea is that the state for each test is specific to that test only—meaning the test can be run in a separate process alongside other tests, and so the tests run faster. See https://github.com/avajs/ava for more.

Next, we'll go up the testing stack and look at functional testing.

16.3 *Functional testing*

Functional testing is similar in style to unit testing, but the key difference is that you test how functions work together in a component. You could argue that the example you did for unit testing is technically a functional test, because, although you tested just one function, that function depends on a number of other functions (the reset-Index function, the addToIndex function, and behind all that, the Lunr.js library) working properly. That said, functional testing is about checking that a group of functions work together as expected, whereas a unit test cares only about how a single function works. Functional testing is like checking that the disc brakes on a car are installed correctly and work when the brake pedal is applied.

You need to track where changes to functions in one module impact functions in other modules. To illustrate, say you have a desktop publishing tool. New features arrive, other members of the team implement those features, and there's a chance that existing code needs to change to accommodate those features. For example, the introduction of an extensions feature into the app allows third-party developers to create extensions that put buttons in the toolbar. Then, someone else comes along and refactors the toolbar implementation, changing the access API. This breaks the third-party extensions because the API for adding buttons to the toolbar has changed. These are the kinds of breaking changes that functional testing is designed to reveal.

16.3.1 *Functional testing in practice*

The challenge of functional testing is being able to track which components interact with each other across modules/contexts and knowing how to go about testing them. In the example for the unit test for the search function, you stubbed out the window object, which would be available by default in the browser. In functional testing, you'll use as many the real-world components as possible. In the Lorikeet file explorer app, most of the modules have been architected so as to be unaware of each other. The app.js file is the point at which the interactions between modules occur, so this is the part you're interested in testing.

You'll continue on the theme of search and test that the search field in the toolbar filters the files that are displayed in the main area. This tests the following elements of the app:

- The userInterface.js file's bindSearchField, resetFilter, and filterResults functions
- The search.js file's find function

You'll need to test this in an environment where the app is running (rather than attempt to stub out environment parts like the DOM). You need a way to test this in the app and a way to automatically fill in the search field and inspect the results visible in the main area.

16.3.2 Testing with ChromeDriver and NW.js

Testing NW.js apps via ChromeDriver is a complicated and developer-unfriendly experience. It requires a lot of tinkering. In older versions of NW.js (0.12), there was a functioning example of testing NW.js apps with ChromeDriver, but since then, updates to various libraries have led to a state where existing test suites have broken, and fixing them is prohibitively time-consuming. You don't want to fight with supporting tools and libraries when you're trying to develop and test apps. In light of this, I won't talk about how to do functional testing with NW.js, and instead will opt to solely cover Electron.

Hopefully, in the future, testing NW.js apps will become easier.

16.4 Testing Electron apps with Spectron

Some developers find that trying to get ChromeDriver and WebDriver set up to play ball is a painful process, especially in terms of finding documentation and a working example. In the Electron community, dedicated tooling has evolved that combines ChromeDriver and WebDriver in a Node.js module, providing a relatively easy way to test desktop apps. This tool is Spectron, and its documentation can be found at http://electron.atom.io/spectron/.

Spectron is available as an npm module and can be installed with the following command in the lorikeet-electron app:

```
npm install spectron --save-dev
```

Now, you can create a file for testing one of the Lorikeet app's functions: double-clicking folders to see their contents. You'll put this file in the test folder and name it folderExplorer.test.js.

To use Spectron, you need to require it in the test code and do some setup to get the app booting up. In the folderExplorer.test.js file, add the code shown next.

Listing 16.5 Getting the folderExplorer.test.js file started

```
'use strict';

const Application = require('spectron').Application;     ◁─── Loads Spectron as
const assert = require('assert');                             module dependency
const osenv = require('osenv');                               in test file
const path = require('path');

let app;                                                              Creates reference
let electronPath = path.join(__dirname, '../node_modules/.bin/electron');  ◁─── to path where
let entryPointPath = path.join(__dirname, '../main.js');   ◁───         Electron binary is
if (process.platform === 'win32') electronPath += '.cmd';  ◁───
```

If on Windows, appends .cmd file extension for Electron binary path

Creates reference to entry point (main.js) for app

In the preceding listing you load dependencies for the file, which includes Node.js's assert module as well as the path module. The Spectron library is loaded as a module, and you use the Application module to help with booting up the app with Chrome-Driver and WebdriverIO behind the scenes. The following listing shows the code that handles booting up the Electron app.

Listing 16.6 Booting the Electron app with Spectron

```
describe('exploring folders', () => {

  beforeEach(() => {
    return app = new Application({        ◁── Initializes instance
      path: electronPath,                      of Spectron's
      args: [entryPointPath]                   Application class
    });                           ◁──────── Path to Electron
  });                                           binary is passed
});                   ◁── Absolute file path to the
                          app's entry point is passed
                          to Application class
```

This is essentially a wrapper around loading the app via ChromeDriver, with the Electron binary path and app entry point passed to it. This is the bare minimum required to set up the functional test loading the app, but more options are available for configuring (see https://github.com/electron/spectron#application-api).

Now, you need the app to run the code that checks if you can double-click a folder and navigate to that folder path. The app instance returned from Spectron's Application class is a wrapper around WebDriver's client API (see http://webdriver.io/api.html for more). It's worth a brief glance at the documentation to get a feel for what the code in the test will do. The API methods let you carry out a number of user actions.

You want to boot up the app, double-click a folder named Documents, and check that you've navigated to that Documents folder. If all those conditions are satisfied, the test passes. You'll write the test using Mocha's syntax style and combine it with Spectron's approach, which involves using Promises. The next listing shows the code for the test.

Listing 16.7 Testing that folders can be navigated with a double click

```
it('should allow the user to navigate folders by double-clicking on them',
    function (done) {

  function finish (error) {        ◁── Creates convenience
    app.stop();                        function to stop error and
    return done(error);                execute Mocha's callback
  }

  let documentsFilePath = path.join(osenv.home(),'/Documents');

  this.timeout(10000);
  app.start().then(() => {
    return app.browserWindow.isVisible();
```

Documents path used to find image folder to double-click and verify the test ◁──

Triggers starting app ◁──

Sets 10-second timeout (for slower machine boots) ──▷

Checks that app loads app window and you can see it ◁──

```
}).then((isVisible) => {
  assert.equal(isVisible, true);
}).then(() => {
  return app.client.doubleClick(`//img[@data-
  filepath="${documentsFilePath}"]`);
}).then(() => {
  return app.client.getText('#current-folder');
}).then((currentFolder) => {
  assert.equal(documentsFilePath, currentFolder);
})
.then(finish)
.catch(finish);
});
```

Finds img element with Documents folder path and double-clicks it

Gets text for current folder element in toolbar

Checks text is same as double-clicked folder path

If condition satisfied, test passes, and finish function called

If not, throws error, intercepted by finish function

If you now use `npm test` to run the test, you'll find that the app opens, double-clicks on a folder, checks that the folder is being viewed in the app, and then closes down again after the test has finished. This shows you how relatively easy it is in Electron to implement a functional test that actually opens the app and uses it the same way a real user would, allowing you to create tests that check real-world conditions.

Now, let's look at the top level—integration testing.

16.5   Integration testing

Also called end-to-end testing (E2E), integration testing is a level of testing where the entire user journey is turned into a set of tests that examine how the entire solution runs, with nothing stubbed and nothing isolated. Everything runs and everything is tested. It's the most comprehensive form of testing that can be done on an app. In some cases, integration testing is the *only* form of testing done on an app (functional and unit tests are ignored because more of the app's code can be covered by an integration test).

What's an example of an integration test? Well, for example, a Lorikeet user might want to find an image file and open it using their preferred image-editing app. They'll need to open the app, possibly type in the name of the image, and then double-click it. This tests a number of features across the app and, like functional testing, needs to run as close to the real scenario as possible.

As mentioned and demonstrated earlier, it's possible to use a combination of Mocha, Selenium, and WebDriver to help automate this testing, but one problem with this approach is that developers are the only ones who'll understand this method. A middle ground is needed to help product owners, users, and developers come to a common understanding of what the app does and how it can be acceptance tested. Enter Cucumber.

16.5.1   Introducing Cucumber

Cucumber is referred to as "the world's most misunderstood testing tool" by its creator, Aslak Hellesøy. Cucumber is a tool for helping developers describe how a piece of software should work, using plain English. The goal is to provide a common understanding among developers, product owners, and users (among other stakeholders) about how that software should function. This provides a source of software documentation clearly defining customer expectations and developer specifications.

What does Cucumber look like to a developer? Well, the starting point usually stems from feature requirements defined by the project-management process, from the perspective of the user/consumer. Returning to the earlier example, say you want to test the feature of opening image files in a folder. You could capture those requirements in the following user story:

```
In order to see photos that I'm currently interested in
As a User
I want to open images from the application
```

This user story captures the context around the feature: who it's for, what it's aiming to achieve, and finally, what feature is needed to achieve this. From that, you can create a feature file that will describe what the feature does.

In the folder containing the Lorikeet electron app, create a folder called features. This folder will contain Cucumber feature files that will be used to document how the software tests, drive automated tests, and provide a shared, common understanding of how the app should work.

Now, to create your first Cucumber feature file, create a file named images.feature and insert the following text into that file:

```
Feature: Images
    In order to see photos that I'm currently interested in
    As a User
    I want to open images from the application

    Scenario: Open a PNG image
        Given I have the application open and running
        When I search for "Pictures"
        And I click on the "Pictures" folder
        And I double click on "Pictures/app with set icons.png"
        Then I should see the "Pictures/app with set icons.png" file
        ➥ opened in a photo app
```

Here, you can read the text and see what looks like plain English instructions on how to use an app feature—hopefully, they make sense straight off the bat. The idea is that regardless of whether you're a developer, product owner, user, or other stakeholder in the project, you'll be able to read this and have the same understanding of the feature as everyone else.

With this feature in place, you can now look at using this plain English document to test the app feature.

16.5.2 *Automatically testing your Electron app with Cucumber and Spectron*

This section shows you how to use Cucumber.js to run integration tests for your app via Spectron. The code for the Cucumber example is available in the GitHub repository for the book, but I'll also walk you through the code here to help you understand how it works.

First off, install cucumber.js; run the command to install the module via npm:

```
npm install cucumber --save-dev
```

Once you have Cucumber.js installed in the development dependencies for the Lorikeet Electron app, you can set up the required files for the app. You already have the images.feature file inside the features folder, so next you want to set up a hooks.js file inside the features/support folder. This hooks.js file in the following listing contains the code that's responsible for the setup and teardown of the Spectron library booting the app.

> **Listing 16.8 The hooks.js file for the Lorikeet Electron app**

```
'use strict';

const Application = require('spectron').Application;
const path = require('path');
let electronPath = path.join(__dirname, '../../node_modules/.bin/electron');
const entryPointPath = path.join(__dirname, '../../main.js');
if (process.platform === 'win32') electronPath += '.cmd';
const {defineSupportCode} = require('cucumber');

defineSupportCode(function ({Before, After}) {        ← Before hook is called
                                                        before Cucumber
  Before(function (scenario, callback) {                feature files run and
    this.app = new Application({                         boots app via Spectron
      path: electronPath,
      args: [entryPointPath]
    });
    callback();
  });
                                                      ← After hook is called when
  After(function (scenario, callback) {                 Cucumber feature file is
    this.app.stop();                                    finished and closes app
    callback();
  });
});
```

The hooks.js file contains code that's used to drive booting the app with Spectron, as well as to shut the app down once it has finished running the Cucumber feature files. Binding the Spectron app instance on the context for the Cucumber scenario means that you can reference the app variable not only in the `After` hook when it comes to shutting the app down, but also when you want to flesh out the step definitions and use the app instance to do things like click UI elements in the app. This leads to the next file that you want to add in the features/step_definitions folder: the image_steps.js file.

The image_steps.js file, shown in the next listing, is used to store the step definitions that you want to match in the Cucumber feature file.

Listing 16.9 The image_steps.js file for the Lorikeet Electron app

```
'use strict';

const assert = require('assert');
const fs = require('fs');
const osenv = require('osenv');
const path = require('path');
const {defineSupportCode} = require('cucumber');

defineSupportCode(
    function({Then, When, Given}) {

            Given(/^I have the app open and running$/, {timeout: 20 * 1000},
    function (callback) {
        const self = this;

        self.app.start().then(() => {
          return self.app.browserWindow.isVisible();
        }).then((isVisible) => {
         assert.equal(isVisible, true);
          callback();
        })

      });

     When(/^I search for "([^"]*)"$/, function (term, callback) {
       this.app.client.setValue('#search', term)
       .then(() => { callback(); });
     });

     When(/^I double click on the "([^"]*)" folder$/, function (folderName,
    callback) {
        const folderPath = path.join(osenv.home(),folderName);
        this.app.client.doubleClick(`//img[@data-filepath="${folderPath}"]`)
        .then(() => { callback(); });
     });

     When(/^I double click on "([^"]*)"$/, function (fileName, callback) {
        const filePath = path.join(osenv.home(),fileName);
        this.app.client.doubleClick(`//img[@data-filepath="${filePath}"]`)
        .then(() => { callback(); });
     });

     Then(/^I should see the "([^"]*)" file opened in a photo app$/,
    function (fileName, callback) {
        const filePath = path.join(osenv.home(),fileName);
        setTimeout(function () {
          fs.stat(filePath, function (err, stat) {
            const timeDifference = Date.now() - stat.atime.getTime();
            assert.equal(null, err);
            assert(timeDifference < 3000);
```

```
        callback(err);
      });
    }, 3000);
  });

  When(/^I wait (\d+) seconds$/, (numberOfSeconds, callback) => {
    setTimeout(callback, numberOfSeconds * 1000);
  });

}
);
```

You'll notice that the API for triggering UI interactions is simple. With this code in place, you're able to run the tests via running this command in the Terminal:

```
NODE_ENV=test node_modules/.bin/cucumber-js
```

If you're using Windows to run the tests, you'll want to run the cucumber-js.cmd command that's present in the same .bin folder. To allow for running tests in either a Unix/Linux or Windows environment, you can write a simple script that will handle both. Create a file called cuke.js, and put the following code in it:

```
'use strict';

const exec = require('child_process').exec;
const path = require('path');

let command = 'node_modules/.bin/cucumber-js';
if (process.platform === 'win32') command += '.cmd';

exec(path.join(process.cwd(), command), (err, stdout, stderr) => {
  console.log(stdout);
  console.log(stderr);
});
```

That code snippet uses Node.js's child_process module to allow you to execute a command in a separate process. The command that you want to run is called `cucumber-js`, and it's in the node_modules/.bin folder. On the line following the definition of the command, check whether the script is running on a Windows computer. If it is, add the .cmd to the command, which then points to running the Windows binary for Cucumber.js. Execute this command and log its contents out to the Terminal. If you want to run this command, you now run the following in the Terminal:

```
NODE_ENV=test node cuke.js
```

If all goes well, you should see the tests passing on your terminal, and that means it worked.

Given all the available tools for testing your desktop apps, it's fair to ask, "So, what tools should I use for my app"? This is a tricky one because there's no single right answer—you have to discover what works best for you and your team. My advice is try unit testing first, because it's the easiest form of testing to implement. Once you become comfortable with it, you can proceed up the levels of the testing stack, and do functional testing to check that components work together as you expect. Eventually, you can progress to integration testing.

Alternatively, if your biggest concern is checking that everything works at the level of the UX, I recommend starting with integration testing first. It will take a bit more to get to grips with, but the end result is worth it, and usually you can then filter down to performing unit testing only if it's needed. Testing is about making sure software works—never forget that.

16.6 Summary

There's a lot in this chapter, but the key things to take away from it are as follows:

- Writing tests for your apps from the start is the best way to avoid spending your time fixing bugs and to prevent an unfavorable UX.
- Unit testing individual functions is the quickest and easiest way to learn how to test.
- The best way to provide the greatest level of test coverage for your app is to start with integration testing.
- If you want to involve stakeholders in helping to document and test your app, use tools like Cucumber.
- Mocha is a great tool for writing your unit and functional tests due to its simple API and semantic syntax.

In chapter 17, we'll explore ways to sort out weird issues and avoid performance problems through the power of debugging tools available toó NW.js and Electron.

Improving
app performance
with debugging

This chapter covers

- Debugging errors on the client with Chrome Developer Tools
- Debugging errors on the server in Node.js
- Profiling UI performance and memory usage
- Using flame graphs to spot performance bottlenecks
- Debugging Electron apps with Devtron

Humans write programs, and humans make mistakes, even ones that automated testing tools won't capture. If you're lucky, you'll be able to get ahold of a stack trace that reports what error occurred and where it happened in the code.

However, some bugs are subtler and won't necessarily result in an error. To find these bugs, you need to use tools that can help to diagnose what's going on in the code, as well as how the app is performing on the computer. Performance is a feature.

In this chapter, I'll take you through how to use the available debugging tools; I'll show how to identify and resolve bottlenecks in your front-end code with the developer tools available in both Electron and NW.js, as well as debugging tools for

264

Node.js that can be used to debug errors and analyze performance. I'll also show you tools for tracking errors that are occurring in your apps as customers use them. Let's murder some bugs (code ones, not the ones with legs).

17.1 *Knowing what you're debugging*

The first thing you must do when debugging a Node.js desktop app is identify what the problem is before you can determine where it's happening in your app. Various techniques can be deployed to identify the problem, such as root cause analysis using the five whys, or trying to read the stack trace of the bug (if you're lucky enough to get one).

Debugging a Node.js desktop app is an interesting challenge because the bug/performance issue could be in any of the following areas:

- Quirks with Chromium's browser and its approach to rendering and executing HTML, CSS, and JavaScript
- Front-end bugs and performance issues
- Node.js bugs and performance issues
- If you're using NW.js, the way NW.js handles sharing state between the app windows and the app process
- If you're using Electron, the way Electron keeps state separate between the app windows
- The bugs, quirks, and performance issues of each of those desktop frameworks
- The app's source code

That's quite a lot of ground to cover, and unless you're a memory champion, chances are you won't have a complete and comprehensive knowledge of all the issues in all those areas. In that case, your best course of action is to apply *root cause analysis.*

Let's walk through an example. Say you spot a bug in a CRM app; clicking a contact's email does not open up the computer's email client with a new message for the contact. In this case, you know what the expected result is, and because you know what action would trigger it, you can begin a process of working through it, as illustrated in figure 17.1.

You can establish how to go about debugging the issue based on working through a set of questions. The questions in figure 17.1 are tailored to the questions a developer would ask when debugging the issue, but a more generic approach would be to ask "Why?" at least five times, in order to establish what's going wrong.

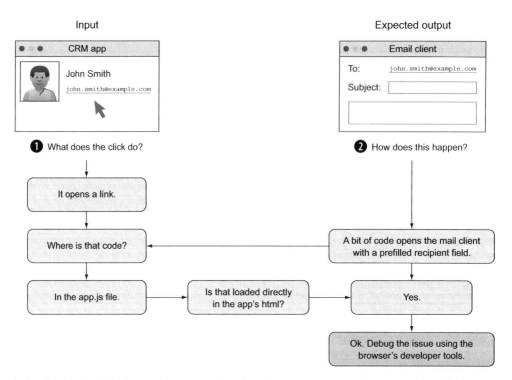

Figure 17.1   Identifying the location of the issue's root cause so you can choose which tool to debug it with

17.1.1 *Identifying the location of the root cause*

Debugging a Node.js desktop app is an interesting scenario, because the Node.js context is shared between the client-side and server-side parts of your app. The best way to work in this scenario is to identify what the root cause is—and where it is—before you open any debugging tools and start poking around. Knowing where in the code the root cause is will help you to determine which debugging tool you should use to diagnose the problem.

If the code is directly loaded by the app's HTML in a script tag, then you'll want to debug the problem using the front-end developer tools (Chrome's Developer Tools). However, if the code is not directly loaded by the client (say, it's a Node.js module, or a script loaded via `require`), then you might want to use Node.js debugging tools to get to the root cause.

When you know where your root cause lies, you can begin debugging it. Let's move on to how to debug a client-side error with the browser developer tools.

17.1.2 *Debugging with the browser developer tools*

As you develop a desktop app using NW.js, you'll notice there's a pesky little toolbar that displays above the app, much like the toolbar shown in a web browser (because that's effectively what the app is running in—a custom web browser). This toolbar contains a few goodies that you'll now appreciate. If you don't see this toolbar, check that the setting for the window toolbar in your app's package.json file is set to true, as in the following code snippet:

```
{
  "window": {
    "toolbar": true
  }
}
```

With the app window toolbar enabled, you now have access to the app window's debugging tools, which are identical to the developer tools available in Google Chrome. To access them, click the cog icon to the right of the address field, as shown in figure 17.2.

Figure 17.2   The toolbar in an NW.js app. Notice the cog icon to the right of the address field. When things are slow or broken in your NW.js app, this cog is your friend.

Clicking the cog icon brings up the developer tools window, which looks like figure 17.3.

This is how debugging works in NW.js. As for Electron, there's a different approach. In keeping with Electron's modular architecture, to load the Chrome Developer Tools in an Electron app, you need to make a call on the app's browser window, like so:

```
new BrowserWindow({width: 800, height: 600})
.webContents.openDevTools();
```

This will show Google Chrome's Developer Tools, similar to what you see in figure 17.3.

Tabs for
different tools

The app's CSS

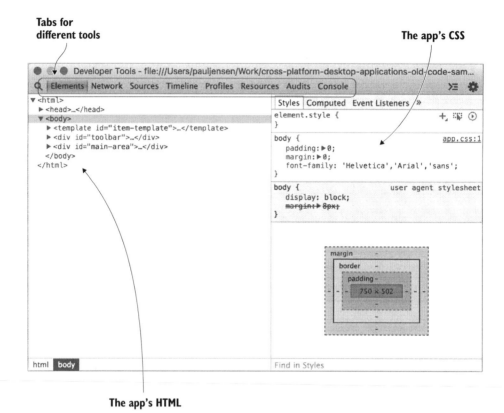

The app's HTML

Figure 17.3   The Developer Tools window for an NW.js app. If you've done front-end web development before, this window might look familiar to you. It's identical to the developer tools that you get in Google Chrome.

What if my app doesn't have a window?

Luckily, there's another way to run the debugger without needing to click the cog icon. You can run the NW.js app with remote debugging enabled by passing the following parameters when running your app from the command line:

```
--remote-debugging-port=PORT
```

This will enable you to open a web browser on the port you specified, and you'll be able to view the Developer Tools from that page.

The Developer Tools window provides a number of handy little tabs, as shown in figure 17.4, that enable the following:

- The Elements tab allows you to browse the HTML of the app and see what CSS styling and JavaScript events are attached to HTML elements in the page.

- The Network tab shows you the time it takes and the order in which the files are loaded by the app.
- The Sources tab allows you to edit the source files live, so that you can debug your app code as the app is running.
- The Timeline tab lets you see how much time is spent by the browser executing different parts of the JavaScript, or rendering elements in the page, or the amount of memory consumed.
- The Profiles tab profiles the CPU to see where in the code the most CPU cycles are being spent.
- The Resources tab explores what data resources are used by the app, such as local storage data.
- The Audits tab performs an audit of the app to find ways you can improve the app's performance.
- The Console tab allows you to access the current JavaScript context via a console.

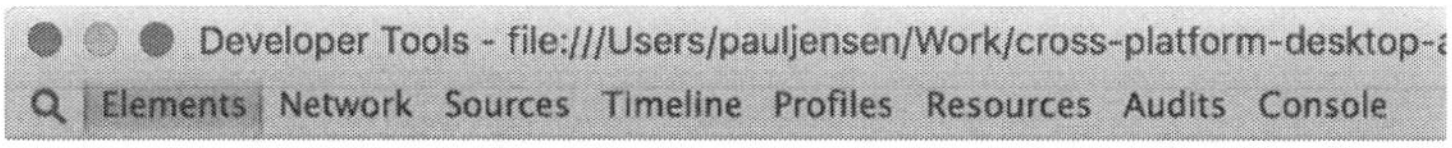

● ● ● Developer Tools - file:///Users/pauljensen/Work/cross-platform-desktop-a

Q | Elements | Network Sources Timeline Profiles Resources Audits Console

Figure 17.4   The tabs in the Developer Tools window

Table 17.1 shows a breakdown of what each tab in figure 17.4 does and how it can be used.

Table 17.1   What the Developer Tools tabs do

Developer Tool tab	What it does
Elements	Allows you to inspect and edit the DOM of the app. Useful for making visual changes on the fly and for fixing visual bugs (usually involving CSS).
Network	Shows how long the app's files take to load, and the order that they load in. Useful for optimizing app load times.
Sources	Shows the source code of the files that are loaded by your app and allows you to insert breakpoints and edit the source code live, rather than having to reload the app after making the change in your text editor or IDE.
Timeline	Allows you to see how much time the browser spends doing low-level tasks for the app, from executing the JavaScript code to rendering different DOM elements on the page. Great for deep-level analysis of your app's performance.
Profiles	Records profiling data about your app's CPU profile or memory usage. Good for spotting processing bottlenecks in your app's code, or memory leaks that can occur as well.
Resources	Shows you both the contents of files loaded by the app and data that's stored by the app, such as local storage, cookies, session information, and even Web SQL (though that's a deprecated standard). Good for inspecting data stored by the app.

Table 17.1   What the Developer Tools tabs do *(continued)*

Developer Tool tab	What it does
Audits	Analyzes your app to see if there are any changes you can make to improve performance, and makes recommendations. A handy tool for helping you make improvements, and it's free.
Console	Provides a console for running JavaScript code. Useful for testing some lines of JavaScript, inspecting the DOM, and checking out the app state.

Table 17.1 gives you an idea of the available options in the Developer Tools window when debugging issues in the client-side code. Later in the chapter, you'll dive into using these tools to help spot performance issues in your code so that you can resolve them. For now, we'll turn our attention to the first purpose of debugging: fixing bugs.

> **CAN'T I USE DEVELOPER TOOLS TO DEBUG THE WHOLE APP?**   Yes, but only if your app isn't loading any other Node.js modules. If it is, then you have to use other debugging tools to see what's going on inside them. This is because there's a bug in the Developer Tools toolbar where the Sources tab isn't able to show Node.js modules that have been loaded. This bug is known by the NW.js team.

17.2   *Fixing bugs*

Bugs are a part of software. In an ideal world, they'd never exist because the humans who wrote the code wouldn't make mistakes. But we do make mistakes (ask anyone who's accidentally filled up their car with the wrong kind of gasoline), so we have to spot them, and then we have to fix them.

When it comes to building desktop apps with Electron or NW.js, if your bug raises a JavaScript error object, then you're in luck. You'll be able to debug it from either the Console tab on the app window's Developer Tools window, or from the command-line output that appears when running the app locally (if your app is running with NW.js). Say you add a file called beetle.js to an app that you're currently working on, and the file has faulty code that reads like this:

```
check.line;
```

Then, you load the beetle.js file into the app.js file via a simple `require` statement:

```
require('./beetle');
```

Load the app from the command line as shown in figure 17.5 (the `nw` command), and note the output from the app.

The stack trace in the Terminal can be a bit of an eyeful to read and figure out. Thankfully, you can also see the error in the Console tab in a more readable format, as shown in figure 17.6.

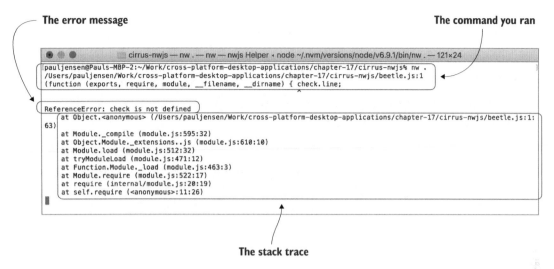

Figure 17.5 The error occurring in an app, and the stack trace that it produces

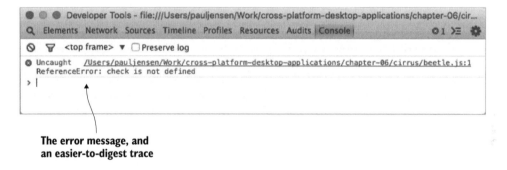

Figure 17.6 The same error as displayed by the Console tab on the Developer Tools window

In this simple example, the error is easy to spot because it raises a JavaScript error object. If you're lucky, any bugs that you encounter in your desktop apps will raise JavaScript errors, providing you with a stack trace that you can read, and therefore debug the error easily.

But not all bugs will raise a JavaScript error. In those cases, you need to have a few more tools at your disposal to determine what's going on. The next section shows extra tools to help you do this.

17.2.1 *Using Node.js's debugger to debug your app*

In NW.js, you can implement debugging either from the command line or from the Developer Tools, depending on whether the code you're looking to debug is loaded via the client or via Node.js. In Electron, you can debug the Node.js process with either Node.js's debugging support or by using the Node Inspector module.

As frameworks that run Node.js, both NW.js and Electron provide the added benefit of the debugging tools available in the Node.js ecosystem. Over the years, the tooling has evolved to enable developers to get a good understanding of what exactly is going on under the hood, providing stack traces at a simple level, and going right down to flame graphs at a more in-depth level.

Table 17.2 shows what tools are on offer, what they work with, and what they're used for.

Table 17.2 Node.js debugging tools

Node.js debugging option	Works with	Used for
Node Debug	NW.js, Electron	Back-end code
Node Inspector	NW.js, Electron	Back-end code
React Inspector	Electron	Isomorphic React apps

NODE DEBUG

Node.js ships with debugging tools by default. These tools let you pause the execution of your code by adding breakpoints in the code, and you can iterate the execution of your code step by step. This is useful when you're investigating your code, and when the cause of a bug isn't clear.

For standard vanilla Node.js apps, if you want to use the debugger, first append this line of code in the place where you'd like the debugger to pause code execution:

```
debugger;
```

Then, when executing your Node.js app, pass the following commands to the command line:

```
node debug <NAME_OF_FILE>
```

This brings up an interactive REPL once the app has reached the `debugger` call. You then have the ability to step through the code by passing the commands shown in table 17.3 to the interactive REPL.

Table 17.3 Commands to pass to the interactive REPL

Key	Command	What it does
c	Continue	Continues executing the code
n	Next	Steps to the next line of execution
s	Step in	Steps into the line of execution to see where it goes
o	Step out	Steps out of the line of execution to where it is called
pause	Pause	Pauses execution of the program

You can use these commands to control the flow of execution in the app and see step by step what the program's doing, which is handy with a hard-to-spot bug.

The difficulty with this approach is that there may be a point deep in your code where you would like to pause execution, but to stop at each line of code being executed before reaching it will take a lot of time (and a lot of key presses). Imagine a fairly small app with 20 files, each being 100 lines of code—you probably wouldn't want to have to press c for *continue* that many times. Plus, if you try to press c for *continue*, then you may end up going past the line where you wanted the program to pause. For this job, you need breakpoints.

Breakpoints are a way of getting the code to stop at a particular point in the codebase. Rather than step through the code line by line to debug an app at different points of execution, you can insert breakpoints to pause execution, allowing you to inspect the state of the code.

When you're debugging the app in the interactive debugger REPL, you'll have extra global functions available to you, listed in table 17.4.

Table 17.4 Available global functions

Function	What it does
setBreakpoint()	Sets the breakpoint on the current line that the app is on
setBreakpoint(line)	Sets the breakpoint on a given line number in the current file
setBreakpoint(fn())	Sets the breakpoint on the calling of a named function
setBreakpoint(filename, line)	Sets the breakpoint on a given filename and line number
clearBreakpoint(filename, line)	Clears the breakpoint on the given filename and line number

This is a brief overview of what's involved with using Node.js's built-in debugging tools. In the context of NW.js, debugging involves a bit more work. That's because when you execute an NW.js app, multiple Node.js processes are happening in the background. You can connect to an existing Node.js process with the debugger, but which process should you connect to, and how do you connect to it remotely?

DEBUGGING THE APP REMOTELY

Node.js's debugger doesn't necessarily have to run inside the same process as the app; it can be attached to an external Node.js process that's already running. You can do this by running the following command:

```
node debug -p PROCESS_ID
```

This allows you to connect a debugger to a running Node.js app. You need to get the process ID of the app that NW.js runs and pass it into the preceding command, in place of the PROCESS_ID text. There are a couple of ways to do it on Mac OS/Linux platforms, and one on Windows:

- On Windows, use Task Manager
- On Mac OS, use Activity Monitor
- On Linux, use Task Manager (or ps from the command line)

The easiest way to get the process ID (regardless of what OS you're on) is to open up the tool that shows the list of running apps/processes. On Windows, this is the Task Manager app; on Mac OS, it's the Activity Monitor app; on the various flavors of Linux Gnome, users know it as the System Monitor app; and for KDE users, it's the System Activity app.

On Mac OS's Activity Monitor app, type in the name *node*, and you'll see a list of processes running that match that term, as shown in figure 17.7. The process ID in this figure shows that the NW.js app's node process is running with a process ID of 10169. Put this process ID into the node debug command, which lets you attach the debugger to the running NW.js app's node process:

```
node debug -p 10169
```

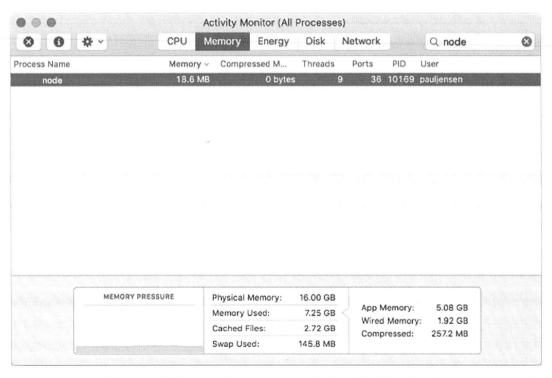

Figure 17.7   Mac OS's Activity Monitor app. The app's process that's running is highlighted, and you can record the process ID in the PID column (10169 in this case).

This means you can go debug the NW.js app's node process remotely. In the next section, we'll look at ways in which you can debug errors on the client.

17.2.2 *Using NW.js's developer tools to debug your app*

The Developer Tools window in NW.js is identical to Google Chrome's Developer Tools. Google Chrome's Developer Tools have gone a long way toward helping developers debug their web apps, and reuse knowledge and techniques to debug their NW.js apps.

To use the developer tools with NW.js, install the SDK version of NW.js. You can either visit the NW.js website and install the SDK version of NW.js from there, or install the SDK version of NW.js via npm:

```
npm install nwjs --nwjs_build_type=sdk
node_modules/.bin/nw install 0.16.1-sdk
node_modules/nw/bin/nw
```

Originally, with versions 0.12 of NW.js and earlier, the SDK was a built-in part of NW.js, but latter versions of NW.js separated this component out. Although this means there are extra steps involved in developing your NW.js app, the benefit is that you can build a smaller version of your app for the binary that doesn't include the developer tools, saving megabytes on the binary size.

Once you have the SDK version of the app installed, you can run your app and open the developer tools by either pressing F12 on your keyboard for Windows and Linux, or by pressing the Command-Alt-I on Mac OS. You can expect to see the Developer Tools window shown in figure 17.8.

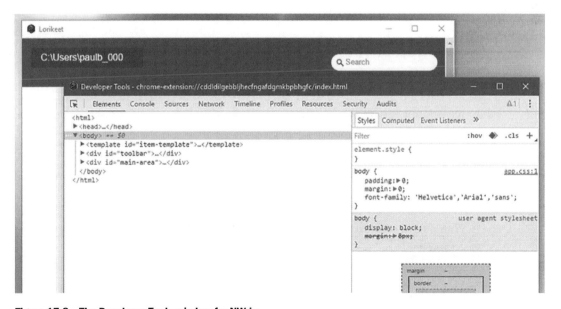

Figure 17.8   The Developer Tools window for NW.js

ELEMENTS TAB

When you bring up the Developer Tools window on an NW.js app, the Elements tab is selected by default, as shown in figure 17.8. This tab lets you inspect the DOM, in case there's a bug in the HTML, a mistyped path for an asset, or a styling bug on the app (see figure 17.9).

Figure 17.9   The Element tab on the Developer Tools window. On the left, you see the HTML for the app, and on the right are the CSS styles that affect the selected DOM element (in this case, the `body` tag).

The Elements tab also allows you to inspect the CSS styles that are applied to a DOM element and edit them inline so that you can fix visual bugs that are occurring in the app. You can edit the DOM here as well, so you can try out changes before making them in the app code.

If you're trying to debug an issue with the JavaScript code, you have two options:

- You can use the Console tab to interact with the app and inspect the JavaScript context there.
- You can use the Sources tab to insert breakpoints and watch variables to see what values they have at different points of the app's execution.

CONSOLE TAB

If you've ever done any form of front-end web development and needed to debug an issue with the JavaScript on the front end, chances are you've seen the Console tab and played with it a bit. Figure 17.10 shows what you can expect to see.

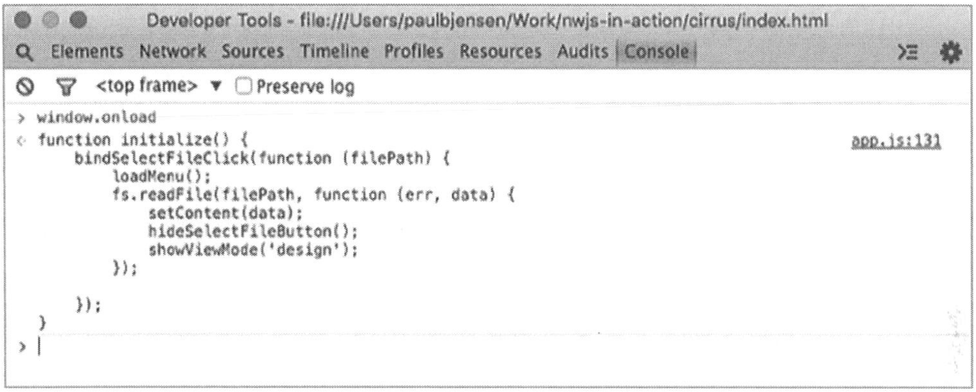

Figure 17.10 The Console tab in the Developer Tools window. If you call `window.onload` in the Console tab, you can see the code for that function on display. Also, any `console.log` statements in the code will output their content here.

The purpose of the Console tab is to be able to interactively debug your app's JavaScript state without needing to resort to inserting breakpoints and pausing/resuming the app's execution.

If you open up the developer tools for the Cirrus app and click the Console tab, you can type in statements to execute and see what happens.

SOURCES TAB

The Sources tab has a lot of handy features crammed into it for debugging, as you can see in figure 17.11.

The key debugging tools in the Sources tab are on the right-hand panel. Here, you can insert breakpoints to stop code execution when it reaches a particular point. The other nice thing you can do is look out for the value of variables in the code, such as the value of the `currentFile` variable in the app.js file, which is used to store the file path for the HTML file that's opened by the WYSIWYG editor. If you wanted to check for the current value of that variable, you could add a watch expression to the app by clicking the + button on the Watch Expression header and then typing `currentFile` as the variable name to watch out for.

After doing this, if you've used the app, you should see the value of the `current-File` variable set to the file path of the file that you were editing in the WYSIWYG editor. In this case, my screen looks like figure 17.12.

**Your application's
files are here.**

**The file source
code is displayed
and editable here.**

**Debugging options
are here in the right-
hand panel.**

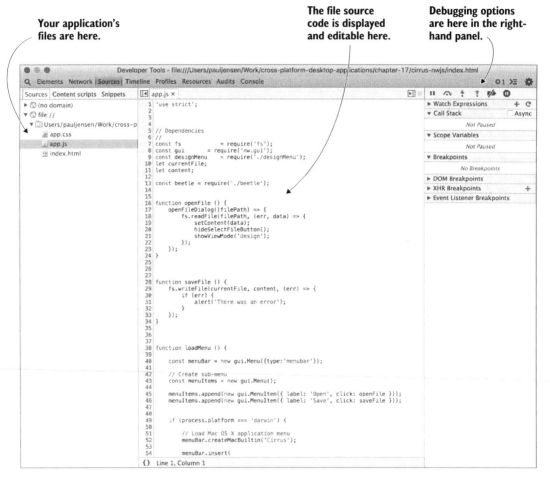

Figure 17.11   The Sources tab on the Developer Tools window

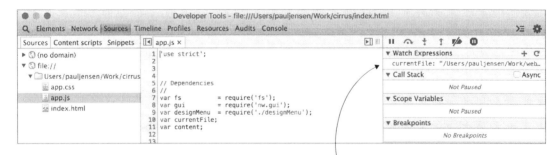

**With the Watch Expressions tool, you
can look at the current value of the
currentFile variable, and see if it is
what you expect.**

Figure 17.12   Observing a variable's current value

As you run the app, you can click the refresh button in the Watch Expressions header to show what the current value of a variable is at intervals.

A nice touch to the developer tools is that in Chrome you can edit your source code directly from the Source tab; but, unfortunately, this feature doesn't work on NW.js, so for the moment you'll need to make do with editing the files in your text editor of choice.

Being able to add breakpoints, inspect for JavaScript errors, and observe the value of variables allows developers to spot bugs in their app and resolve them. The other kind of issue that can occur isn't necessarily a bug (depending on whom you ask), but more an issue of speed: performance. The next section looks at ways you can diagnose performance issues and how to resolve them.

17.3 Resolving performance issues

The issues that affect the performance of desktop apps are the same issues that affect the performance of web apps:

- How quickly content assets are loaded by the browser
- How much memory and CPU are consumed by executing the JavaScript
- The frame rate at which the browser is able to render the page

Performance optimization tends to be an afterthought until the app is live and performance issues are impacting app usability. The plus is that it's easy to spot the error, resolve it quickly, and deploy the changes to users quickly.

With a desktop app, the user is stuck with that version, unless it has self-updating functionality enabled. Either way, there's a greater pressure to get it right the first time (because your users might not be as patient). In this section, we'll explore what each of the tabs on the Developer Tools window does and what it's useful for when you're trying to spot performance issues with your desktop app.

17.3.1 Network tab

With performance issues, the first place to look is how long it takes to load the HTML, CSS, and JavaScript files that make the app. In the Developer Tools window, the Network tab shows how long it takes for those assets to load, be parsed, and render in the browser, as shown in figure 17.13.

For web apps, the Network tab is useful because it shows you how long it takes for the assets to load and gives you a benchmark to measure against. As you can see in figure 17.13, the app looks like it loads pretty quickly (128 ms—the blue, right-most line), which is due in part to the fact that the assets are being loaded from the computer's hard disk, rather than from a web server on the internet. Nevertheless, the Network tab is useful for building desktop apps:

- You can see the size of the files, whether they're getting too big, and whether they should be minified and gzipped to reduce their size.
- You can see how many assets are being loaded by the app and check whether concatenating them together will improve the performance of the app.

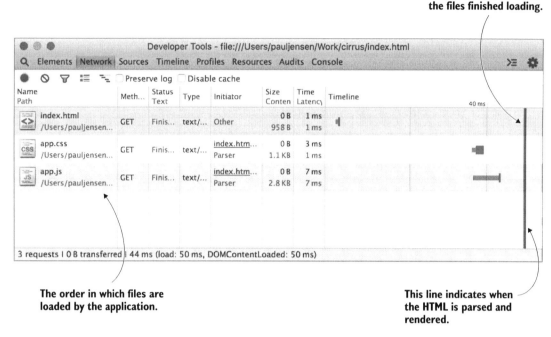

This line indicates when the files finished loading.

The order in which files are loaded by the application.

This line indicates when the HTML is parsed and rendered.

Figure 17.13   The Network tab panel

This tab gives a good indication of whether your app is becoming bloated; if so, you'll notice the number of assets loaded by the app grows and begins to impact the loading time. Keep an eye on the loading metric as your app grows.

Once the app has loaded, the next step is to look at how it performs. For this, you have some other tabs in the Developer Tools window that can help out.

17.3.2   *Timeline tab*

Next to the Network tab is the Timeline tab—the Swiss army knife of the Developer Tools window because it has so many ways to display performance data. It's a helpful tab when it comes to optimizing the performance of your app with regard to the following:

- Tracking how much memory is used in the JS heap
- Seeing how long the app spends performing various browser-based tasks
- Seeing what browser-rendering events are causing jank

This tab provides lots of data-visualization features to explore, but you need to record the performance data first. Click the Timeline tab, and then click the red record button, as shown in figure 17.14.

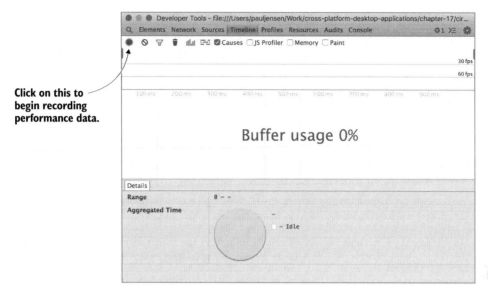

Click on this to begin recording performance data.

Figure 17.14   The record button on the Timeline tab

Once you've clicked the record button, you're recording performance data. At this point, you can use the app like you normally would, or if there's a particular action that you've noticed is slow or janky, perform that action in the app.

> **WHAT IS JANK?**   *Jank* refers to when the browser animation and rendering drops below 60 frames per second and you begin to notice that the page rendering judders and has some stutter in rendering elements on the screen.

When you're happy that you've recorded the relevant performance data for what you wanted to measure, click the record button again to stop recording the performance data, and you should now see a screen with lots of data, like in figure 17.15.

You'll now have a lot of data to play with and inspect. Figure 17.15 has drilled down on a particular point in the timeline where the JS heap jumps up rapidly, indicating that there's a point where something happens to cause this. If you explore the events that occur during the use of the app, you'll see that clicking from the design view to the code view is responsible for triggering the spike. You now have enough information to target where you explore the code and optimize it.

As you check and uncheck different options in the Timeline tab, different visualizations of the data are displayed for you. I recommend browsing those tools to get a feel for them, as there's a lot to do in that tab alone. Next, we'll check out the Profiles tab.

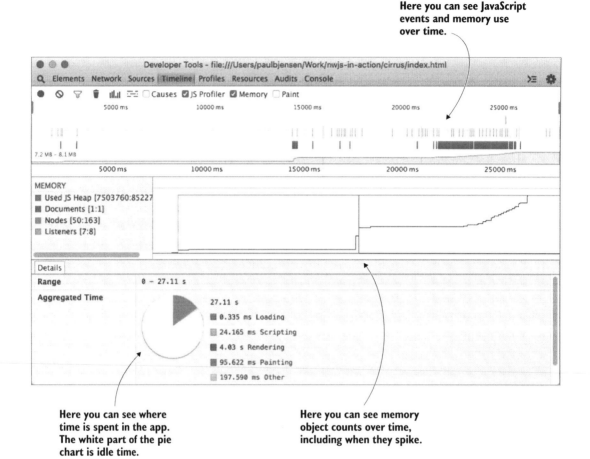

Here you can see JavaScript events and memory use over time.

Here you can see where time is spent in the app. The white part of the pie chart is idle time.

Here you can see memory object counts over time, including when they spike.

Figure 17.15   The Timeline tab displaying performance data

17.3.3 *Profiles tab*

The Profiles tab offers the ability to trace the following performance areas:

- Where the app is spending its time (in terms of CPU cycles) executing code
- What the memory usage is like as the app is used, and what kinds of memory objects are being created over time
- Where potential memory leaks may be occurring in the code

When you click the Profiles tab, you're presented with three options, shown in table 17.5.

Table 17.5   Profile tab options

Option	What it does
Collect JavaScript CPU Profile	Shows where your app is spending time executing code
Take Heap Snapshot	Takes a snapshot of the current memory heap in the app
Record Heap Allocations	Records memory heap over a period of time

Depending on the nature of your performance problem, you'll want to try out the different options and see what data you get back. To use one of the options listed on the tab, click the Start button shown on the tab (let's choose the CPU profile in this case) and use the app. When you're finished, you'll see something like figure 17.16.

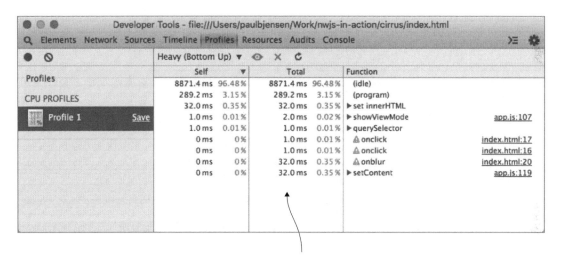

Here you can see where the CPU
spends its time executing functions
in the application's code

Figure 17.16   The Profiles tab with the CPU profile results

The results from doing a CPU profile analysis can also be displayed as a flame chart. Click the toolbar drop-down to change how the results are displayed, and you should see something like figure 17.17.

The flame graph shows you where time is being spent by your app and helps to spot any bottlenecks.

Being able to analyze the performance qualities of your desktop app comes in handy when you're trying to make sure that your product works for your customers before it goes out there.

Having now covered NW.js's developer tools, let's look at what Electron has to offer.

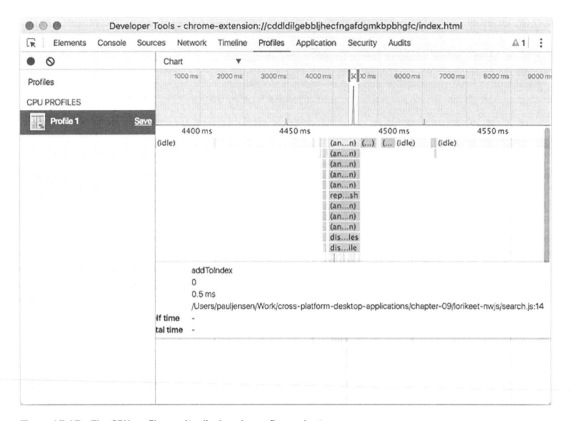

Figure 17.17   The CPU profile results displayed as a flame chart

17.4   *Debugging Electron apps*

Like NW.js, Electron uses Chrome's Developer Tools under the hood. Electron provides access to the developer tools either from the View menu in the app's main menu or by pressing Ctrl-Shift-I (Command-Shift-I on Mac OS).

If you try to open the developer tools in one of your Electron apps, you'll see a new window pop up, looking like figure 17.18.

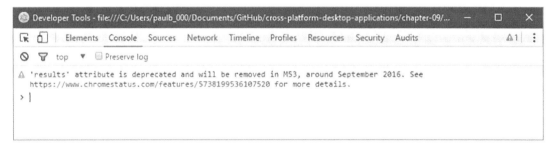

Figure 17.18   Electron's Developer Tools window. The nice thing about Chrome's Developer Tools is that it detects browser features used in your app and emits warnings in the console about them being deprecated in the near future.

The Developer Tools window is almost the same as the one shown in NW.js, but the order of the tabs is different, though they're the same as the ones in NW.js. In that respect, it's nice because you can use the same tools to debug both NW.js and Electron apps.

That said, Electron's approach to rendering app windows as separate processes rather than all in a single app process makes it a bit more involved in terms of debugging what's happening in each app window. Fear not, though—Electron has a dedicated debugging tool for handling this, called Devtron.

17.4.1 *Introducing Devtron for debugging Electron apps*

Devtron is a debugging tool for Electron apps that allows you to inspect some of the more intricate aspects of your Electron apps, such as the following:

- How your app loads dependencies in both the main back-end process and in each renderer front-end process
- Inspecting data messages that are passed between the main and renderer processes
- Linting the code to make sure you haven't incorrectly scoped a variable or omitted a break command in a case statement
- Showing what events are occurring in the Electron app so you can see whether certain things are happening, such as when a window is closed or when an app registers itself as being ready

Devtron is built on top of Chrome's Developer Tools, so installing it is a two-step process. First, install it as a development dependency for your Electron app via npm:

```
npm i devtron --save-dev
```

Next, complete the installation process by running your Electron app. Once you've got your Electron app up and running, open the developer tools, either by pressing Ctrl-Shift-I (Command-Alt-I for Mac OS) to view the tools, or by clicking the View menu and selecting Toggle Developer Tools, as shown in figure 17.19.

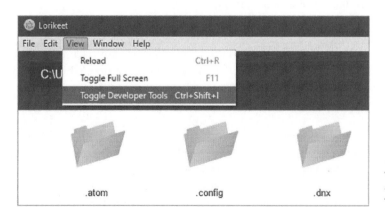

Figure 17.19 Opening the developer tools from an Electron app's main toolbar

With the developer tools open, click the Console tab and run the following command:

```
require('devtron').install()
```

You should see a new tab appear (the Devtron tab) in the Developer Tools window, as shown in figure 17.20.

Figure 17.20   The Devtron tab at the end of the Developer Tools

The Devtron tab is built as an extension of the developer tools, which means you can run it alongside the rest of the Developer Tools for the app. If you click it, you can expect to see something like figure 17.21.

Figure 17.21   The Devtron tab in the Developer Tools

In the sidebar on the left of the Developer Tools window, you have five menu items. You'll go through each of them one by one, with the exception of the last menu item (which is information and not a debugging option).

REQUIRE GRAPH

The Require Graph item is used to list how npm module dependencies are loaded in the renderer and main processes by the app. The idea is that by looking at the dependency graph information, you can see not only the order in which the modules are loaded by the main/renderer process, but also see how big they are (and therefore how much they contribute to the whole size of the app). You can also search through the modules by their name and filename with the search input field at the top.

To begin using Require Graph, you first need to check whether you want to visualize the dependency graph for the main process or the renderer process, and click the tab that represents the process you choose. Then, click Load Graph in the top right of the window. When you do this on the renderer process for the Lorikeet app, you can see the information presented in the dependency graph shown in figure 17.22.

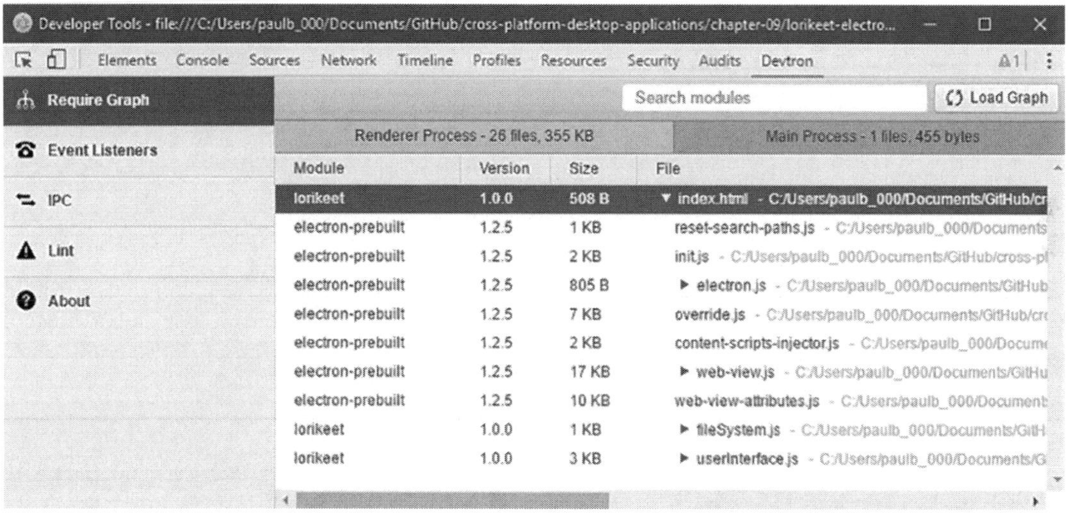

Figure 17.22 The dependency graph for the renderer process in Lorikeet Electron. Notice that the app's total file size is 355 KB—not bad for a simple file explorer app.

The Require Graph tab shows that the index.html file loads first, followed by Electron loading its required files, and then the rest of Lorikeet's files are loaded. The size of the files is also relatively small, which is nice because it shows that you can pack quite a bit of functionality into the desktop app without making it monolithic.

EVENT LISTENERS

The Event Listeners menu item shows events emitted during the app's lifecycle and allows you to see what the code looks like for binding on them. The idea is that you can see what events are occurring and where they're triggered in terms of Electron's APIs.

To view them, click the Event Listeners menu item in the left sidebar and then click the Load Listeners button in the top right of the window. The Developer tools window should then look like figure 17.23.

In the window, you can see the names of the events that are being emitted on each part of Electron's APIs, as well as events that are being emitted by Node.js. This allows you to check that the events you expect to be happening in the app are in fact happening.

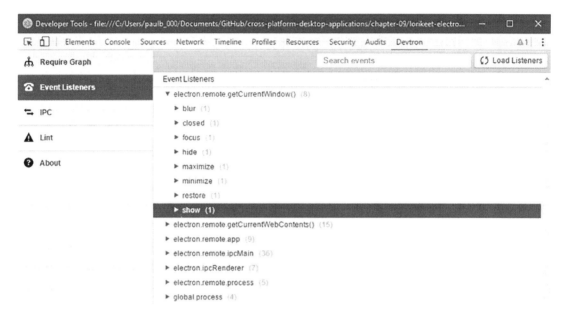

Figure 17.23   The Event Listeners pane in the Devtron tab

IPC

The IPC menu item shows what inter-process communication is occurring between the main process and the renderer process of the Electron app. It's useful when you want to see what data messages are being passed between the processes.

When you want to see what's happening, click the IPC menu item in the left sidebar of the Devtron tab pane and then use the buttons in the top-right pane to handle recording IPC messages and clearing them, as shown in figure 17.24.

Figure 17.24   The IPC buttons for the IPC pane in the Devtron tab. The idea is that you can record IPC messages that occur when the app is running.

The Record button handles recording IPC messages occurring in the app, including the ones used by Electron's internal modules to transmit data between the main process and the renderer process. To start recording these IPC messages, click the Record button in the top right, and when you use the app, you should start to see IPC messages pouring into the window, as in figure 17.25.

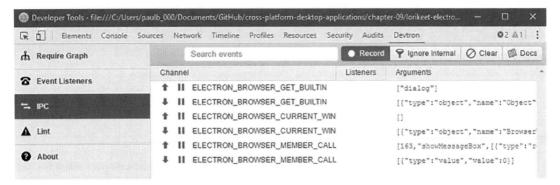

Figure 17.25   IPC messages being recorded in the Lorikeet app. In this case, some internal Electron messages are being sent on three different channels with various data arguments.

The IPC messages can be used to see how Electron triggers internal features, such as displaying a dialog on the renderer process with a message to the user when an error occurs. To filter out Electron's internal IPC messages, click the Ignore Internal button to hide them; and to clear all messages, click Clear. Also, don't forget to click Record again to stop recording IPC messages.

LINTING

The Linting menu item is useful for doing some cleanup tasks on your Electron app. It will do the following:

- Check what version of Electron you're running and inform you if there's a more up-to-date version available to use
- Check whether you're using an asar archive or not to load your app quicker
- Check whether you're handling exceptions in your app or ignoring them
- Check whether your app has crash handling installed to capture when your app crashes
- Check whether the app window has an event handler for when the app window becomes unresponsive

Click Linting in the left sidebar, and then click the Lint App button at the top right. The Linting pane will then flag up useful suggestions, as figure 17.26 illustrates.

You can think of the Linting tab as a way of sweeping through issues in the app before you start preparing it for shipping.

We've covered a number of Devtron features that can be used to debug parts of Electron, such as its use of IPC messages and the way it uses events. When it comes to building Electron apps, Devtron is a handy tool for debugging and improving your app. To find out more about Devtron, check out the project at http://electron.atom.io/devtron/.

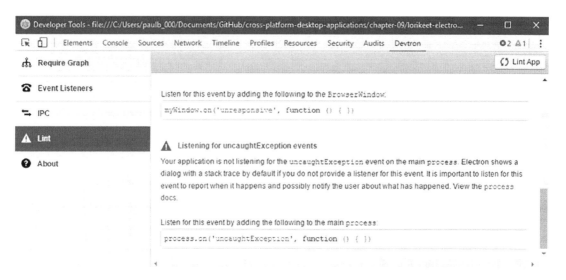

Figure 17.26   The Linting pane in the Devtron tab. The Lorikeet app can make improvements to be that little bit better.

17.5   *Summary*

In this chapter, we've looked at the tools available to use when you're fixing bugs in your apps, as well as tools that can help you spot performance problems and see how to address them. Here are some of the key takeaways from the chapter:

- Root cause analysis is the first tool you should use when trying to diagnose the cause of a problem, as you will want to save time by avoiding going down dead ends in your analysis.
- The developer tools at your disposal are the same ones available in the Google Chrome web browser (the Chrome Developer Tools), and will come in handy if you work with web apps as well as desktop apps.
- You can use Node.js's remote debugging capabilities to debug a live running app on the fly without having to close it down and then painstakingly replicate the conditions in which a bug has occurred.
- Try to keep the number of assets that your app must load to a minimum.
- The Sources tab in the Developer Tools window is handy for analyzing an app's state when you need to fix a bug.
- The Profiles tab is handy for analyzing the performance of your app.
- Devtron is a great tool for debugging your Electron apps.

In chapter 18, we'll look at how you can package the app for shipping to the wider world on Mac OS, Windows, and Linux.

Packaging the application for the wider world

Once you've gotten to a stage with your app where it's ready for people to use, the next step is to consider how you want to package it for running on your users' computers so that users can install it. There are lots of different ways to do this, and depending on the app you're building and who your audience is, it's good to know which options exist and how you can make use of them.

In this chapter, we'll explore those options and show how to package your app as executable binaries for Mac OS, Microsoft Windows, and Linux (Ubuntu), including creating Windows installers for your Electron apps.

First, we'll look at some options for protecting your source code and the pros and cons of those approaches.

18.1   Creating executables for your app

When you're ready to ship your app to the wider world, start by making sure it's available in a format for users to download and run on their computer. For this, you need to create executables for each OS you want to support. The good news is that you can do this from a single codebase, and the only negative is that there's a bit of fiddly work to produce executables for all the OSs. Luckily, there are some tools out there to take care of this work, and this section shows you how to use them to create executables for each OS.

We'll start by looking at creating apps for Microsoft Windows.

18.1.1   Creating an NW.js app executable for Windows

The world's most popular OS, Microsoft Windows, has had quite a journey in the last few years. Following the release of Windows 7, Microsoft was trying to compete with Apple in the tablet market. It released Windows 8, a version of Windows with a touch-friendly UI that could work on both personal computers and tablets. It was a bold move, but unfortunately it didn't go down well with users of Windows; the removal of the Start button from the desktop was a major stumbling block. Windows 8.1 shortly came out and reintroduced the much-loved Start button back to the desktop, and last year Windows 10 was introduced as a free upgrade to existing users of Windows 7, 8, and 8.1.

Although Windows isn't as dominant as it was in the 1990s and early 2000s, the OS still has the largest market share out there, with Windows 7 being the frontrunner. There are quite a few versions of the OS in use today (including, believe it or not, Windows XP), but building a .exe file for Windows tends to work seamlessly across the major versions of the OS.

For the sake of simplicity, I'll assume you have Windows 10 running on your computer. It's a free upgrade for users, but if you're running Mac OS or even Linux, don't despair, because there are other options. You can install virtual machine software and images that will allow you to run a copy of Windows 10 to test your app against.

18.1.2   Installing a virtual machine

Table 18.1 lists some virtual machine software and image options.

Table 18.1   Popular virtual machine software

Virtual machine	Platform	URL	Cost
VirtualBox	Windows/Mac/Linux	virtualbox.org	Free
VMware Fusion	Mac	vmware.com/products/fusion	$89
Parallels	Mac	parallels.com	$95

Once you have virtual machine software you're happy with, find a virtual machine image running the version of Windows that you want to test against. A quick search on Google will reveal options for you.

When you've got a virtual machine running Windows (or you have a computer running Windows natively), you can proceed to build and test an executable version of your app for that OS.

18.1.3 Building a .exe of an NW.js app for Windows

For this exercise, you'll turn to one of the existing apps you built earlier in this book—a file explorer app called Lorikeet—and look at how to turn that into an executable app. In chapter 4, you covered generating a Windows version of the NW.js app using a tool called nw-builder. You could repeat that step here, but instead I'll show you what's going on when you create a binary executable of the app on Windows. That way, you can understand how the sausage is made, rather than getting the sausage and eating it.

Let's grab a copy of the Lorikeet app that you built from GitHub:

```
git clone git://github.com:/paulbjensen/cross-platform-desktop-
applications/chapter-04/lorikeet-nwjs
```

Now, install the dependencies, and you'll be ready to build a copy of the app as a Windows executable:

```
cd lorikeet-nwjs
npm install
```

Start by creating a zip file of the contents of the Lorikeet folder. This can be done easily in Windows by selecting all the contents of the folder name and choosing Send to > Compressed (zipped) folder, as shown in figure 18.1.

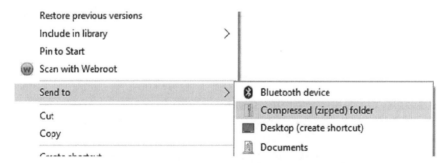

Figure 18.1   Creating a zip file of the contents of the Lorikeet folder. Make sure you create a zip folder of the contents of the Lorikeet folder, rather than of the Lorikeet folder itself.

Next, name the zip file package.nw, rather than a name followed by .zip. You should see a dialog asking if you want to do this, warning that the file may become unusable. Click Yes to the dialog shown in figure 18.2.

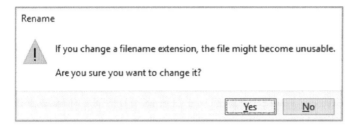

Figure 18.2   Renaming the zip file to package.nw so the app can be packaged right for the Windows executable.

You now need to combine package.nw with the NW.exe file. Assuming you have a globally installed copy of NW.js sitting on your computer (via having run `npm install -g nw`), copy the package.nw file to the same location as the nw.exe file (mine is shown here):

```
C:\Users\paulb_000\AppData\Roaming\npm\node_modules\nw\nwjs\nw.exe
```

Copy the package.nw app to the same folder as the nw.exe file, and then run the following command to generate the exe file:

```
copy /b nw.exe+package.nw lorikeet.exe
```

This should generate a standalone lorikeet.exe file that you could put on another Windows machine and run right off the bat. That's all it takes to make an NW.js app into a Windows executable file.

The next section looks at how to create a Windows executable for an Electron app.

18.1.4 *Creating an Electron app executable for Windows*

Electron follows a similar pattern for creating standalone executable versions of an app for Windows. The first thing to do is get ahold of the source code for an Electron app. You can take an example app from this repository on GitHub: https://github .com/paulbjensen/cross-platform-desktop-applications.

Grab the Hello World Electron app from chapter 1, and you'll turn that into a standalone .exe file. After you've grabbed the source code for the app, you'll install a utility library for Electron called asar. Asar is a tool for packaging your app into an asar archive, which resolves the following issues:

- It makes sure that long file paths are shortened so you don't run into issues with Windows' 256-character limit on file paths.
- It speeds up Node.js's `require` function a bit.
- It doesn't expose all your files in the app to anyone who wants to poke around in the source code.

First, install asar via npm on the command line:

```
npm install -g asar
```

Now, you'll be able to turn your app's source code into an asar archive. As an example, you'll take the Hello World Electron app's source code and turn it into an asar archive. `cd` the folder containing the app's folder, and then run the asar archive command in the Command Prompt/Terminal:

```
cd cross-platform-desktop-applications/chapter-01
asar pack hello-world-electron app.asar
```

The second command listed will generate an app.asar file that's an asar archive consisting of the contents of the hello-world-electron directory. After this, you'll combine the app.asar file with the Electron app.

Grab a copy of the prebuilt binary for Electron from the GitHub repository for Electron from https://github.com/electron/electron/releases. Download a copy that corresponds to the OS and CPU version, which in the case of this example is v1.4.15-win32-x64.zip, available at http://mng.bz/yH23.

Unzip the file, and you should have a folder named electron-v1.4.15-win32-x64. The folder will contain another folder called resources. Put the app.asar file inside the resources folder. Then, you can change directory into the parent folder and double-click the electron.exe file to run the app. You should then see something like figure 18.3.

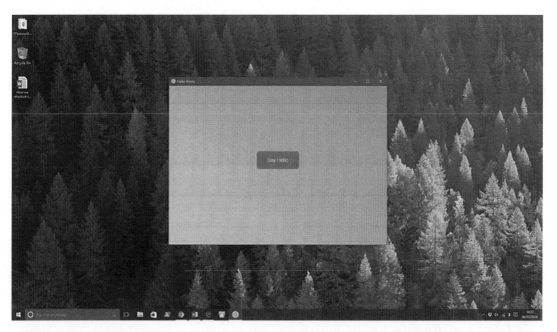

Figure 18.3 The Hello World app running as a standalone executable. Note that the Windows app doesn't have the default menu toolbar that shows when the app is running from the Electron command line, and the Electron icon shows in the taskbar.

This is good, but you'll probably want to rename the electron.exe file to one that matches your app name (for example, hello-world.exe) and change the app icon. To change the app icon, you can use a tool called rcedit (a command-line resource editor). Install rcedit via the command line with npm:

```
npm install –g rcedit
```

You can now edit the icon and version numbers for the app. Provided you have an app icon available in .ico format, you can run the following command on your command-line prompt to change the app icon used on the electron.exe file:

```
rcedit electron.exe --set-icon "my-app-icon.ico"
```

Using rcedit, you can then give the app its own unique look and feel.

> **ARE THERE ANY OTHER PACKAGING TOOLS THAT CAN HELP?**   Yes, there's a good tool for Electron called electron-packager that you can install via npm. It allows you to create builds of your Electron app for Windows, Mac OS, and Linux. It's similar to NW.js's nw-builder library, and details of its full API and capabilities can be found at www.npmjs.com/package/electron-packager.

This covers setting up a standalone executable app on Windows, but what if you want to create a setup installer for your Windows app? Well, good news—you can. The next section walks through how to do that.

18.2   *Creating a setup installer for your Windows app*

Although standalone executables for Windows run fine, most users of Windows apps are used to installing them via setup installers. Setup installers take care of putting the app and its contents in the right places on the user's computer, as well as making sure that Desktop and Start menu shortcuts are installed for the app. Setup installers work by double-clicking the setup.exe file and clicking through the setup installer to make sure the app is installed in the right place and with the right user permissions.

What are the options for NW.js and Electron?

18.2.1   *Creating a Windows setup installer with NW.js*

Creating a Windows setup installer for a standalone NW.js app is a little bit of a dance, but the good news is that it is possible. Here are the various options that exist for creating a Windows setup installer:

- NSIS from Nullsoft
- Inno Setup
- WinRAR

I'll show you how to create a Windows installer with Inno Setup. I've found it to work absolutely fine, and it's not too difficult to use. The software tool is available at www .jrsoftware.org/isinfo.php. Visit the website and download a copy to run on Windows.

Once you've installed Inno Setup on your Windows computer, you can begin the process of creating a Windows installer for your app. Run Inno Setup on your computer. You should see a screen like figure 18.4.

Figure 18.4   Inno Setup's initial screen

In Inno Setup's Welcome dialog box, the New File section shows two options:

- Create a new empty script file
- Create a new script file using the Script Wizard

For new users, the second option is best. Select the second option and click OK. You should see the Inno Setup Script Wizard dialog, as shown in figure 18.5.

Click Next to proceed to the Application Information screen. Here, you'll provide information about the app such as its name, version number, the app publisher's name, and the app's website, as shown in figure 18.6.

Figure 18.5   The Inno Setup Script Wizard

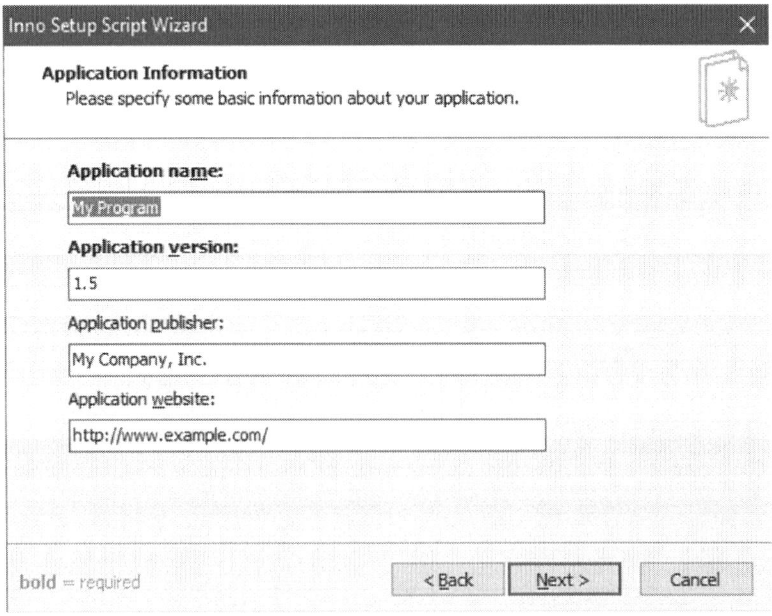

Figure 18.6   The Application Information screen in the Script Wizard

Fill in your app's information, and click Next to proceed with the Application Folder screen. Here, you'll configure what the app's folder is named and where it will be installed on the user's computer by default (usually in the Program Files folder in the C: drive). You should see a screen like figure 18.7.

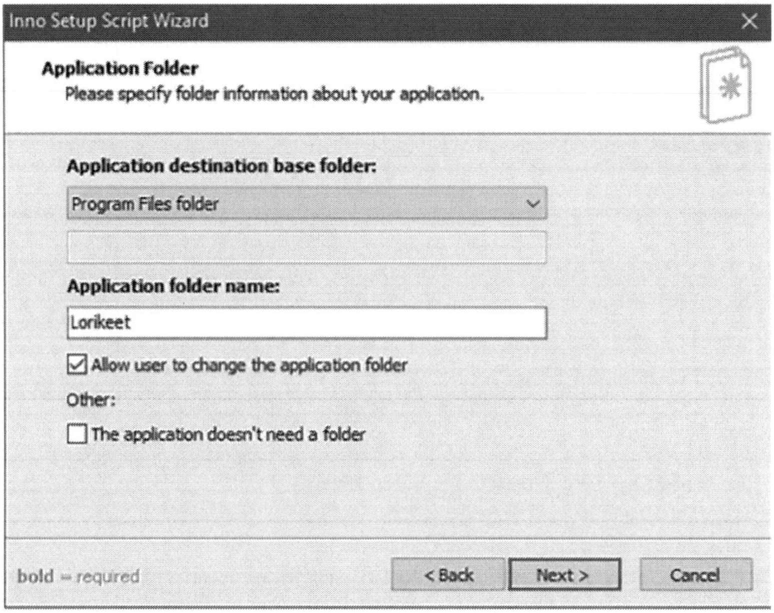

Figure 18.7   The Application Folder options screen in the Setup Wizard

I've decided to use the Windows version of the Lorikeet app, so I'll name the folder Lorikeet. You can also configure whether the app needs a folder in the Program Files folder, as well as whether the user will be allowed to change the name of the folder when installing the app.

Once you've provided the name of the app folder you want, click Next to proceed to the next screen, which in this case is the Application Files screen shown in figure 18.8. Here is where you provide the files that make up your built NW.js app, so the Setup Wizard will be able to compile those into the setup.exe file created by Inno Setup.

The dialog in figure 18.8 shows a few options:

- The app's main executable file
- Whether the user should be offered the chance to run the app immediately after they have installed it
- Whether to include other files and folders to be installed in the setup installer

Figure 18.8   The Application Files screen in the Setup Wizard

The first and third options are the most important because this is where you add the files/folders of your NW.js's Windows app. If you built the Windows app as a single executable, you can select that .exe file for including in the setup installer. But if you've built your Windows app with nw-builder and you find that there are multiple files to go with the Windows app, then you can include those by adding the folder that contains all those files.

Once you've added the app's main file (and any other additional files), click Next to move on to the next screen in the Setup Wizard, the Application Shortcuts screen, shown in figure 18.9.

The Application Shortcuts screen shows configurations options for the icon shortcuts being placed in various places on the user's computer, such as the Start Menu, the Desktop, and even in the Quick Launch bar on older computers.

The default options specified here are fine (though you're welcome to adjust them as you like for your app). Once you've made your choices, click Next to move on to the next screen. The Wizard presents the configuration options for displaying licensing information to the user as they install the app. Figure 18.10 shows the options.

You don't necessarily have to provide anything here, but it's recommended that you include software licensing information in your app. Here is where you can provide licensing information for the user to agree to before they can use the software, as well as release notes and other information to display before the software gets installed (and after).

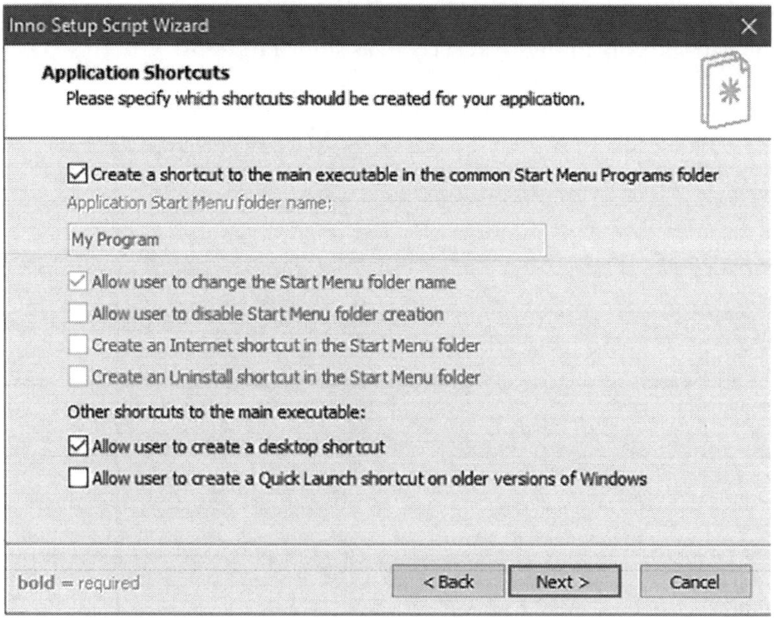

Figure 18.9   The Application Shortcuts screen in the Setup Wizard

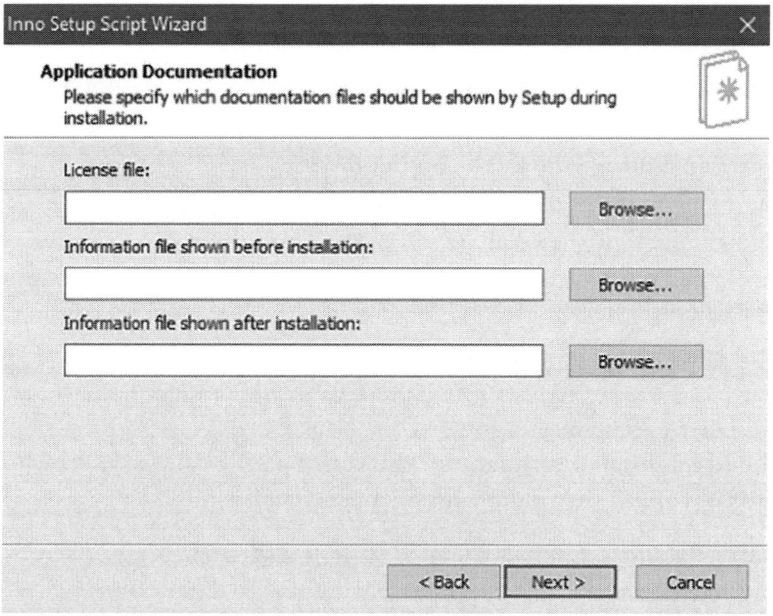

Figure 18.10   Application Documentation configurations in the Script Wizard

If you're happy to proceed, click Next to see options for the languages you want the setup installer to support in the next screen, as shown in figure 18.11.

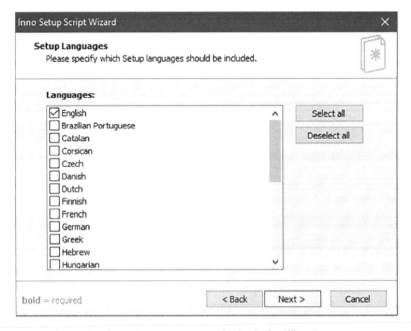

Figure 18.11   The Setup Languages screen in the Script Wizard

When you're happy with your language options, click Next to see the Compiler Settings screen, shown in figure 18.12. There you can configure the following:

- Where the setup.exe file will be output to
- What the filename of the setup installer will be
- What icon the setup installer should have (if any)
- Whether the setup installer should require the user to input a password before the installer will install software.

When you've filled in this screen, click Next again and click through to the end of the Script Wizard as shown in figure 18.13, where you can compile the script and create the setup installer executable.

With the setup installer created, you can distribute that file to users who want to install your NW.js app via a Windows installer executable.

COULD I USE THE SAME TECHNIQUE FOR ELECTRON .EXE APPS?   Yes. There's no reason you can't use Inno Setup 5 for creating a Windows installer for an Electron app. That said, Electron has a lot of packaging tools that enable you to use some of Electron's more advanced features, such as being able to automatically update apps through Electron's Squirrel framework.

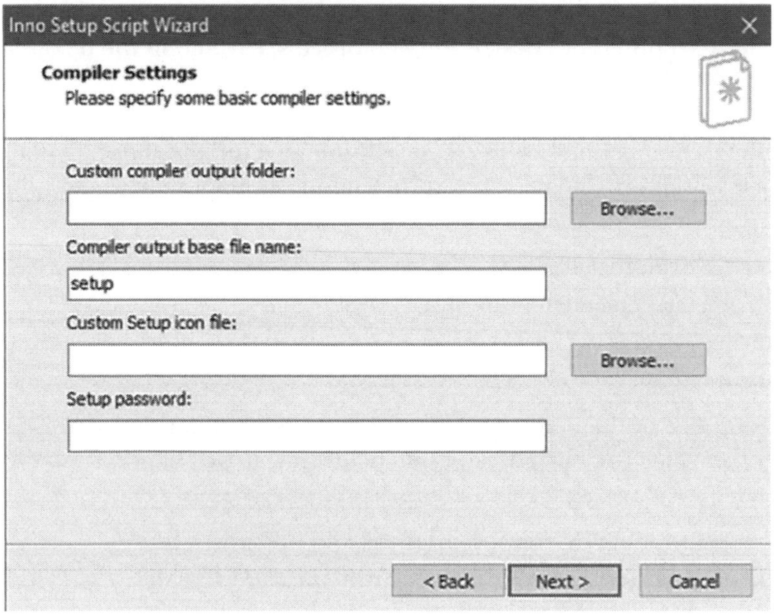

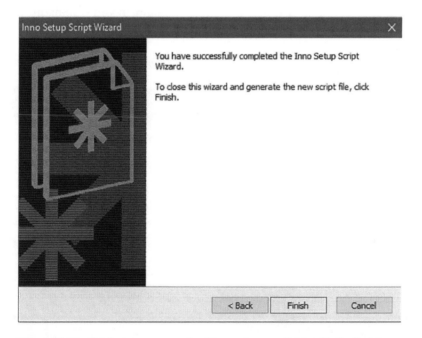

Figure 18.12   The Compiler Settings screen in the Script Wizard

Figure 18.13   The last screen you should see when you finish with the Script Wizard

This pretty much covers how to set up a Windows setup installer for an NW.js app. For Electron, there is a different, though simpler, process, covered in the next section.

18.2.2   *Creating a Windows setup installer with Electron*

Electron offers a number of ways to create a Windows setup installer for your Electron app. A quick search on Google will return a number of approaches and libraries to install. Here are some libraries available to help build a Windows installer:

- Grunt-Electron-Installer
- Electron-installer-squirrel-windows
- electron-packager
- electron-builder

I'll cover using one of them, the npm module electron-builder. It not only takes care of building your Electron app for multiple platforms, it also handles some platform-specific issues:

- Packaging your app to support applying app updates
- Being able to sign the code as a security measure for Mac and Windows app stores
- Managing versioned builds of the app
- Compiling native modules for each OS platform

To install electron-builder, run the following command in the Command Prompt/Terminal:

```
npm install -g electron-builder
```

This will install electron-builder on your computer as a global npm module. Now, let's walk through an example of using it to help you generate a Windows installer for an Electron app.

First, grab a copy of the Hello World Electron app from GitHub:

```
git clone https://github.com/paulbjensen/book-examples.git
cd book-examples/chapter-18/hello-world-electron
```

The Electron app is going to be packaged with electron-builder so you can create a version of the app that has a Windows installer.

electron-builder relies on build configuration information being present in the app's package.json file, like how NW.js and Electron look for their configuration information in that file. electron-builder requires that the following fields are present in the package.json file:

- Name
- Description
- Version
- Author

Here's an example of what those fields should look like:

```
{
  "name": "hello-world",
  "description":"A hello world Electron application",
  "version": "1.0.0",
  "author" : "Paul Jensen <paul@anephenix.com>"
}
```

In the Hello World Electron app's package.json file, the description and author fields are not present. Add those to the package.json file (and amend as you'd like). The next step is to add some more build configuration information to the package.json file about the Windows icon to be used.

When specifying the Windows .ico file for the app, you need to provide a public URL to access the file, rather than a local file. You can put the file in a number of places:

- As a file that's served from Amazon S3
- As a file that's served from a Dropbox folder
- As a file that exists in a public GitHub repository

Wherever you choose to host that file, make sure anyone can reach it (test in a web browser running in private/incognito mode). Here's a URL for a .ico file that you can use for this walkthrough: https://github.com/paulbjensen/lorikeet/raw/master/icon.ico.

In the package.json file for the app, insert the following code:

```
{
  "build": {
    "iconUrl":" https://github.com/paulbjensen/lorikeet/raw/master/icon.ico"
  }
}
```

Make sure that a copy of that icon file is present inside a build folder in the app. After doing that, add these script commands to the package.json file:

```
"scripts": {
  "pack": "build",
  "dist": "build"
}
```

These script commands can be run using npm run on the command line. Finally, you need to ensure that Electron is installed as a development dependency. You can do that by running the following command:

```
npm i electron -save-dev
```

If you were to run npm run pack at the command-line prompt, you'd see that the app executables are packaged in the newly created dist folder. When you browse the dist folder, you'll see that the Electron app has been turned into .exe files for different processor architectures (ia32 and x86-64).

At this point, electron-builder then wraps another npm module that handles building the Electron app as a Windows installer. This is a module called electron-windows-installer, with documentation here: https://github.com/electronjs/windows-installer#usage.

If you rename the name field of the package.json file to hello and run `npm run dist`, electron-builder creates the following Windows-based installer items for the app:

- A nupkg file for installing the app via the NuGet package manager
- A .exe file
- A Microsoft Setup Installer (.msi) file named setup.msi

With these files, you can install the app on other computers via a single file.

That covers creating a Windows setup installer for Electron. Now, we'll look at options for creating both executable versions of the app for Mac OS.

18.3   *Creating an NW.js app executable for Mac OS*

You have a few options for how to proceed, but by far the simplest is to use nw-builder to create the executable, and for another npm module called appdmg to wrap that executable as a .dmg file for ease of installation on Macs.

I'll show you how nw-builder works first, and then how to turn the executable app into a .dmg file with appdmg.

18.3.1   *Creating the Mac executable app*

nw-builder is a tool for creating different executables of your NW.js app for different OSs. If you haven't got it installed already, run the following command on your command line:

```
npm install -g nw-builder
```

Now, you can use nw-builder to build a Mac executable app. Find an NW.js app that you want to build an executable copy of, and you'll create an executable for it. I'll resort to building a copy of the Lorikeet app that you created earlier in the book.

Once you've checked out a copy of the app, you can use nw-builder with it by passing a series of arguments to the command-line command. Let's say you've checked out a copy of the Lorikeet app's source code on your computer. `cd` into the app folder, and then run the following commands to generate the app's Mac OS executable:

```
nwbuild lorikeet-nwjs -p osx64
```

The first command goes to the directory where Lorikeet's source code is, and the second handles building the app for the 64-bit version of Mac OS. When the command has finished, you should have a new build folder. Inside the build folder is another folder named lorikeet, and inside that folder is the 64-bit build, which contains an executable of the app.

The next step is to turn these executable builds of the app into .dmg files, which are visual installers that make installing Apple Mac software easy. This is where the appdmg module comes in handy.

To install appdmg, run the following command in the Terminal:

```
npm install -g appdmg
```

Running that command installs the appdmg module as a global npm module. This means you can use it to create .dmg files for all the Mac OS builds across all of your NW.js and Electron apps.

To use appdmg, pass two arguments to the command line, like so:

```
appdmg <json-path> <dmg-path>
```

Here, the first argument passed to the appdmg command is a path to a JSON file containing configuration information for appdmg. The second argument passed is the path where you want the created .dmg to be placed.

The JSON file contains configuration information for appdmg, and you can give it any filename. I've given it the name app.json. An example of the app.json that you might want to use for the Lorikeet app is shown in the following listing.

Listing 18.1 The app.json file for the appdmg image creator

```
{
    "title": "Lorikeet",
    "icon": "icon.icns",
    "background": "background.png",
    "icon-size": 80,
    "contents": [
        { "x": 448, "y": 220, "type": "link", "path": "/Applications" },
        { "x": 192, "y": 220, "type": "file", "path":
"build/lorikeet/osx64/lorikeet.app" }
    ]
}
```

Annotations:
- Title to display in window → "title": "Lorikeet"
- Relative path to icon to display when mounting app → "icon": "icon.icns"
- Background to display in setup installer window → "background": "background.png"
- Size of icons in setup installer windows → "icon-size": 80
- Files to be displayed in setup installer window → "contents"

When you have this configuration set up in the app.json file, you can run the appdmg command on your Mac OS computer, like so:

```
appdmg app.json ~/Desktop/lorikeet.dmg
```

When you run this command, the output .dmg file will be placed in your Desktop folder and therefore it will be visible on your desktop screen. The Terminal output should look something like figure 18.14.

When the process has finished and you have a .dmg file on your desktop, double-click to open it, and something like figure 18.15 should appear.

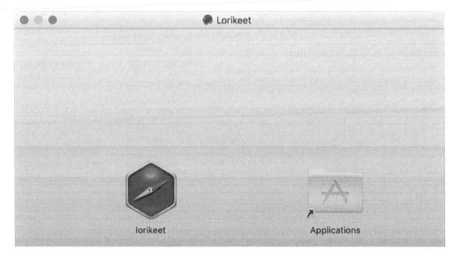

```
Pauls-MBP:lorikeet pauljensen$ appdmg app.json ~/Desktop/lorikeet.dmg
[ 1/20] Looking for target...                  [[object Object]]
[ 2/20] Reading JSON Specification...          [[object Object]]
[ 3/20] Parsing JSON Specification...          [[object Object]]
[[ 4/20] Validating JSON Specification...      [[object Object]]                    ]
[ 5/20] Looking for files...                   [[object Object]]
[ 6/20] Calculating size of image...           [[object Object]]
[ 7/20] Creating temporary image...            [[object Object]]
[ 8/20] Mounting temporary image...            [[object Object]]
[ 9/20] Making hidden background folder...     [[object Object]]
[10/20] Copying background...                  [[object Object]]
[11/20] Reading background dimensions...       [[object Object]]
[12/20] Copying icon...                        [[object Object]]
[13/20] Setting icon...                        [[object Object]]
[14/20] Creating links...                      [[object Object]]
[15/20] Copying files...                       [[object Object]]
[16/20] Making all the visuals...              [[object Object]]
[17/20] Blessing image...                      [[object Object]]
[18/20] Unmounting temporary image...          [[object Object]]
[19/20] Finalizing image...                    [[object Object]]
[20/20] Removing temporary image...            [[object Object]]

[object Object]
/Users/pauljensen/Desktop/lorikeet.dmg
Pauls-MBP:lorikeet pauljensen$
```

Figure 18.14   Running appdmg on Mac OS. If all goes well, you can expect to see an itemized breakdown of the tasks being performed to create the .dmg file, and they should all be green.

Figure 18.15   The .dmg file in action, showing the app installer

In figure 18.15, you'll see the .dmg file's app installer window, where the user can drag and drop the Lorikeet app into the Applications folder to install it on their computer.

This covers how to create a standalone NW.js app for Mac OS and package it as a .dmg for users to easily install on their computer. The next section shows how to do the same for Electron apps.

18.3.2 Creating an Electron app executable for Mac OS

Electron offers a number of npm modules that can take care of creating the app executable on Mac OS, including electron-builder, mentioned earlier. You'll use the electron-builder module because it provides a good UX for creating packaged app builds of Electron apps.

First, grab the Electron Hello World app to create a Mac .dmg for. When you have a copy of the source code for the app checked out, cd into the directory containing the app and run this command on the Terminal to install electron-builder as a development dependency:

```
npm i electron-builder --save-dev
```

Once you've installed electron-builder as a development dependency for the app, take a look at the app's package.json file and make sure it has the following required fields:

- Name
- Version
- Author
- Description

Once you've got those fields populated in the package.json file, the next thing to do is add the build configuration to the package.json file, as in the next listing.

Listing 18.2   Adding the build configuration information to the package.json file

```
{
  "name": "hello-world",
  "version": "0.0.1",
  "main": "main.js",
  "description":"A hello world application for Electron",
  "author": "Paul Jensen <paul@anephenix.com>",
  "scripts": {                                    ◁── Adds some scripts for
    "pack": "node_modules/.bin/build",                handling creation of
    "dist": "node_modules/.bin/build"                 .app and .dmg files
  },
  "build": {                     ◁── Include build
    "mac": {                         configuration
      "title": "Hello World",        info here
      "icon": "icon.icns",
      "background": "background.png",
      "icon-size": 80,
      "contents": [
        {
          "x": 448,
          "y": 220,
          "type": "link",
          "path": "/Applications"
        },
```

```
      {
        "x": 192,
        "y": 220,
        "type": "file",
        "path": "dist/hello-world-darwin-x64/hello-world.app"
      }
    ]
  }
},
"devDependencies": {
  "electron-builder": "^13.5.0",
  "electron ": "1.4.15"
}
}
```

If you take a close look at the package.json file, you'll notice that the `build` property looks remarkably similar to the configuration used for creating the .dmg file for the NW.js app with appdmg. This is because electron-builder uses appdmg under the hood and passes the configuration to that library here, instead of through a separate JSON file.

Once you have the script in place, you want to make sure you have the following image assets in place for the app:

- An icon.icns file for the app's icon
- A background.png image to be displayed in the background of the app installer

When you have both of those items in the app's source code, you can run the npm commands that will generate the .app and .dmg files. In the Terminal, run the following commands:

```
npm run pack && npm run dist
```

This code uses the Unix `&&` operator to run two commands in sequential order. Once the first command (`npm run pack`) has finished, it triggers the second command (`npm run dist`). `npm run pack` will create the .app file that contains all the app's source code as a standalone executable, and `npm run dist` does the following:

- Creates the .dmg file for users to install the app on their computer
- Creates a mac.zip file for supporting automatic updates via Squirrel

The first file is the one you want to offer to new users to install your app. The zip file is the one for existing users of your app and is the package that's used to provide them with automatic updates. When you run the .dmg file, you can expect to see a result like the one shown in figure 18.16.

This shows how you can create setup installers for Mac OS using a variety of tools. The key thing to take away from this is that appdmg is a great tool for handling the creation of .dmg files, but when it comes to creating those .dmg files for Electron

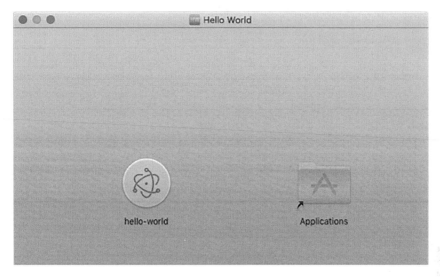

Figure 18.16 The .dmg installer for the Hello World Electron app

apps, you're better off using the electron-builder npm module, because it takes care of a lot more things.

The next section shows how to create standalone executables for Linux.

18.4 Creating executable apps for Linux

When it comes to creating executable apps for Linux, bear in mind that there are multiple distributions of Linux, some of which are quite common and popular (Linux Mint, Ubuntu, Fedora, and openSUSE come to mind), and some of which are smaller, more niche distributions. To install software for Linux distributions, there are a number of different software package management tools:

- Yum (used by Red Hat, Fedora, CentOS)
- YaST (used by OpenSUSE)
- Synaptic (used by Ubuntu, Linux Mint)

You can always serve your software as a tarball and let Linux users run `make` and `make install` on their computer, but not all Linux users will know how to do that, and Linux is making inroads into all kinds of areas, including education and local government. In order to best support your Linux users, do the following:

- Identify what Linux distributions are supported by your app framework
- Find out (if you can) what Linux OSs your customers are using
- If you can't identify that, find out what the most popular Linux OSs are and support those

18.4.1 Creating NW.js standalone apps for Linux

One of the options available to you for NW.js is to use nw-builder, which has been used earlier in the book. If you haven't already, you can install nw-builder by running the following command:

```
npm install -g nw-builder
```

Next, you need an app to convert into a Linux standalone executable and run nw-builder on with configuration details specific to Linux. In the chapter so far, we've used the Lorikeet app, but to add some variety, you'll use one of the other apps that you worked on earlier in the book, a WYSIWYG app called Cirrus.

Grab a copy from GitHub at https://github.com/paulbjensen/cirrus/archive/master .zip. Once you've downloaded the zip file and extracted the contents into a folder, cd into the folder and run the following command to install software dependencies:

```
npm install
```

Now, you can build the Linux standalone executables with nw-builder. Run the following command in the Terminal to build both 32-bit and 64-bit versions of app for Linux:

```
nwbuild cirrus -p linux32,linux64
```

This will create two builds of the app for Linux—one for 32-bit architecture, and another for 64-bit architecture. When nw-builder finishes building the packages, you'll find a build folder. The build folder contains another folder with the name of the software (Cirrus, in this case), and inside that are two folders: linux32 and linux64. These are the folders for the different builds of the app that you specified earlier.

As the app stands, you could take the files produced from the build and run them on Linux, as shown in figure 18.17.

The software at this point is a collection of these files:

- Cirrus (a binary executable that takes the name of the app)
- icudtl.dat (a binary data file for NW.js)
- libffmpegsumo.so (a file used by Chromium for multimedia support)
- locales folder (a folder containing files for localization info for different countries)
- nw.pak (a file for NW.js)

When you want to bundle these files into packages for RPM, Yum, Apt, and dpkg, you'll want to include all of them and make the binary executable named after your app the main executable.

This covers what to do for an NW.js project. How about for Electron?

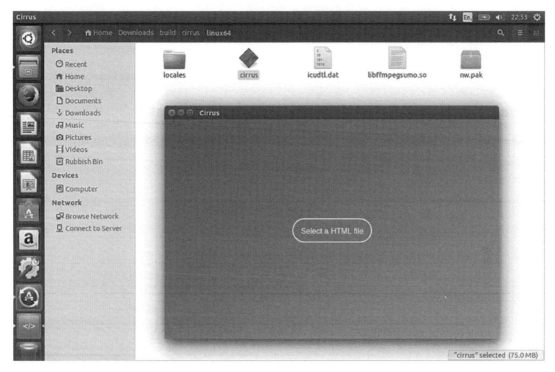

Figure 18.17   Cirrus running on Ubuntu Linux 14.04 LTS. Cirrus is running in the foreground, and in the background are the files that make up the app. You may also notice the app icon in the bottom-left corner.

18.4.2 *Creating Electron standalone apps for Linux*

Electron has a number of tools available for building an Electron app as a standalone Linux executable:

- Grunt-build-atom-shell (grunt plugin: https://github.com/paulcbetts/grunt-build-atom-shell)
- electron-packager (npm module: www.npmjs.com/package/electron-packager)
- electron-builder (npm module: https://github.com/electron-userland/electron-builder)

You used electron-builder for the Mac OS and Windows builds earlier in the chapter, so this time you'll take electron-packager for a spin instead. electron-packager is in the Electron-userland organization on GitHub, and is maintained by a number of major contributors within Electron's community.

You'll start by installing electron-packager on your computer as a global dependency:

```
npm install -g electron-packager
```

cd into the directory where the app's source code is (in this case, you'll use the Hello World Electron app as an example), and then run the electron-packager command:

```
cd hello-world-electron
electron-packager FULL_PATH_TO/hello-world-electron --name=hello-world
--platform=linux --arch=x64 --version=1.4.15
```

This will take the source in the hello-world-electron directory, turn it into an Electron app called hello-world with Electron version 1.4.15, and build that app for Linux on the 64-bit x86 architecture.

After running that command, you should have a new folder called hello-world-linux-x64. Inside that folder will be the following set of files:

- content_shell.pak (a file for Electron)
- hello-world (a binary executable that takes the name of the app)
- icudtl.dat (a binary data file for Electron)
- libffmpeg.so (a file used by Chromium for multimedia support)
- libnode.so (a file for Electron)
- LICENSE (a text file containing license information for the software)
- LICENSES.chromium.html (an HTML file containing license information about the software used in Chromium, the open source version of Chrome that Electron uses)
- locales folder (a folder containing files for localization info for different countries)
- natives_blob.bin (a file for Electron)
- resources folder (a folder containing the app's source code)
- snapshot_blob.bin (a file for Electron)
- version (a text file containing the software version

When you run the app and its files on a Linux machine (say, a machine running Ubuntu 14.04), you'll see something like figure 18.18.

This shows you how you can use electron-packager to package an Electron app as a standalone Linux executable. The ability to do this for both NW.js and Electron means you have the flexibility to choose which desktop app framework you want to use for the app. That said, do bear in mind one major caveat when choosing Electron with regard to Windows support: if you need to support Windows XP (which still has a statistically significant customer base in China), then Electron isn't supported.

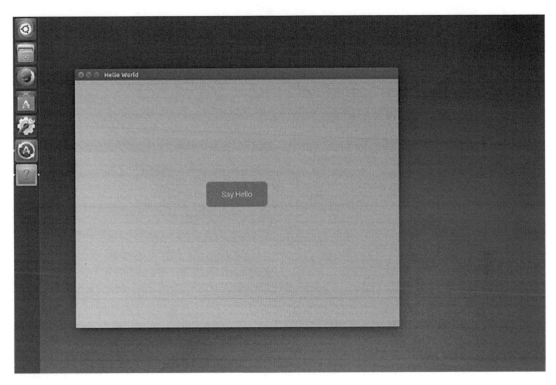

Figure 18.18   The Hello World Electron app as a standalone app on Ubuntu

18.5 *Summary*

In this chapter, we've looked at the different ways in which you can build your NW.js and Electron apps for the different OSs out there.

Consider which OSs your customers are likely to use so you can spend your time working on supporting the platforms that need to be supported. Being able to build Windows and Mac OS executables for the app with tools like nw-builder, electron-builder, and electron-packager ensures that you can reduce the amount of time spent packaging the app—and spend more time creating features for your app.

You also explored how to create setup installers for the executables of your app so that users of your app can install them with ease. You'll find that Inno Setup 5 is a great tool for creating setup installers and is easy to use, so that will help you with creating setup installers for your Windows apps.

As for Mac OS, appdmg is the tool of choice for creating .dmg files for your Mac OS apps.

These tools go a long way toward helping you to provide a smooth installation experience for your users. Bear in mind that there currently aren't any major building tools in the NW.js and Electron space that simplify turning built Linux executables into packages for Yum, YaST, and Apt. That's something you'll have to do manually.

appendix
Installing Node.js

There are a couple of different ways to install Node.js, but the simplest way to get it installed is by visiting https://nodejs.org and clicking the Downloads link in the top navigation bar. You'll see a page of download options for different operating systems. If you're running Windows or Mac OS, you can choose to download one of the installers available. If you're running Linux, you can either download a tarball of the source code and compile it or install it via a package manager. For instructions on using a Linux package manager to install Node.js, take a look at https://nodejs.org/en/download/package-manager.

INSTALLING MULTIPLE VERSIONS OF NODE.JS WITH NVM Another option for developers running Mac OS X or Linux is to use nvm (Node Version Manager) to handle installing Node.js. nvm allows you to install multiple versions of Node.js on your computer and then switch between the different versions. This is very useful when you want to test how your code runs against newer versions of Node.js. It also enables you to work on multiple Node.js applications that are running different versions of Node.js. For more on nvm, visit https://github.com/creationix/nvm.

index

MORE TITLES FROM MANNING

Secrets of the JavaScript Ninja,
Second Edition

by John Resig, Bear Bibeault, and Josip Maras

ISBN: 9781617292859
464 pages
$44.99
August 2016

Get Programming with JavaScript

by John R. Larsen

ISBN: 9781617293108
432 pages
$39.99
August 2016

Sails.js in Action

by Mike McNeil and Irl Nathan

ISBN: 9781617292613
488 pages
$49.99
January 2017

For ordering information go to www.manning.com

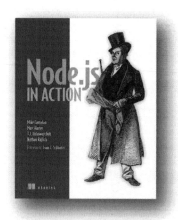

Node.js in Action

by Mike Cantelon, Marc Harter,
  T.J. Holowaychuk, and Nathan Rajlich

ISBN: 9781617290572
416 pages
$44.99
October 2013

Node.js in Practice

by Alex Young and Marc Harter

ISBN: 9781617290930
424 pages
$49.99
December 2014

*Getting MEAN with Mongo, Express,
Angular, and Node, Second Edition*

by Simon D. Holmes

ISBN: 9781617294754
450 pages
$44.99
March 2018

For ordering information go to www.manning.com

MORE TITLES FROM MANNING

Express in Action

Writing, building, and testing Node.js applications

by Evan M. Hahn

ISBN: 9781617292422
256 pages
$39.99
April 2016

Angular 2 Development with TypeScript

by Yakov Fain and Anton Moiseev

ISBN: 9781617293122
456 pages
$44.99
December 2016

Grokking Algorithms

*An illustrated guide for programmers
and other curious people*

by Aditya Y. Bhargava

ISBN: 9781617292231
256 pages
$44.99
May 2016

For ordering information go to www.manning.com